taste of home

Favorite Brand Name Recipes

2009

taste of home
BOOKS

REIMAN MEDIA GROUP, INC.
Editor in Chief: Catherine Cassidy
Vice President & Executive Editor/Books: Heidi Reuter Lloyd
Creative Director: Ardyth Cope
Food Director: Diane Werner, R.D.
Senior Editor/Books: Mark Hagen
Art Directors: Gretchen Trautman, Rudy Krochalk
Content Production Supervisor: Julie Wagner
Recipe Asset Systems: Coleen Martin, Sue A. Jurack
Premedia Supervisor: Scott Berger
Editorial Assistant: Barb Czysz

Chief Marketing Officer: Lisa Karpinski
Vice President/Book Marketing: Dan Fink
Creative Director/Creative Marketing: Jim Palmen

Cover Photography: Taste of Home Photo Studio
Photographer: Jim Wieland
Food Stylist: Sarah Thompson
Set Stylist: Melissa Haberman

THE READER'S DIGEST ASSOCIATION, INC.
President and Chief Executive Officer: Mary G. Berner
President, RDA Food & Entertaining: Suzanne M. Grimes
President, Consumer Marketing: Dawn Zier

Pictured on the front cover (*top to bottom):* Carrot Ginger Cupcakes (*page 186*) and Asian Pork Ribs with Spicy Noodles (*page 130*).
Pictured on the back cover (*clockwise from top left):* Amazin' Crab Rice Cakes (*page 127*), Greek-Style Tortellini (*page 45*) and Brickle Bundt Cake (*page 202*).

ISBN-13: 978-1-4127-1955-1
ISBN-10: 1-4127-1955-0

ISSN: 1554-0111

Manufactured in U.S.A.

8 7 6 5 4 3 2 1

Microwave Cooking: Microwave ovens vary in wattage. Use the cooking times as guidelines and check for doneness before adding more time.

taste of home
Favorite Brand Name Recipes
2009

Dig into Hundreds of Taste Sensations from America's Most Trusted Name Brands

Serving unbeatable meals has never been easier than it is with this edition of *Favorite Brand Name Recipes 2009*. After all, with the 352 family-friendly specialties this book offers, finding a dinnertime solution is always a snap!

Taste of Home, the world's No. 1 cooking magazine, is known for sharing heartwarming dishes that fit the schedules, budgets and tastes of today's family cooks…and this colorful collection is no exception. That's because the *Taste of Home* team selected each dish.

The days of running to specialty stores and spending money on unique ingredients are over! Each of the recipes in *Favorite Brand Name Recipes 2009* relies on everyday ingredients you likely have on hand. Best of all, many of the dishes come from the brand names you depend on, so you know that everything will turn out perfectly.

Linguine with Herbs, Tomatoes and Capers, p. 170

Best of the Best

Take a look at the recipes inside, and you'll recognize dozens of the name brands you've relied on for years.

• When we wanted to include an ideal potato salad in this book, we turned to the experts at IDAHO® potatoes. We knew they would have the perfect solution, and Loaded, Baked Potato Salad fit the bill. (Check out the recipe on page 26 of the "Salads" chapter.)

• Looking for a fun twist to a Southwestern standby? So were we, and we knew just whom to ask. ORTEGA® shared a recipe for Double Cheeseburger Tortillas that's sure to become a staple in your home. You'll find the details on page 165.

• There's always room for dessert, and this book has plenty to offer with dozens of cookies, pies,

cakes and more. So when we wanted a chocolate sensation, we asked NESTLÉ® TOLL HOUSE® for some input, and they shared the secrets behind Triple-Chocolate Cupcakes. (Turn to page 209 in the "Desserts" chapter to read about these glorious goodies!)

And That's Not All!

Take a look inside, and you'll discover dishes that fit all of your culinary needs. Want a no-fuss appetizer? Consider Slow-Cooked Mini Pulled Pork Bites on page 7. The tangy snacks come together with CAMPBELL'S® soup and PEPPERIDGE FARM® dinner rolls.

Rounding out meals has never been easier than with *Favorite Brand Name Recipes 2009*. For instance, turn to page 60 and you'll find Kettle Cooked Baked Beans With Smoked Sausage. This specialty relies on VAN CAMP'S® pork and beans as well as HUNT'S® tomato paste and GULDEN'S® mustard. Or surprise your gang with golden squares of Focaccia (see page 122). The colorful loaf bakes up effortlessly with RED STAR® or QUICK•RISE™ yeast.

In addition, more than 100 color photographs and over 300 tips make it a cinch to serve the perfect menu…whether you're planning a weeknight supper or a weekend dinner party.

Finding Your Favorites

When trying to decide what to prepare, simply turn to page 213. There you'll find a general index that lists every recipe by food category, major ingredient and/or cooking method.

For instance, if you have some chicken in the refrigerator that you'd like to serve tonight, turn to "chicken" in the general index. You'll find several incredible dishes to choose from.

The alphabetical index is another good reference. Starting on page 221, it's a great way to find recipes by name.

We hope that *Taste of Home Favorite Brand Name Recipes 2009* becomes your most-used kitchen helper. It was a true delight bringing it to you!

Top to bottom: Triple-Chocolate Cupcakes (p. 209), Chopped Mexican Salad (p. 37), Spicy Squash & Chicken Soup (p. 68)

Appetizers & Snacks

Slow-Cooked Mini Pulled Pork Bites

(pictured at left)

    1 can (10-3/4 ounces) CAMPBELL'S® Condensed
        Tomato Soup
1/2 cup packed brown sugar
1/4 cup cider vinegar
    1 teaspoon garlic powder
    4 pounds boneless pork shoulder
    1 package (13.9 ounces) PEPPERIDGE FARM® Soft Country
        Style Dinner Rolls
    Hot pepper sauce (optional)

1. Stir the soup, brown sugar, vinegar and garlic powder in a 6-quart slow cooker. Add the pork and turn to coat.

2. Cover and cook on LOW for 6 to 7 hours* or until the pork is fork-tender.

3. Remove the pork from the cooker to a cutting board and let stand for 10 minutes. Using 2 forks, shred the pork. Return the pork to the cooker.

4. Divide the pork mixture among the rolls. Serve with the hot pepper sauce, if desired.   *Makes 16 mini sandwiches*

Or on HIGH for 4 to 5 hours.

Clockwise from top left: *Slow-Cooked Mini Pulled Pork Bites, Bacon Appetizer Crescents (p. 19), Refried Bean and Corn Cakes (p. 10), Hot "Crab" and Artichoke Dip (p. 8)*

Crunchy-Fruity Snack Mix

Crunchy-Fruity Snack Mix

(pictured above)

1 cup (4 ounces) roasted and salted soy nuts
1 cup broken-in-half pretzel sticks (about
    1-1/2 ounces)
2/3 cup white chocolate chips
2/3 cup dried pineapple, cut into 1/2-inch pieces
2/3 cup dried cranberries

1. Combine soy nuts, pretzels, chocolate chips, pineapple and cranberries in large bow; mix well.

2. Store in tightly covered container.

Makes 4 cups

Crunchy Fruit Snack: Try Crunchy-Fruity Snack Mix on hot or cold cereal for breakfast, sprinkle it on waffles or pancakes, or use it as an ice cream topper. Also try it mixed into muffin, quickbread, or cookie doughs or batters.

Hot "Crab" and Artichoke Dip

(pictured on page 6)

1 (8-ounce) package cream cheese, softened
1/2 cup mayonnaise
1/2 cup shredded Cheddar cheese
1/4 cup CREAM OF WHEAT® Hot Cereal (Instant,
    1-minute, 2-1/2-minute or 10-minute cook
    time), uncooked
1 teaspoon TRAPPEY'S® Red Devil™ Cayenne
    Pepper Sauce
1 teaspoon Worcestershire sauce
1 teaspoon Chesapeake seasoning
1 (9-ounce) jar artichoke hearts, drained,
    coarsely chopped
8 ounces pasteurized surimi (imitation
    crabmeat), coarsely chopped
1 teaspoon ground paprika
    Vegetables, crackers or tortilla chips (optional)

1. Preheat oven to 350°F. Stir cream cheese in medium mixing bowl until softened. Add mayonnaise, Cheddar cheese, Cream of Wheat, pepper sauce, Worcestershire sauce and Chesapeake seasoning; mix well. Fold in artichoke hearts and surimi.

2. Pour into 1-quart casserole dish. Sprinkle on paprika. Bake 30 minutes. Serve warm with vegetables, crackers or tortilla chips, if desired.

Makes 6 to 8 servings

Tip: Spread leftover dip on English muffins, and place under the broiler for a few minutes until bubbly and browned. Cut into quarters and serve.

Everything Ham Dip

1 (3-ounce) package cream cheese, softened
1/2 cup sour cream
1 tablespoon sherry
1 (5-ounce) can HORMEL® chunk ham, drained
    and flaked
2 tablespoons chopped water chestnuts
2 tablespoons minced onion
1/2 teaspoon dried dill weed
3 slices HORMEL® bacon, cooked and crumbled
3 tablespoons finely chopped pecans
    Melba toast, if desired

Beat cream cheese until light and fluffy. Add sour cream and sherry. Beat until smooth. Stir in ham, water chestnuts, onion and dill weed. Cover and refrigerate until chilled, about 1 hour. Stir in bacon and pecans just before serving. Serve with Melba toast, if desired.

Makes about 2 cups

Mini Taco Cups

(pictured at bottom right)

24 wonton wrappers
1 pound lean ground beef
1 packet (1.25 ounces) ORTEGA® Taco
   Seasoning Mix
1/2 cup plus 2 tablespoons ORTEGA® Thick
   & Chunky Salsa, divided
1 cup (4 ounces) shredded Mexican-blend
   cheese
   Additional ORTEGA® Thick & Chunky Salsa
   Sour cream (optional)
   B&G® Sliced Black Olives (optional)

Preheat oven to 425°F. Coat 24 mini muffin cups with nonstick cooking spray. Press wrappers into cups.

Cook and stir beef in medium skillet over medium heat until browned. Drain excess fat and discard. Stir in seasoning mix and 2 tablespoons salsa. Spoon mixture evenly into wonton cups. Top evenly with remaining 1/2 cup salsa and cheese.

Bake 8 minutes or until wontons are golden brown. Serve with additional salsa. Garnish with sour cream and olives, if desired. *Makes 24 servings*

Tip: For a deliciously different light lunch, press refrigerated rolls or biscuits into regular muffin cups, then fill with the seasoned ground beef mixture. Bake at the time and temperature suggested on the refrigerated roll package.

Karo Fiesta Krunch

8 cups popped corn
4 cups corn flakes
2 cups corn chips
1 cup tortilla chips
1 cup roasted peanuts
1/2 cup KARO® Light or Dark Corn Syrup
1/2 cup margarine
1/4 cup brown sugar, packed
1 package (1-1/4 ounces) taco seasoning mix

Preheat oven to 250°F. In large roasting pan, combine popped corn, corn flakes, corn chips, tortilla chips and peanuts.

In medium saucepan, combine corn syrup, margarine, brown sugar and taco seasoning. Bring to boil over medium-high heat, stirring constantly.

Pour over cornflake mixture; toss to coat well. Bake 60 minutes, stirring every 15 minutes. Cool, stirring frequently. Store in tightly covered container.
Makes 16 cups

Cheesy Quichettes

12 slices bacon, crisp-cooked and crumbled
6 eggs, beaten
1/4 cup milk
1-1/2 cups refrigerated shredded hash brown
   potatoes
1/4 cup chopped fresh parsley
1/2 teaspoon salt
1-1/2 cups (6 ounces) shredded Mexican cheese
   blend with jalapeño peppers, or sharp
   cheddar cheese

1. Preheat oven to 400°F. Lightly coat 12 standard (2-1/2-inch) muffin cups with nonstick cooking spray. Sprinkle bacon evenly into muffin cups.

2. Beat eggs and milk in large bowl. Add potatoes, parsley and salt; mix well. Spoon equal amounts into muffin cups. Bake 15 minutes or until knife inserted into centers comes out almost clean.

3. Sprinkle evenly with cheese. Let stand 3 minutes or until cheese melts. (Egg mixture will continue to cook while standing.*) To remove from pans, gently run knife around outer edges; lift out with fork.
Makes 12 quichettes

*Standing also allows for easier removal of quichettes from pan.

Mini Taco Cups

2. Combine turkey, onion mixture, bread crumbs, cream, egg, mint, salt and cayenne pepper in large bowl. Mix well; form 40 meatballs. Place meatballs on prepared baking sheets. Cover with plastic wrap; chill 1 hour.

3. Meanwhile, prepare Yogurt-Cucumber Sauce. Preheat oven to 400°F. Brush meatballs with remaining tablespoon oil. Bake 15 to 20 minutes, turning once during baking for even browning. Serve with sauce. *Makes 40 meatballs*

Yogurt-Cucumber Sauce

- 1 cup *or* 1 container (about 7 ounces) plain Greek-style yogurt
- 1/2 cup peeled, seeded and finely chopped cucumber
- 2 teaspoons chopped fresh mint
- 2 teaspoons grated lemon peel
- 2 teaspoons lemon juice
- 1/4 teaspoon salt

Combine all ingredients in small bowl. Refrigerate until ready to serve. *Makes about 1 cup*

Refried Bean and Corn Cakes

(pictured on page 6)

- 1 can (16 ounces) ORTEGA® Refried Beans
- 1 cup crushed ORTEGA® Taco Shells
- 1 egg
- 1 tablespoon ORTEGA® Fire-Roasted Diced Green Chiles
- 1/4 cup vegetable or corn oil
- 1/2 cup ORTEGA® Black Bean and Corn Salsa
  Sour cream (optional)
  Chopped fresh cilantro (optional)

Combine refried beans, taco shells, egg and chiles in large mixing bowl; stir well. Let stand 5 minutes.

Heat oil in large skillet. Drop bean mixture into pan by heaping tablespoonfuls; do not crowd pan. Mash into flat cakes with spatula. Fry cakes about 4 minutes; turn over and fry 4 minutes longer. Drain on paper towels. Cook remaining bean mixture in batches.

Spoon sour cream, if desired, and 1 tablespoon salsa on each cake. Garnish with cilantro, if desired. Serve warm or at room temperature.

Makes 6 to 8 servings

Turkey Meatballs with
Yogurt-Cucumber Sauce

Turkey Meatballs with Yogurt-Cucumber Sauce

(pictured above)

- 2 tablespoons olive oil, divided
- 1 cup finely chopped onion
- 2 garlic cloves, minced
- 1-1/4 pounds ground turkey or ground lamb
- 1/2 cup plain dry bread crumbs
- 1/4 cup whipping cream
- 1 egg, lightly beaten
- 3 tablespoons chopped fresh mint
- 1 teaspoon salt
- 1/8 teaspoon cayenne pepper
  Yogurt-Cucumber Sauce (recipe follows)

1. Line 2 baking sheets with parchment paper. Heat 1 tablespoon oil in medium skillet over medium-high heat. Cook and stir onion 3 minutes or until softened. Add garlic; cook and stir 30 seconds. Let cool slightly.

Apricot Brie en Croûte

(pictured below)

1 sheet frozen puff pastry (half of 17-1/4-ounce package)
1 round (8 ounces) Brie cheese
1/4 cup apricot preserves

1. Unfold puff pastry and thaw 20 minutes on lightly floured work surface. Preheat oven to 400°F. Line baking sheet with parchment paper.

2. Roll out puff pastry to 12-inch square. Place Brie in center of square; spread preserves over top of Brie.

3. Gather up edges of puff pastry and bring together over center of Brie, covering cheese entirely. Pinch pastry edges together to seal. Transfer to prepared baking sheet.

4. Bake 20 to 25 minutes or until golden brown. (If top of pastry browns too quickly, cover loosely with small piece of foil.) Serve warm.

Makes 6 servings

Extra: For added flavor and texture, sprinkle 2 tablespoons sliced almonds over the preserves. Proceed with wrapping and baking the Brie as directed above.

Edamame Frittata

2 tablespoons olive oil
1/2 cup frozen shelled edamame
1/3 cup frozen corn
1/4 cup chopped shallot (1 shallot)
5 eggs
3/4 teaspoon Italian seasoning
1/2 teaspoon salt
1/2 teaspoon pepper
1/4 cup chopped green onions (about 4)
1/2 cup crumbled goat cheese

1. Preheat broiler. Heat olive oil in large broilerproof skillet over medium-high heat. Add edamame, corn and shallot. Cook and stir 6 to 8 minutes or until shallot is brown and edamame is hot.

2. Meanwhile, beat eggs, seasoning, salt and pepper in medium bowl. Stir in green onions. Pour egg mixture over vegetables in skillet. Sprinkle with cheese. Cook over medium heat 5 to 7 minutes or until eggs are set on bottom, lifting up mixture to allow uncooked portion to flow underneath.

3. Broil 7 inches from heat about 1 minute or until top is puffy and golden. Loosen frittata from skillet with spatula; slide onto small platter. Cut into wedges to serve.

Makes 4 servings

Apricot Brie en Croûte

Hot Cheesy Chili Dip

Hot Cheesy Chili Dip

(pictured above)

1 pound lean ground beef
1/2 cup chopped onion
1 package (1 pound) pasteurized process cheese
    spread with jalapeño pepper, cut into cubes
1 can (15 ounces) kidney beans, drained
1 bottle (12 ounces) HEINZ® Chili Sauce
1/4 cup chopped fresh parsley
    Tortilla chips or crackers

In large saucepan, cook beef and onion until onion is tender; drain. Stir in cheese, beans and chili sauce; heat, stirring until cheese is melted. Stir in parsley. Serve warm with tortilla chips or crackers.

Makes about 5 cups

Guacamole

2 avocados, mashed
1/4 cup red salsa (mild or hot, according to taste)
3 tablespoons NEWMAN'S OWN® Salad
    Dressing
2 tablespoons lime or lemon juice
1 clove garlic, finely minced
    Salt and black pepper

Combine all ingredients and mix well. Chill for 1 to 2 hours tightly covered. Serve with tortilla chips.

Makes about 2 cups

Blue Cheese Mushrooms

1 pound medium fresh mushrooms
1/4 cup sliced green onions
1 tablespoon butter or margarine
1 package (4 ounces) ATHENOS Crumbled Blue
    Cheese
3 ounces PHILADELPHIA® Cream Cheese,
    softened

PREHEAT broiler. Remove stems from mushrooms; chop stems. Cook and stir stems and onions in butter in small skillet on medium heat until tender.

ADD blue cheese and cream cheese; mix well. Spoon evenly into mushroom caps; place on rack of broiler pan.

BROIL 2 to 3 minutes or until golden brown. Serve warm. *Makes about 2 dozen or 24 servings, 1 mushroom each.*

Sweet 'N' Salty Clusters

1 bag popped JOLLY TIME® Blast O Butter
    Microwave Pop Corn (about 10-12 cups)
1 cup mini pretzel twists
10 ounces white chocolate or almond bark,
    chopped
3/4 cup semi-sweet chocolate chips

1. Place popped pop corn in large bowl; remove any unpopped kernels. Stir in pretzels.

2. Microwave white chocolate in large glass measuring cup on HIGH 1 to 1-1/2 minutes, or until chocolate is shiny. Stir until completely melted. Pour over pop corn and pretzels; mix until evenly coated. Spread mixture onto cookie sheet.

3. Microwave semi-sweet chocolate chips in clean glass measuring cup on HIGH 30 seconds, or until chocolate is shiny. Stir until smooth. Drizzle over pop corn mixture; cool completely. Break into clusters. Store tightly covered.

Makes 8 servings

helpful hint

Instead of serving snacks and nut mixes in one big bowl, fill several small bowls and place them around the room for easy access by guests.

Southwestern Popcorn Shrimp Dip

1 carton (20 ounces) SEAPAK® Popcorn Shrimp
1 cup mayonnaise
1 chipotle pepper in adobo sauce, minced (about 1 tablespoon)
2 cups frozen corn, thawed
1 large red pepper, diced (about 1-1/2 cups)
1 bunch of green onions, thinly sliced (about 1 cup)
   Crackers or crostini

Prepare the shrimp according to package directions. Roughly chop shrimp and set aside.

Stir mayonnaise and chipotle pepper in adobo sauce in large bowl. Add the chopped cooked shrimp, corn, red pepper and green onions. Toss to coat.

Scoop shrimp mixture into a serving bowl and serve with crackers or crostini.   *Makes 8 servings*

Rustic Tuscany Bread

1 loaf (1 pound) frozen bread dough
   PAM® Original No-Stick Cooking Spray
1 tablespoon olive oil
1/4 teaspoon salt
1/4 teaspoon cracked black pepper
1 can (14.5 ounces) HUNT'S® Diced Tomatoes with Basil, Garlic & Oregano, well drained
1/2 cup (2 ounces) shredded Cheddar cheese
1/2 cup (2 ounces) shredded mozzarella cheese

1. Thaw bread dough according to package directions. Preheat oven to 400°F. Spray baking sheet with cooking spray; set aside.

2. Pat out dough into 12×10-inch rectangle on prepared baking sheet. Brush lightly with olive oil; sprinkle evenly with salt and pepper. Spoon tomatoes lengthwise down center third of dough; sprinkle evenly with Cheddar cheese and mozzarella cheese. Fold long sides of dough over filling; press seams together to seal. Using sharp knife, cut 3 diagonal slices, about 2 inches apart, in top of dough, cutting through first layer. Repeat with second set of cuts in opposite direction, criss-crossing first cuts, to form diamond pattern.

3. Bake 25 minutes, or until golden brown. Cool slightly. Cut into 12 slices to serve.
          Makes 6 servings

Chipotle-Spiced Nuts

(pictured below)

1 pound mixed nuts
4 tablespoons butter, melted
2 tablespoons ORTEGA® Chipotle Taco Seasoning Mix
1 tablespoon light brown sugar

Preheat oven to 325°F. Toss nuts, butter, seasoning mix and brown sugar in large bowl until well combined.

Spread nut mixture on baking pan. Bake 20 minutes, stirring after 10 minutes. Serve warm, if desired. To store, allow to cool, and place in airtight container for up to 2 weeks.   *Makes 1 pound*

Tip: Try sprinkling these nuts over your favorite ice cream for a flavorful "hot" and cold dessert.

Note: For gift-giving to friends and family, pack these deliciously spicy nuts in a decorative tin can. You can share the recipe on a gift tag, too!

Chipotle-Spiced Nuts

Beef Empanadas

(pictured at right)

1 tablespoon olive oil
3 tablespoons finely chopped onion
1 garlic clove, minced
1/4 pound ground beef
2 tablespoons chopped pimiento-stuffed green olives
2 tablespoons raisins
2 tablespoons ketchup
1 tablespoon chopped fresh parsley
1/2 teaspoon ground cumin
1 sheet frozen puff pastry (half of 17-1/4-ounce package)
1 egg yolk

1. Preheat oven to 400°F. Line baking sheet with parchment paper.

2. Heat olive oil in large skillet over medium-high heat. Add onion and garlic. Cook and stir 2 to 3 minutes. Crumble ground beef into skillet. Brown beef 6 to 8 minutes, stirring to break up meat. Drain fat. Add olives, raisins, ketchup, parsley and cumin; cook and stir 1 to 2 minutes.

3. Roll out pastry sheet to 12×12-inch square on lightly floured surface. Cut square into nine 4-inch squares. Place rounded tablespoonful of filling on each square. Fold over to form triangle; seal edges with fork. Place on baking sheet. Bake 18 to 20 minutes or until golden brown. Serve immediately.   *Makes 9 empanadas*

Crispy Baked Potato Wedges

2 medium baking potatoes
2 tablespoons unsalted butter
1 tablespoon MRS. DASH® Original Blend
2 tablespoons grated Parmesan cheese

1. Preheat oven to 375°F.

2. Scrub potatoes and pat dry. Cut each potato lengthwise to make eight wedges.

3. Combine butter and MRS. DASH® Original Blend in small saucepan and heat until butter is melted.

4. Dip potato wedges in butter mixture, turning to coat all sides. Arrange potato wedges cut side down in a single layer in 15×10-inch jelly-roll pan. Spoon remaining butter mixture over potatoes. Sprinkle evenly with cheese.

5. Bake 30 minutes or until golden brown and edges are crisp. Drain on paper towels.

Makes 4 servings

Cool Veggie Pizza Appetizer

2 cans (8 ounces each) refrigerated crescent dinner rolls
1 package (8 ounces) PHILADELPHIA® Cream Cheese, softened
1/2 cup MIRACLE WHIP® Dressing
1 teaspoon dill weed
1/2 teaspoon onion salt
1 cup broccoli florets
1 cup chopped green bell pepper
1 cup chopped seeded tomato
1/4 cup chopped red onion

PREHEAT oven to 375°F. Separate dough into 4 rectangles. Press onto bottom and up side of 15×10×1-inch baking pan to form crust.

BAKE 11 to 13 minutes or until golden brown; cool.

MIX cream cheese, dressing, dill and onion salt until well blended. Spread over crust; top with remaining ingredients. Refrigerate. Cut into squares.
Makes 32 servings.

Great Substitute: Substitute chopped cucumbers, shredded carrot and/or red bell peppers for any of the chopped vegetables.

Hawaiian Pizza Bites

1 canister (13.9 ounces) refrigerated pizza crust dough
3/4 cup pizza sauce
1-1/2 cups (6 ounces) shredded mozzarella cheese
3 ounces sliced Canadian bacon, cut into small pieces
1 can (8 ounces) DOLE® Pineapple Tidbits or 1 can (20 ounces) DOLE® Pineapple Chunks, drained

• Unroll dough onto lightly floured surface. Cut 15 to 16 circles with 3-inch cookie or biscuit cutter and place them on cookie sheet sprayed with nonstick vegetable cooking spray.

• Bake at 400°F., 8 minutes. Remove from oven. Top crusts with pizza sauce, one-half cheese, Canadian bacon and pineapple tidbits. Top with remaining cheese.

• Bake an additional 6 to 10 minutes or until crusts are golden brown.   *Makes 15 to 16 pizza bites*

Lawry's® Grilled Chicken Nachos

2. Meanwhile, in medium bowl, combine tomatoes, chili, LAWRY'S® Garlic Salt and LAWRY'S® Seasoned Pepper; set aside.

3. Remove chicken and onion from Marinade, discarding Marinade. Grill chicken and onion, turning once and brushing with additional 1/4 cup Marinade, 10 minutes or until chicken is thoroughly cooked and onion is tender. Shred chicken and chop onion.

4. In medium bowl, combine chicken, onion and remaining 2 tablespoons Marinade. In center of double layer (18×18-inch pieces) heavy-duty aluminum foil, arrange tortilla chips, then top with chicken mixture and cheese. Grill 1 minute or until cheese is melted. To serve, top with tomato mixture, drained if desired, avocado and lime juice.

Makes 6 servings

Party Cheese Ball

2 packages (8 ounces each) PHILADELPHIA®
    Cream Cheese, softened
1 package (8 ounces) KRAFT® Shredded Sharp
    Cheddar Cheese
1 tablespoon finely chopped onions
1 tablespoon chopped red bell peppers
2 teaspoons Worcestershire sauce
1 teaspoon lemon juice
    Dash ground red pepper (cayenne)
    Dash salt
1 cup chopped PLANTERS® Pecans

BEAT cream cheese and Cheddar cheese in small bowl with electric mixer on medium speed until well blended.

MIX in all remaining ingredients except pecans; cover. Refrigerate several hours or overnight.

SHAPE into ball; roll in pecans. Serve with assorted NABISCO Crackers.

Makes 24 servings, 2 tablespoons each.

Variation: Mix cream cheese mixture as directed; shape into log or 24 small balls, each about 1 inch in diameter. Roll in pecans until evenly coated. Serve as directed.

Substitution: Substitute pimientos for the red bell peppers.

Lawry's® Grilled Chicken Nachos

(pictured above)

3/4 cup plus 2 tablespoons LAWRY'S® Herb
    & Garlic Marinade With Lemon Juice
1 pound boneless, skinless chicken breasts
1 medium onion, cut into 1/2-inch thick slices
3 medium tomatoes, chopped
1 serrano chili, seeded and finely chopped
1/2 teaspoon LAWRY'S® Garlic Salt
1/4 teaspoon LAWRY'S® Seasoned Pepper
1 bag (11 ounces) plain tortilla chips
2 cups shredded cheddar or Monterey Jack
    cheese (about 8 ounces)
1 avocado, diced
1 tablespoon lime juice

1. In large resealable plastic bag, pour 1/2 cup LAWRY'S® Herb & Garlic Marinade With Lemon Juice over chicken and onion; turn to coat. Close bag and marinate in refrigerator 30 minutes.

Spicy Polenta Cheese Bites

3 cups water
1 cup corn grits
1/2 teaspoon salt
1/4 teaspoon chili powder
1 tablespoon butter
1/4 cup minced onion or shallot
1 tablespoon minced jalapeño pepper*
1/2 cup shredded sharp cheddar cheese or fontina cheese

Jalapeño peppers can sting and irritate the skin, so wear rubber gloves when handling peppers and do not touch eyes.

1. Grease 8-inch square pan. Bring water to a boil in large nonstick saucepan over high heat. Slowly add grits, stirring constantly. Reduce heat to low. Cook, stirring frequently, until grits absorb water and become tender. Stir in salt and chili powder.

2. Melt butter in small saucepan. Add onion and jalapeño. Cook and stir over medium-high heat 3 to 5 minutes or until tender. Add to corn mixture; stir to mix well. Spread in prepared pan. Set aside 1 hour or until cool and firm.

3. Preheat broiler and set rack 4 inches from heat. Cut polenta into 16 squares. Sprinkle with cheese. Carefully lift out squares; arrange on nonstick baking sheet. Broil 5 minutes or until cheese melts and becomes slightly browned. Remove immediately. Cut each square in half. (Polenta will become firm as it cools.) *Makes 32 appetizers*

Tip: For spicier flavor, add 1/8 to 1/4 teaspoon crushed red pepper flakes to the onion-jalapeño mixture.

Crunchy Coconut Shrimp

1-1/3 cups *French's®* French Fried Onions
1/3 cup flaked, sweetened coconut
1 pound large shrimp, shelled and deveined
2 egg whites, beaten

1. Place French Fried Onions and coconut into plastic bag. Lightly crush with hands or rolling pin.

2. Dip shrimp into egg whites. Coat with onion mixture, pressing firmly to adhere.

3. Bake shrimp at 400°F for 10 minutes until shrimp are fully cooked and crispy. *Makes 4 servings*

Variation: Add 1 teaspoon curry powder to crushed onions.

Mini New Potato Bites

1-1/2 pounds new potatoes (about 15 potatoes)
4 ounces (1/2 of 8-ounce package) PHILADELPHIA® Cream Cheese, softened
2 tablespoons BREAKSTONE'S® or KNUDSEN® Sour Cream
2 tablespoons KRAFT® 100% Grated Parmesan Cheese
4 slices OSCAR MAYER® Bacon, cooked, crumbled
2 tablespoons snipped fresh chives

PLACE potatoes in large saucepan; add enough water to cover. Bring to boil. Reduce heat to medium-low; cook 15 minutes or until potatoes are tender.

MIX cream cheese, sour cream and Parmesan cheese; cover. Refrigerate until ready to use.

DRAIN potatoes. Cool slightly. Cut potatoes in half; cut small piece from bottom of each potato half so potato lies flat. Place on serving platter. Top each potato half with 1 teaspoon of the cream cheese mixture. Sprinkle with bacon and chives.
Makes 15 servings, 2 topped potato halves each.

Make Ahead: These potatoes are delicious served hot or cold.

Substitution: Substitute PHILADELPHIA Chive & Onion Cream Cheese Spread for the regular cream cheese for added flavor.

Avocado Lime Cream Bites

2 medium ripe avocados
1 tablespoon MRS. DASH® Garlic & Herb Seasoning Blend
2 tablespoons fresh lime juice
1/2 teaspoon hot sauce
20 small round tortilla chips
10 cherry tomatoes

1. Peel, pit, dice and mash avocados. Add MRS. DASH® Garlic & Herb, lime juice and hot sauce; mix well.

2. Cover mixture and chill until ready to serve.

3. Spoon avocado mixture on small round corn chips. Slice cherry tomatoes and place on top.
Makes 5 servings

Deviled Ham Finger Sandwiches

Deviled Ham
Finger Sandwiches

(pictured above)

**1 package (8 ounces) PHILADELPHIA® Cream
Cheese, softened
1 can (4.25 ounces) deviled ham
1/4 cup KRAFT® Mayo Real Mayonnaise
10 small stuffed green olives, finely chopped
36 slices white bread, crusts removed**

MIX cream cheese, ham, mayo and olives until well
blended.

SPREAD each of 18 of the bread slices with about
2 tablespoons of the cream cheese mixture. Cover
with remaining bread slices to make 18 sandwiches.

CUT each sandwich into quarters.
Makes 18 servings, 4 sandwich quarters each.

Make Ahead: Prepare cream cheese mixture
as directed. Cover and refrigerate up to 5 days.
Spread onto bread slices and continue as directed.
For easier spreading, mix 1 tablespoon milk with
chilled cream cheese mixture before spreading
onto bread slices. Or prepare sandwiches as
directed, but do not cut into quarters. Wrap in
plastic wrap. Refrigerate until ready to serve. Cut
into quarters just before serving.

Substitution: Substitute **MIRACLE WHIP** Dressing
for the mayo.

Potato and Cheese Filled
Pot Stickers

**2 cups SIMPLY POTATOES® Mashed Potatoes
1/3 cup CRYSTAL FARMS® Finely Shredded
Cheddar cheese
3 tablespoons finely chopped red bell pepper
2 tablespoons finely chopped green onion
1 package (12 ounces) pot sticker wraps
3 to 4 tablespoons vegetable oil**

**DIPPING SAUCE INGREDIENTS
1/2 cup soy sauce
1 teaspoon sesame oil
1 teaspoon sesame seeds**

1. Combine Simply Potatoes®, cheese, red pepper
and green onion in medium bowl; mix well. Place
10 pot sticker wraps on work surface. Spoon
2 generous teaspoons mashed potato mixture in
center of each wrap. Lightly brush edges of each
wrap with water. Fold wrap in half forming a half
moon; press edges together to seal.

2. Continue working in batches of 10, filling all pot
sticker wraps. (Pot stickers can be assembled,
covered and refrigerated up to 4 hours before
frying.)

3. To fry: Heat 1 tablespoon oil in 12-inch nonstick
skillet over medium-high heat. Swirl pan to evenly
spread oil in bottom of skillet. Place 10 pot stickers
in single layer in skillet. Cook 2 to 3 minutes or until
one side is light golden brown. Flip each pot sticker;
continue cooking 1 to 2 minutes or until light golden
brown on other side. Continue cooking pot stickers
in batches of 10, using more oil as needed.

4. Meanwhile, combine all sauce ingredients in small
bowl. Serve pot stickers with dipping sauce.
Makes 40 pot stickers

helpful hint

*How many appetizers will you need? Plan on
4 to 6 servings per person before dinner. For an
appetizer buffet, plan on 8 to 10 servings
per person.*

Bacon Appetizer Crescents

(pictured on page 6)

      1 package (8 ounces) PHILADELPHIA® Cream
         Cheese, softened
      8 slices OSCAR MAYER® Bacon, crisply cooked,
         crumbled
  1/3 cup KRAFT® 100% Grated Parmesan Cheese
  1/4 cup finely chopped onion
      2 tablespoons chopped fresh parsley
      1 tablespoon milk
      2 cans (8 ounces each) refrigerated crescent
         dinner rolls

PREHEAT oven to 375°F. Mix cream cheese, bacon,
Parmesan cheese, onion, parsley and milk until well
blended; set aside.

SEPARATE each can of dough into 8 triangles.
Spread each triangle with 1 rounded tablespoonful
of cream cheese mixture. Cut each triangle
lengthwise into 3 narrow triangles. Roll up, starting
at wide ends. Place point-side down on greased
baking sheet.

BAKE 12 to 15 minutes or until golden brown. Serve
warm.   *Makes 4 dozen or 24 servings,*
                           2 crescents each.

Jazz It Up: Sprinkle lightly with poppy seeds
before baking.

Tangy Baked Wings

(pictured at right)

      1 pouch CAMPBELL'S® Dry Onion Soup and
         Recipe Mix
  1/3 cup honey
      2 tablespoons spicy-brown mustard
    18 chicken wings (about 3 pounds)

1. Stir the soup mix, honey and mustard with a
spoon in a large bowl.

2. Cut the chicken wings at the joints into 54 pieces.
Discard the tips or save for another use. Put the
wings in the bowl. Toss to coat with the soup
mixture. Place the wings on a large shallow-sided
baking pan.

3. Bake at 400°F. for 45 minutes or until the wings
are cooked through, turning halfway during cooking.
                         Makes 36 appetizers

Wisconsin Three-Cheese Taco Dip

     12 ounces cream cheese, softened
   1/2 cup dairy sour cream
       2 teaspoons chili powder
 1-1/2 teaspoons ground cumin
   1/8 teaspoon ground red pepper
   1/2 cup salsa
       2 cups shredded lettuce or lettuce leaves
       1 cup (4 ounces) shredded Wisconsin Cheddar
          cheese
       1 cup (4 ounces) shredded Wisconsin Monterey
          Jack cheese
   1/2 cup diced plum tomatoes
   1/3 cup sliced green onions
   1/4 cup sliced ripe olives
   1/4 cup pimiento-stuffed green olives
          Tortilla chips and blue corn chips

Combine cream cheese, sour cream, chili powder,
cumin and red pepper in large bowl; mix until
well blended. Stir in salsa. Spread onto 10-inch
serving platter lined with lettuce. Top with cheeses,
tomatoes, green onions and olives. Serve with chips.
                              Makes 10 servings

Favorite recipe from **Wisconsin Milk Marketing
Board**

Tangy Baked Wings

The Cheese Tray

Timeless cheese and crackers are the easiest and most welcome addition to any appetizer buffet or party. Go beyond the store-brand cheddar and serve up a cheese tray with a few tasty varieties.

- Select three to four cheeses. Too many cheeses can confuse the palate.

- Visit a specialty cheese shop or deli to check out the array of cheese selections. Ask the manager for suggestions on which cheeses to select for a cheese tray sampler.

- The most important rule is to serve cheese at room temperature so the rich flavors can be appreciated. Take the cheese out of the refrigerator at least 30 minutes before serving.

Ideas for Cheese Tray Samplers

- Serve several types of cheddar, such as one each from England, Oregon and Vermont.

- Always include a variety of textures—from creamy to firm—and a variety of flavors—from mild to sharp.

- Create cheese trays from a particular country like a French or Italian sampler.

Cracker & Bread Pairings

- Choose crackers that won't compete with very flavorful cheeses. For example, crisp and plain water crackers work with almost all cheeses. Wheat crackers are also a good selection because they add texture; however, spicy crackers tend to overtake the flavor of the cheese.

- Fresh, crusty bread is always a good choice for serving with cheese. Choose long narrow loaves or baguettes and cut into thin slices.

- To make French bread toasts or crostini, brush thin bread slices with olive oil, then bake in a 375°F oven for 5 minutes or until they are browned and crispy.

Don't Forget the Fruit, Olives and Nuts

- When in doubt about what type of fruit to serve with cheese, choose grapes, an easy and perfect fruit for a cheese tray.

- For a contrast in texture, serve crisp carrot or celery sticks or even apple or pear slices with softer cheeses.

- When serving salty cheeses such as Parmesan or Asiago, pair them with something sweet like fresh or dried fruit, especially apricots and figs.

- Look for tangy fruit pastes like quince or plum. Top a wheat cracker with a thin slice of cheese like white cheddar or manchego. Arrange a thin slice of fruit paste over the cheese for a fruit and cheese combination that everyone will love.

- Stop by the olive bar at the supermarket and pick up a variety of olives, the perfect addition to cheese samplers. (Don't forget to serve with a small dish for the pits.)

- If you pick herbed olives, try heating them to bring out their flavor. Heat in the oven at 350°F for 15 to 20 minutes and serve warm.

- For yet another classic addition, choose toasted nuts (see page 13) or a snack mix (see page 8).

Dips

Dips are very easy to make at the last minute without heading to the store. Just get out the food processor or blender and combine ingredients you already have in the refrigerator for a hasty, tasty dip.

- For creamy dips, start with a base such as cream cheese, sour cream or even cottage cheese. Add a handful of fresh herbs, roasted peppers or onions, blue cheese or olives. Heighten the flavor with fresh garlic and thin with a little olive oil, milk or cream. Serve with any type of chips, crackers or sliced crusty bread you have available.

- For chunky dips, chop avocados, mangos or apples. Add chopped tomatoes, celery or diced red peppers. Toss with a little citrus juice or olive oil for a refreshing crunchy treat.

- Purée or coarsely mash a can of beans. Combine with garlic, olive oil and herbs for another instant dip or spread.

- To keep a dip warm, serve in a microwavable container so you can reheat it if it gets cold during the party. Or, serve in a small slow cooker set on LOW heat.

- To make dips more healthful, use reduced-fat sour cream or mayonnaise.

Dippers

Most dips can be paired with a wide variety of dippers. Dipper possibilities include:

- **Crispy snacks:** Potato, bagel or tortilla chips, or even breadsticks, pita bread wedges or toast points.

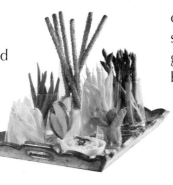

- **Crudités:** Generous amounts of cut-up fresh vegetables such as carrot sticks, celery sticks, broccoli or cauliflower florets, Chinese pea pods or snow peas, radishes and asparagus. To keep them crispy, plunge in ice water one hour before serving. Drain well and keep refrigerated until ready to serve.

Make-Ahead Appetizers

Tackling the prep work in advance gives you breathing room for all the other fun cooking before a party.

- Appetizers such as empanadas, made with filling wrapped in pastry (such as those on page 14), can be formed but not baked. Place uncooked empanadas in a single layer on baking sheets and freeze. Transfer frozen empanadas to resealable freezer food storage bags; seal and freeze up to one month. To serve, place frozen empanadas on ungreased baking sheets. Bake as directed in the recipe.

- Homemade meatballs are another great appetizer to make ahead. Place cooked meatballs in a resealable freezer food storage bag and freeze up to one month. Thaw in the refrigerator and cook until thoroughly heated.

- Dips make wonderful make-ahead appetizers—after all, most dips taste better as they sit. Most creamy dips and spreads can be stored in an airtight container and chilled for up to one week. To serve, let stand at room temperature 30 minutes and stir before serving.

- Addictive nut mixes are terrific snacks that can be prepared at least a week in advance. Be sure to make more than you think—they always go quickly and it's hard not to munch on them before the party.

Salads

Grilled Chicken & Veggie Macaroni Salad

(pictured at left)

1/2 cup LAWRY'S® Herb & Garlic Marinade With
    Lemon Juice
3/4 pound boneless, skinless chicken breasts
    1 medium sweet onion, cut into 1/2-inch slices
    1 medium red bell pepper, quartered and seeded
    2 stalks celery
    1 cup HELLMANN'S® or BEST FOODS® Real Mayonnaise
    2 tablespoons white vinegar
1-1/2 teaspoons LAWRY'S® Seasoned Salt
    1 teaspoon sugar
1/2 teaspoon LAWRY'S® Seasoned Pepper
    8 ounces elbow macaroni, cooked, rinsed with cold water
    and drained

1. In separate large resealable plastic bags, pour 1/4 cup LAWRY'S® Herb & Garlic Marinade With Lemon Juice over chicken and 1/4 cup Marinade over vegetables; turn to coat. Close bags and marinate in refrigerator 30 minutes.

2. Remove chicken and vegetables from Marinade; discard Marinade. Grill or broil chicken and vegetables, turning once, 10 minutes or until chicken is thoroughly cooked and vegetables are tender; cool slightly, then chop.

3. In large bowl, combine remaining ingredients except macaroni. Stir in macaroni, chicken and vegetables. Serve chilled or at room temperature. *Makes 8 servings*

Note: Also terrific with any of your favorite LAWRY'S® Marinades.

Tip: For creamier salad, add additional Mayonnaise.

Clockwise from top left: *Ravioli Panzanella Salad (p. 24), Festive Cranberry Pineapple Salad (p. 38), Grilled Chicken & Veggie Macaroni Salad, Bulgur, Tuna, Tomato and Avocado Salad (p. 32)*

Santa Fe BBQ Ranch Salad

(pictured at right)

1 cup *Cattlemen's®* Golden Honey Barbecue
    Sauce, divided
1/2 cup ranch salad dressing
1 pound boneless, skinless chicken
12 cups washed and torn Romaine lettuce
1 small red onion, thinly sliced
1 small ripe avocado, diced 1/2-inch
4 ripe plum tomatoes, sliced
2 cups shredded Monterey Jack cheese
1/2 cup cooked, crumbled bacon

1. Prepare BBQ Ranch Dressing: Combine 1/2 cup
barbecue sauce and salad dressing in small bowl;
reserve.

2. Grill or broil chicken over medium-high heat
10 minutes until no longer pink in center. Cut into
strips and toss with remaining 1/2 cup barbecue
sauce.

3. Toss lettuce, onion, avocado, tomatoes, cheese
and bacon in large bowl. Portion on salad plates,
dividing evenly. Top with chicken and serve with
BBQ Ranch Dressing.   *Makes 4 servings*

Ravioli Panzanella Salad

(pictured on page 22)

1 package (9 ounces) refrigerated fresh cheese
    ravioli or tortellini
2 tablespoons olive oil
2 teaspoons white wine vinegar
1/8 teaspoon pepper
1 cup halved grape tomatoes *or* 1 large tomato,
    chopped
1/2 cup sliced pimiento-stuffed olives
1/4 cup finely chopped celery
1 large shallot, finely chopped *or* 1/4 cup finely
    chopped red onion
1/4 cup finely chopped Italian parsley

1. Cook ravioli according to package directions;
drain well. Transfer to large serving bowl; set aside
to cool 10 minutes.

2. Whisk oil, vinegar and pepper in small bowl until
well blended. Add to ravioli with tomatoes, olives,
celery and shallot; toss gently. Sprinkle with parsley.
          Makes 4 to 6 servings

Turkey, Mandarin and Poppy Seed Salad

1/4 cup orange juice
1-1/2 tablespoons red wine vinegar
1-1/2 teaspoons poppy seeds
1-1/2 teaspoons olive oil
1 teaspoon Dijon-style mustard
1/8 teaspoon ground pepper
5 cups torn stemmed washed red leaf lettuce
2 cups torn stemmed washed spinach
1/2 pound honey roasted turkey breast, cut into
    1/2-inch julienne strips
1 can (10-1/2 ounces) mandarin oranges,
    drained

In small bowl, combine orange juice, vinegar, poppy
seeds, oil, mustard and pepper. Set aside. In large
bowl, toss together lettuce, spinach, turkey and
oranges. Pour dressing over turkey mixture and
serve immediately.   *Makes 4 servings*

Favorite recipe from **National Turkey Federation**

Nutty Pear Slaw

3 cups (8 ounces) coleslaw mix, packaged
1 can (15 ounces) Bartlett pear halves, chopped
1/2 cup dry roasted peanuts
DRESSING
1/4 cup olive or vegetable oil
2 tablespoons orange juice
2 tablespoons white wine vinegar
1-1/2 teaspoons Dijon-style mustard
1/2 teaspoon onion salt
1/4 teaspoon black pepper, coarsely ground

In small bowl, combine dressing ingredients, whisk
until blended. In large bowl, combine coleslaw mix
and pears. Add dressing; toss lightly to coat. Add
chopped peanuts; re-toss just before serving.
          Makes 8 servings

Favorite recipe from **Pacific Northwest Canned
Pear Service**

helpful hint

*The classic ratio for vinaigrette is 3 parts oil
to 1 part acid (vinegar, lemon or lime juice). For
a milder dressing, use 4 parts oil to 1 part acid.*

Greek Pasta Salad

(pictured at right)

6 cups cooked rotini or penne
1-1/2 cups diced cucumber
2 medium tomatoes, diced
1 medium green bell pepper, diced
2 ounces feta cheese, finely crumbled
12 medium pitted black olives, sliced into thirds
1/4 cup chopped fresh dill *or* 2 teaspoons
    dried dill
Juice of 1/2 lemon
1/4 teaspoon salt
1/8 teaspoon pepper

Mix all ingredients together in large bowl. Chill until ready to serve.   *Makes 8 servings*

Chicken Pear Salad with Blue Cheese

6 cups salad greens
1-1/4 cups cooked chicken or smoked turkey strips
1 yellow or green bell pepper, cut into bite-size
    pieces or cut into strips and halved
1 can (15 ounces) DEL MONTE® Lite Sliced
    Pears, drained
1/2 cup reduced-calorie, fat-free or regular blue
    cheese salad dressing
Cracked black pepper
Crumbled blue cheese

1. In large bowl, toss greens, chicken and bell pepper. Arrange on 4 dinner plates.

2. Arrange pears on top. Drizzle with dressing; sprinkle with black pepper and cheese, if desired.
          Makes 4 servings

Quick Spinach Salad

1 package (10 ounces) spinach leaves, washed
    and torn into bite-size pieces
4 slices bacon, cooked and crumbled
2 hard-cooked eggs, sliced (optional)
3/4 cup blue cheese salad dressing
1 cup PEPPERIDGE FARM® Generous Cut
    Cracked Pepper & Parmesan Cheese
    Croutons

Toss spinach, bacon, eggs and dressing in a large bowl until evenly coated. Top with croutons.
          Makes 6 servings

Loaded, Baked Potato Salad

4 pounds IDAHO® potatoes, peeled
1 pound bacon, crisply cooked, and chopped
    into 1/2-inch pieces (fat reserved, if desired)
2 cups grated or shredded Cheddar cheese
1-1/2 cups sour cream (regular or low-fat)
4 ounces unsalted butter, softened
1/2 cup chopped green onions
1 tablespoon black pepper
1 teaspoon salt

1. Cook whole potatoes in boiling, unsalted water until tender. Refrigerate until chilled, then chop into 1-inch pieces.

2. Transfer the potatoes to a large bowl along with the remaining ingredients and thoroughly combine. Add some of the reserved bacon fat, if desired.

3. Chill at least 2 hours before serving. Adjust the seasoning prior to serving.   *Makes 2 quarts*

Note: Any condiments or toppings typically added to a loaded baked potato may be used for this recipe.

Fruited Turkey Salad

1 cup diced turkey
3/4 cup diced celery
1 tablespoon minced onion
1/2 teaspoon salt
2 cups uncooked salad macaroni (rings,
    juniorettes or shells)
1 cup drained Mandarin oranges
1 cup seedless green grapes
8 ounces pineapple or lemon yogurt
1/2 cup mayonnaise-type salad dressing

Mix turkey, celery, onion and salt. Cover and refrigerate overnight.

Cook macaroni according to package directions; drain, rinse with cold water and drain thoroughly. Add macaroni to turkey mixture; stir in Mandarin oranges and grapes. Mix yogurt and salad dressing. Fold into salad. Refrigerate several hours to allow flavors to blend.   *Makes 4 servings*

Favorite recipe from **North Dakota Wheat Commission**

Pesto Rice Salad

(pictured below)

2 cups MINUTE® White Rice, uncooked
1 package (7 ounces) basil pesto sauce
1 cup cherry tomatoes, halved
8 ounces whole-milk mozzarella cheese,
    cut into 1/2-inch cubes
1/3 cup shredded Parmesan cheese
Toasted pine nuts (optional)

Prepare rice according to package directions. Place in large bowl. Let stand 10 minutes. Add pesto sauce; mix well. Gently stir in tomatoes and cheese. Serve warm or cover and refrigerate until ready to serve. Sprinkle with pine nuts, if desired.

Makes 6 servings

Tip: To toast pine nuts, spread in single layer in heavy-bottomed skillet. Cook over medium heat 1 to 2 minutes, stirring frequently, until nuts are lightly browned. Remove from skillet immediately. Cool before using.

Pesto Rice Salad

Orange Delight

2 packages (4-serving size) orange-flavored
    gelatin
2 cups hot water
2 cups cottage cheese
1 can (20 ounces) crushed pineapple,
    well-drained
1 cup pecans
1 cup orange juice
1 cup pineapple juice
1/2 cup mayonnaise
6 tablespoons sugar
1 pint whipping cream, whipped to stiff peaks

1. Dissolve gelatin in hot water in large serving bowl. Set aside.

2. Meanwhile, place cottage cheese in strainer; drain thoroughly.

3. When gelatin has cooled and thickened, stir in cottage cheese and all remaining ingredients except whipped cream. Refrigerate until cool but not set; fold in whipped cream. Refrigerate 1 hour or until ready to serve.   *Makes 8 to 10 servings*

Potato, Cucumber and Dill Salad

3 large IDAHO® Potatoes, unpeeled and
    thinly sliced
1/4 cup rice wine vinegar
1/4 cup canola or vegetable oil
1-1/2 tablespoons Dijon mustard
1/2 cup chopped fresh dill, or 1 tablespoon
    dried whole dill weed
1/2 teaspoon salt
1 large cucumber, unpeeled and thinly sliced

1. Place potato slices in a 9-inch square microwave-safe baking dish; cover with microwaveable plastic wrap and microwave on HIGH 9 to 11 minutes or until tender, stirring gently every 3 minutes.

2. Combine vinegar, oil, mustard, dill and salt in a small jar. Cover tightly and shake vigorously. Pour vinegar mixture over potatoes. Cover and refrigerate until chilled. Gently mix in sliced cucumber before serving.   *Makes 4 servings*

Tip: A baked potato is done when it reaches an internal temperature of 210°F.

Chicken and Pasta Salad
with Kalamata Olives

Chicken and Pasta Salad with Kalamata Olives

(pictured above)

       4 ounces uncooked rotini
       2 cups diced cooked chicken
   1/2 cup chopped roasted red bell peppers
     12 pitted kalamata olives, halved
1-1/2 tablespoons olive oil
       1 tablespoon dried basil
       1 tablespoon cider vinegar
       1 to 2 garlic cloves, minced
   1/4 teaspoon salt

1. Cook rotini according to package directions. Drain well; cool.

2. Combine chicken, peppers, olives, oil, basil, vinegar, garlic and salt in medium bowl.

3. Add cooled pasta to chicken mixture; toss gently. Divide equally among 4 plates.   *Makes 4 servings*

Classic Rice Salad

       2 cups MINUTE® White Rice, uncooked
   1/2 cup chopped onion
   1/2 cup sweet pickle relish
   1/2 cup light mayonnaise
   1/4 cup chopped pimentos
       2 hard-cooked eggs, chopped
       2 teaspoons mustard
   1/2 teaspoon salt
       Lettuce leaves (optional)

Prepare rice according to package directions. Mix all ingredients. Chill. Serve on lettuce leaves, if desired.
      Makes 6 servings

Tip: For perfect hard-cooked eggs, place the eggs in a single layer in a saucepan. Add enough cold water to cover the eggs by at least 1 inch. Cover and bring to a boil over high heat. Remove from the heat. Let eggs stand, covered, in the hot water 15 to 17 minutes. Immediately pour off the water; cover the eggs with cold water or ice water and let stand until completely cooled before peeling.

Sweet Italian Marinated Vegetable Salad

(pictured at right)

1/2 can (14 ounces) quartered artichoke hearts, drained
5 ounces grape or cherry tomatoes, halved
1/2 cup chopped green bell pepper
1/4 cup finely chopped red onion
2 ounces mozzarella cheese, cut into 1/4-inch cubes
2 tablespoons white or rice wine vinegar
1 tablespoon chopped fresh oregano *or*
1 teaspoon dried oregano
2 teaspoons sugar
1/8 teaspoon salt
1/8 teaspoon crushed red pepper flakes

Stir together all ingredients in medium bowl. For pronounced flavor, serve immediately, or chill 1 hour for more blended flavor.

Makes 4 servings

Pasta Salad with Tomatoes and Grilled Salmon

12 ounces penne pasta
2 yellow bell peppers
1 red bell pepper
3 tablespoons plus additional olive oil
3 tablespoons plus additional MRS. DASH® Garlic and Herb Seasoning Blend
3 tablespoons lemon juice
2 medium tomatoes, seeded and diced
1 pint cherry tomatoes (yellow, if possible), halved
1 large cucumber, peeled, seeded and diced
8 (4-ounce) salmon fillets

1. Cook pasta according to package directions. Set aside.

2. Roast peppers; cool, peel, seed and dice.

3. Combine olive oil, MRS. DASH® Garlic and Herb Seasoning Blend and lemon juice in large bowl. Add prepared vegetables and pasta; toss well and chill.

4. When ready to serve, brush salmon fillets with a little olive oil and sprinkle lightly with MRS. DASH® Garlic and Herb Seasoning Blend.

5. Grill fillets 3 to 4 minutes per side over medium heat. Serve hot with pasta salad.

Makes 8 servings

Fresh Fruit Salad Orange Cups

3 large navel oranges (1-3/4 pounds)
1 cup fresh raspberries
1 cup fresh blueberries
2 tablespoons honey
1-1/2 tablespoons chopped fresh mint
6 small mint sprigs
2 teaspoons confectioners' sugar (optional)

1. Cut oranges in half widthwise. Use small serrated knife or sharp paring knife to cut orange sections from membrane (as you would a grapefruit). Working over large bowl, use knife to pull out sections and drop into bowl. Drain any juice from oranges into bowl. (Do not squeeze orange cups.) Use grapefruit spoon or fingers to pull out and discard membranes from cups. Arrange cups, cut side up, on serving platter.

2. Combine raspberries and blueberries with orange sections. Drizzle honey over fruit. Add chopped mint: toss well. Mound mixture equally into orange cups; top with mint sprigs. (At this point, cups may be covered and chilled up to 2 hours before serving.) If desired, place confectioners' sugar in mesh strainer and sprinkle over fruit cups just before serving.

Makes 6 servings

Hot and Sweet Chicken Salad

1 medium jalapeño pepper,* seeded and minced
2 tablespoons apricot jam
2 tablespoons white wine vinegar
1 tablespoon vegetable oil
2 cups diced cooked chicken breast
1 large stalk celery, thinly sliced, *or* 1/4 cup roasted and salted almonds, *or* 1 cup chow mein noodles

Jalapeño peppers can sting and irritate the skin, so wear rubber gloves when handling peppers and do not touch your eyes.

Combine jalapeño, jam, vinegar and oil in small bowl. Stir well. Place chicken in salad bowl. Pour dressing over chicken. Just before serving, sprinkle with celery. Toss gently.

Makes 4 servings

Lime-Ginger Coleslaw

(pictured at right)

2 cups shredded green cabbage
1 cup shredded red cabbage
1-1/2 cups matchstick-size carrots
1/4 cup finely chopped green onions
3 tablespoons lime juice
2 tablespoons sugar
2 tablespoons chopped fresh cilantro
2 teaspoons vegetable or canola oil
1-1/2 teaspoons grated gingerroot
1/8 teaspoon salt
1/8 teaspoon crushed red pepper flakes

Combine all ingredients in large bowl. Toss well. Let stand 10 minutes before serving.

Makes 4 servings

Bulgur, Tuna, Tomato and Avocado Salad

(pictured on page 22)

2/3 cup water
1/3 cup bulgur wheat
1 cup halved grape tomatoes
1 can (6 ounces) tuna packed in water, drained and flaked
1/4 cup finely chopped red onion
1 large stalk celery, trimmed and thinly sliced
1/4 cup finely chopped avocado
1 tablespoon minced fresh Italian parsley
1 to 2 tablespoons lemon juice
4 teaspoons chicken broth
1 teaspoon olive oil
1/8 teaspoon pepper

1. Bring water to a boil in small saucepan. Stir in bulgur. Cover. Reduce heat to low. Simmer 8 minutes or until bulgur swells and has absorbed most of the water. Remove from heat. Set aside, covered, 10 minutes.

2. Meanwhile, combine tomatoes, tuna, onion and celery in large bowl. Stir in bulgur, avocado and parsley. Combine lemon juice, broth, oil and pepper in small bowl. Pour over salad. Toss gently to mix. Chill 2 hours before serving. *Makes 3 servings*

Note: Bulgur wheat is wheat kernels that have been steamed, dried and crushed. Look for it in the rice and dried beans section or in the natural foods aisle of your supermarket.

Honey Mustard Potato Salad

1-1/2 quarts water
4 cups chopped potatoes, skin-on, no bigger than 1/2-inch cubes
2 tablespoons MRS. DASH® Original Seasoning Blend
1/2 cup light salad dressing
3 tablespoons honey
3 tablespoons mustard
3 eggs, hard cooked and chopped
1/2 cup diced celery
1/2 cup chopped green pepper

1. Combine water and potatoes in a 4-quart saucepan.

2. Cook potatoes over medium heat, 20 to 25 minutes or to desired doneness. Drain.

3. Combine hot potatoes and MRS. DASH® Original Seasoning Blend; toss lightly. Set aside.

4. Combine salad dressing, honey and mustard; mix well.

5. Add salad dressing mixture, eggs, celery and green pepper; mix well. Cover, chill several hours or overnight. *Makes 6 servings*

Spring Greens with Blueberries, Walnuts and Feta Cheese

1 tablespoon canola oil
1 tablespoon white wine vinegar or sherry vinegar
2 teaspoons Dijon mustard
1/2 teaspoon salt
1/2 teaspoon pepper
5 cups mixed spring greens (5 ounces)
1 cup fresh blueberries
1/2 cup crumbled feta cheese
1/4 cup chopped walnuts or pecans, toasted*

To toast nuts, place in nonstick skillet. Cook and stir over medium-low heat until nuts begin to brown, about 5 minutes. Remove immediately to plate to cool.

Combine oil, vinegar, mustard, salt and pepper in large bowl; whisk well. Add greens and blueberries; toss well. Divide evenly among 4 serving plates. Top with cheese and walnuts. *Makes 4 servings*

Watergate Salad

(pictured at right)

1 can (20 ounces) DOLE® Crushed Pineapple, undrained
1 package (4-serving size) instant Pistachio pudding and pie filling
1 cup miniature marshmallows
1/2 cup chopped pecans
1-1/2 cups (1/2 of 8-ounce tub) thawed non-diary whipped topping

• Mix pineapple, dry pudding mix, marshmallows and pecans in large bowl until well blended. Gently stir in whipped topping; cover.

• Refrigerate 1 hour or until ready to serve.

Makes 8 servings

Pear and Orange Salad

4 red Bartlett pears
1 to 2 tablespoons lemon juice
4 small navel oranges
4 Belgian endive, sliced thinly
1 bunch watercress, washed and trimmed
1/2 cup walnuts, broken into pieces
2 tablespoons cut chives
Small clusters of red grapes
2 cups cubed JARLSBERG LITE™ cheese
Citrus Dressing or Chunky Blue Dressing (recipes follow, optional)

Quarter and core pears; slice into wedges. Brush with lemon juice. With sharp knife, peel oranges, removing white membrane (save peel for Citrus Dressing, below). Slice crosswise into thin slices. Line a salad bowl or platter with endive and watercress. Layer fruits over greens. Sprinkle with nuts, chives; arrange clusters of grapes and cheese. Serve with Citrus Dressing or Chunky Blue Cheese Dressing, if desired. *Makes 8 servings*

Citrus Dressing: Whisk together 1/4 cup canola oil, 1/4 cup orange juice, 1 tablespoon minced red onion, grated zest from 2 navel oranges, and salt and pepper to taste.

Chunky Blue Dressing: Mash 8 ounces creamy blue cheese (Saga Blue) without rind. Add 1-1/2 cups plain yogurt and blend well. Stir in 2 tablespoons aquavit or vodka, if desired, and black pepper to taste.

Caesar Salad Tacos

10 ounces romaine lettuce, torn
2 cups (8 ounces) shredded Cheddar cheese, divided
1 avocado, diced
1 can (4 ounces) ORTEGA® Diced Green Chiles
1/2 cup JOAN OF ARC® Black Beans, drained, rinsed
1/4 cup whole-kernel corn
1/3 cup Caesar salad dressing
1/4 cup ORTEGA® Taco Sauce
12 ORTEGA® Taco Shells, warmed
2 cups diced tomatoes

Combine lettuce, 1 cup cheese, avocado, chiles, beans and corn in large bowl.

Combine dressing and taco sauce in small bowl; mix well. Pour over lettuce mixture; toss well to coat.

Fill each taco shell with salad; top with remaining cheese and tomatoes. *Makes 6 servings*

Wilted Spinach Salad with White Beans & Olives

2 thick slices bacon, diced
1/2 cup chopped yellow onion
1 can (15 ounces) navy beans, rinsed and drained
1/2 cup halved pitted kalamata or ripe olives
1 bag (9 ounces) baby spinach
1 cup cherry tomatoes (cut in half if large)
1-1/2 tablespoons balsamic vinegar
Pepper (optional)

1. Cook bacon in Dutch oven or large saucepan over medium heat 2 minutes. Add onion; cook, stirring occasionally, 5 to 6 minutes or until bacon is crisp and onion is tender. Stir in beans and olives; heat through.

2. Add spinach, tomatoes and vinegar. Cover. Cook 1 minute or until spinach is slightly wilted. Turn off heat. Toss mixture lightly. Transfer to serving plates. Season with pepper, if desired.

Makes 4 servings

Chicken, Spinach & Mango Salad with
Warm Tomato Vinaigrette

Chicken, Spinach & Mango Salad with Warm Tomato Vinaigrette

(pictured above)

2 teaspoons olive oil
12 ounces boneless skinless chicken breasts, cut
    into thin strips
1 can (14.5 ounces) HUNT'S® Petite Diced
    Tomatoes, undrained
1/4 cup French dressing
1 tablespoon seasoned rice vinegar
1 bag (5 ounces) fresh baby spinach
2 ripe mangoes, peeled, cut into bite-size pieces
2 medium ripe avocados, peeled, cut into
    bite-size pieces
4 slices fully cooked bacon, heated, crumbled

1. Heat oil in large skillet over medium-high heat.
Add chicken; cook 4 minutes, or until lightly
browned, stirring occasionally.

2. Add tomatoes with their juice; stir. Bring to a boil.
Reduce heat to low. Cook 5 minutes, or until chicken
is no longer pink in center, stirring frequently.
Add dressing and vinegar; cook 2 minutes, or until
heated through, stirring occasionally.

3. Arrange spinach, mangoes and avocados evenly
on each of 4 serving plates. Top with chicken
mixture; sprinkle with bacon. Serve warm.

Makes 4 servings

Shrimp Pasta Caesar Salad

SALAD
8 ounces (2-1/2 cups) uncooked rotelle (twists)
1 pound medium cooked shrimp
4 ounces (1 cup) pea pods, cut in half, blanched
1/2 cup sliced green onions
1 can (2-1/4 ounces) sliced ripe olives, drained
1-1/2 cups garlic croutons
1/2 cup grated Parmesan cheese
6 cups torn romaine lettuce

LEMON CAESAR DRESSING
1 teaspoon grated lemon peel
3 tablespoons lemon juice
1 teaspoon Dijon mustard
1 teaspoon anchovy paste
1 teaspoon Worcestershire sauce
2 garlic cloves, minced
1/2 teaspoon salt
1/4 teaspoon pepper
1/2 cup olive oil
1 tablespoon dairy sour cream

Cook pasta as directed on package. Drain; rinse with
cold water. In large bowl, combine pasta, shrimp,
pea pods, green onions, and olives; toss gently to
combine.

In medium bowl, using wire whisk, blend all dressing
ingredients except oil and sour cream. Gradually
add oil, whisking constantly until smooth. Add sour
cream, whisking until smooth. Pour dressing over
salad; toss gently. Cover; refrigerate 1 to 2 hours to
blend flavors, stirring occasionally. Add croutons
and cheese to salad; toss gently before serving.
Serve over lettuce. *Makes 8 servings*

Favorite recipe from **North Dakota Wheat
Commision**

Chopped Mexican Salad

(pictured below)

3/4 cup LAWRY'S® Mexican Chile & Lime
 Marinade With Lime Juice
1 pound boneless, skinless chicken breasts
1 medium red onion, cut into 1/2-inch slices
1 medium green bell pepper, cored and
 quartered
1 cup sour cream
2 tablespoons milk
1 tablespoon chopped fresh cilantro
8 cups torn romaine or iceberg lettuce leaves
1 cup frozen, thawed or drained canned whole
 kernel corn
1 cup chickpeas or garbanzos, rinsed and
 drained
1 medium tomato, seeded and chopped
1 medium avocado, diced
1 cup crushed plain tortilla chips
1/2 cup crumbled queso fresco cheese or
 Monterey Jack cheese (about 2 ounces)

1. In 2 separate resealable plastic bags, pour 1/4 cup LAWRY'S® Mexican Chile & Lime Marinade With Lime Juice over chicken, then 1/4 cup Marinade over onion and green pepper; turn to coat. Close bags and marinate in refrigerator 30 minutes.

2. Meanwhile, in medium bowl, blend sour cream, milk, cilantro and remaining 1/4 cup Marinade until smooth; chill, if desired.

3. Remove chicken and vegetables from Marinade, discarding Marinade. Grill chicken and vegetables, turning once, 10 minutes or until chicken is thoroughly cooked and vegetables are tender. Thinly slice chicken, then chop onion and green pepper.

4. On serving platter, arrange lettuce. Top with chicken, onion, green pepper, corn, chickpeas, tomato and avocado. Evenly top with tortilla chips and cheese, then serve with sour cream mixture.

Makes 4 servings

Note: Also terrific with LAWRY'S® Mesquite Marinade With Lime Juice or LAWRY'S® Baja Chipotle Marinade With Lime Juice.

Chopped Mexican Salad

Very Verde Green Bean Salad

(pictured at right)

1 tablespoon olive oil
1 pound fresh green beans
1/2 cup water
1/2 teaspoon salt
1/2 teaspoon black pepper
1/2 cup ORTEGA® Salsa Verde
2 tablespoons ORTEGA® Garden Vegetable Salsa

Heat oil in large skillet over medium heat. When oil begins to shimmer, add green beans; toss lightly in oil. Heat about 3 minutes, tossing to coat beans well.

Add water, salt and pepper carefully. Cover; cook 5 minutes or until beans are tender. Add salsas; toss to coat beans evenly. Heat 1 or 2 minutes to warm salsas. Refrigerate or serve at room temperature.

Makes 4 servings

Tip: Try using broccoli or cauliflower florets instead of green beans to make an easy side dish for any meal.

Festive Cranberry Pineapple Salad

(pictured on page 22)

1 can (20 ounces) DOLE® Crushed Pineapple, undrained
2 packages (4-serving size) or 1 package (8-serving size) raspberry- or cherry-flavored gelatin
1 can (16 ounces) whole berry cranberry sauce
1 medium DOLE® Apple, chopped
1/3 cup chopped walnuts

• Drain pineapple; reserve juice. Remove 1 tablespoon crushed pineapple; set aside for garnish. In medium saucepan, combine reserved juice with water to make 3 cups; heat to boiling. Add gelatin; stir at least 2 minutes until completely dissolved. Stir in cranberry sauce. Pour into large bowl. Refrigerate 1-1/2 hours or until slightly thickened (consistency of unbeaten egg whites).

• Stir in remaining pineapple, apple and walnuts; stir gently until well blended. Pour into medium serving bowl.

• Refrigerate 4 hours or until firm. Garnish with reserved crushed pineapple and additional apple slices just before serving. Store leftover gelatin in refrigerator.

Makes 14 servings

Marinated Macaroni Salad

3 tablespoons olive oil
6 cloves garlic, quartered lengthwise
1/3 cup red wine vinegar
2 tablespoons chopped oregano
1 tablespoon chopped thyme
Salt to taste (optional)
1/4 to 1/2 teaspoon crushed red pepper flakes
6 cups cooked elbow macaroni
2 cups (10 ounces) coarsely chopped roasted red bell peppers (1-inch)
2 cups arugula leaves
1 cup California Ripe Olives, cut into wedges
1 cup diced smoked mozzarella (1/4-inch)

Heat oil in a small sauté pan over medium heat. Add garlic, reduce heat to low. Cook for 4 to 6 minutes, stirring occasionally, until evenly golden. Remove from heat; allow to cool for 3 to 4 minutes. Whisk in red wine vinegar, oregano, thyme, salt, if desired, and pepper flakes. Set aside.

In a large mixing bowl, combine macaroni, peppers, arugula, California Ripe Olives and smoked mozzarella. Add red wine-garlic dressing and toss until evenly coated. Marinate for 30 minutes. Serve cold or at room temperature.   *Makes 6 servings*

Favorite recipe from **California Olive Industry**

Asian Apple Slaw

1/2 cup HELLMANN'S® or BEST FOODS® Canola Cholesterol Free Mayonnaise
2 teaspoons sugar
1 teaspoon reduced-sodium soy sauce
1 teaspoon apple cider vinegar
1/2 tablespoon grated fresh *or* 1/2 teaspoon ground ginger
1 bag (16 ounces) coleslaw mix
1 Granny Smith apple, julienned (1/8-×1/8-×3-inch strips)
2 green onions, chopped

In large bowl, combine HELLMANN'S® or BEST FOODS® Canola Cholesterol Free Mayonnaise, sugar, soy sauce, vinegar and ginger. Stir in remaining ingredients. Chill, if desired.   *Makes 8 servings*

Minestrone Salad

(pictured at right)

1 large or 2 medium tomatoes, chopped
1 can (15 ounces) chickpeas, rinsed and drained
2 medium stalks celery, chopped
1 cup cooked macaroni
1/4 cup shredded Parmesan cheese
2 tablespoons Italian dressing
Salt and pepper

Combine tomatoes, chickpeas, celery and macaroni in salad bowl. Add cheese and dressing; toss well. Season with salt and pepper.   *Makes 4 servings*

Rice Tabbouleh

3 cups cooked rice
1 cup chopped Italian flat-leaf parsley
3/4 cup chopped cucumber
3/4 cup chopped tomato
1/4 cup minced mint leaves
1/4 cup olive oil
1/4 cup lemon juice
1 teaspoon salt
1 teaspoon ground black pepper

In a large bowl, combine rice, parsley, cucumber, tomato, mint, olive oil, lemon juice, salt and pepper. Toss well.   *Makes 6 servings*

Favorite recipe from **USA Rice**

Southwest Veggie Salad

4 frozen spicy black bean vegetarian burgers
3/4 cup frozen corn
8 cups torn mixed salad greens
3/4 cup chopped tomato
1/4 cup sliced green onions
1/2 cup salsa
1/2 cup (2 ounces) shredded Monterey Jack cheese
or Mexican cheese blend
1/4 cup sour cream
1-1/2 cups tortilla chips

1. Preheat oven to 375°F. Place frozen burgers on foil-lined baking sheet. Bake 17 to 19 minutes, turning burgers after 8 minutes. Meanwhile, place corn in small microwavable bowl and loosely cover. Cook on HIGH 1 minute or until heated through. Drain off any liquid.

2. Toss greens, tomato and green onions in large bowl. Arrange on 4 serving plates.

3. Cut each burger into 8 thin strips. Top each salad with 8 burger strips and 3 tablespoons of corn. Drizzle with salsa. Sprinkle with cheese. Top with sour cream. Serve with chips.   *Makes 4 servings*

Fiesta Pasta Salad

12 ounces tricolor rotini pasta
1 cup ORTEGA® Garden Vegetable Salsa
1 cup frozen whole-kernel corn, thawed
1 cup JOAN OF ARC® Black Beans, drained
1/2 cup chopped fresh cilantro
1/4 cup mayonnaise
2 tablespoons ORTEGA® Diced Jalapeños
3 green onions, diced

Cook pasta according to package directions. Cool.

Combine pasta, salsa, corn, beans, cilantro, mayonnaise, jalapeños and green onions in large bowl; mix well. Refrigerate at least 30 minutes before serving.   *Makes 6 to 8 servings*

Tip: For an elegant first course or brunch item, serve this salad in stemmed wine or martini glasses, or in lettuce cups made from Bibb or iceberg lettuce.

Sesame Rice Salad

1 can (15 ounces) mandarin orange segments, undrained
1 teaspoon ground ginger
2 cups MINUTE® Brown Rice, uncooked
1 can (8 ounces) sliced water chestnuts, drained and chopped
1/2 cup sliced celery
1/2 cup Asian sesame salad dressing
3 green onions, thinly sliced

Drain oranges, reserving liquid. Add enough water to reserved liquid to measure 1-3/4 cups. Stir in ginger. Prepare rice according to package directions, substituting 1-3/4 cups orange liquid for water. Refrigerate cooked rice 30 minutes. Add water chestnuts, celery, dressing and onions; mix lightly. Gently stir in oranges.   *Makes 4 servings*

Cobb Salad

Grilled Corn & Black-Eyed Pea Salad

3 tablespoons BERTOLLI® CLASSICO™ Olive Oil
1-1/2 teaspoons LAWRY'S® Seasoned Salt
4 ears corn-on-the-cob
1 can (15 ounce) black-eyed peas, rinsed and drained
1 medium tomato, chopped
2 green onions, finely chopped
1 medium jalapeño pepper, seeded and finely chopped
2 tablespoons lime juice
1/2 teaspoon LAWRY'S® Garlic Salt
Hot pepper sauce to taste (optional)

1. In small bowl, combine 2 tablespoons Olive Oil with 1 teaspoon LAWRY'S® Seasoned Salt; evenly brush on corn. Grill, turning occasionally, 8 minutes or until browned; cool. With knife, remove kernels from cobs.

2. In medium bowl, combine corn with remaining Olive Oil, LAWRY'S® Seasoned Salt and remaining ingredients. Serve chilled or at room temperature.

Makes 8 servings

Tip: Serve with tortilla chips for a tasty appetizer.

Cobb Salad

(pictured above)

1 package (10 ounces) torn mixed salad greens
or 8 cups torn romaine lettuce
6 ounces cooked chicken breast, cut into bite-size pieces
1 tomato, seeded and chopped
2 hard-cooked eggs, cut into bite-size pieces
4 slices bacon, crisp-cooked and crumbled
1 ripe avocado, peeled and diced
1 large carrot, shredded
1/4 cup (2 ounces) blue cheese, crumbled
Creamy or vinaigrette dressing

1. Place lettuce in serving bowl. Arrange chicken, tomato, eggs, bacon, avocado, carrot and cheese on top of lettuce.

2. Serve with dressing. *Makes 4 servings*

Strawberry Spinach Salad

SALAD:
1 tablespoon MRS. DASH® Lemon Pepper Seasoning Blend
1/3 pound spinach leaves, washed
1/2 pint fresh strawberries, sliced
1 kiwi, sliced
1 tablespoon slivered almonds

DRESSING:
1 teaspoon MRS. DASH® Original Blend
1 tablespoon raspberry preserves
1 tablespoon vegetable oil
1 tablespoon rice vinegar

1. Place salad ingredients in attractive bowl.

2. Make dressing by mixing remaining ingredients together.

3. Toss spinach with dressing and serve immediately. *Makes 4 servings*

Salad Toppers

A good salad can be much more than lettuce and tomatoes. Salad toppings bring a welcome change of new flavors and textures.

Croutons

- **Homemade croutons:** Cut leftover bread into cubes. Toss in olive oil or melted butter to lightly coat and arrange the cubes on a baking sheet. Bake in a 375°F oven for about 10 to 15 minutes or until the croutons are golden brown and crispy.

- **Garlic croutons:** Sauté fresh garlic in olive oil, then toss with the bread cubes and bake.

- **Herbed croutons:** Combine your favorite combination of dried herbs, coarse salt and freshly ground black pepper with olive oil or melted butter. Toss the bread cubes in the mixture and bake.

- **Parmesan cheese croutons:** Combine grated Parmesan cheese with freshly ground black pepper and melted butter. Toss the bread cubes in the mixture and bake.

- **Pita crisps:** Tear pita bread into small pieces and arrange on a baking sheet. Brush with the garlic, herb or cheese mixture. Bake crisps until golden.

Toasted Nuts

- Cooking nuts in a skillet just until golden makes them extra crunchy and intensifies their flavor. Remove them from the skillet right after toasting to prevent overbrowning.

Cheese Crisps

- Spoon grated cheese such as cheddar or Parmesan in small piles onto a parchment paper-lined baking sheet. Bake in a 375°F oven 8 to 10 minutes or until golden. Let stand 1 minute. Let cool on a wire rack. Serve the crisps whole or break them into bite-size pieces and sprinkle over the salad.

Additional Toppers

- **Crispy & Crunchy:** Crumbled crisp-cooked bacon or pancetta, French-fried onions or shallots, crispy tortilla strips or sunflower seeds.

- **Soft & Tangy:** Parmesan cheese curls, cheese cubes or sliced olives.

Pasta & Potato Salad Pointers

- Since pasta absorbs some of the dressing, cook pasta very al dente to avoid a mushy pasta salad.

- After draining cooked pasta, toss it immediately with a little olive oil. The oil will prevent the pasta from sticking together as it cools down.

- Cool cooked pasta completely before combining it with any dressing. If the pasta is warm, it will absorb too much dressing.

- Use waxy potatoes such as red or Yukon Gold potatoes for potato salad. These potatoes keep their shape better than starchy russet or baking potatoes.

- Toss hot cooked potatoes in a little vinegar and oil to give potato salad a more lively taste. Or, dress the potatoes while still warm, then refrigerate to cool quickly.

- To keep large bowls of potato or any other kind of creamy salad cold, take a small food storage bowl (about 2 or 3 cups), fill it with water, seal and freeze. Put the frozen bowl in the bottom of the salad bowl. Then, pile the salad on top. It will help keep the salad cold and safe to eat.

Side Dishes

Greek-Style Tortellini

(pictured at left)

1 package (9 ounces) refrigerated fresh cheese tortellini
2 tablespoons olive oil
1-1/2 teaspoons red wine vinegar
1 can (14 ounces) quartered artichoke hearts, drained
1 cup halved grape tomatoes *or* 1 large tomato, chopped
1/4 cup finely chopped green onions
1/8 teaspoon dried oregano
1/8 teaspoon pepper

1. Cook tortellini according to package directions. Drain well. Spoon into large serving bowl. Let cool 10 minutes.

2. Whisk together oil and vinegar in cup or small bowl. Add to tortellini. Mix gently. Add artichoke hearts, tomatoes, green onions, oregano and pepper. Toss gently.

Makes 4 to 6 servings

Variation: Add 1 cup diced grilled chicken breast to the salad. Increase vinegar to 1 tablespoon and oil to 2-1/2 tablespoons.

Clockwise from top left: *Bacon and Cheese Brunch Potatoes (p. 46), Cajun Dirty Rice (p. 46), Greek-Style Tortellini, Grilled Ratatouille (p. 60)*

Mushroom Sage Stuffing

(pictured at right)

1/4 cup (1/2 stick) butter
2 cups sliced shiitake mushroom caps
1 small onion, chopped
1 stalk celery, chopped
2 teaspoons minced fresh sage
1 teaspoon grated orange peel
1/4 teaspoon salt
1/4 teaspoon pepper
6 cups 1/2-inch cubes French or sourdough bread, toasted
1 cup chicken broth

1. Preheat oven to 325°F. Grease 8-inch square baking dish.

2. Melt butter in large saucepan or Dutch oven over medium-high heat. Add mushrooms, onion and celery; cook and stir 5 minutes or until vegetables are tender. Stir in sage, orange peel, salt and pepper. Stir in bread. Gradually add broth, stirring constantly to moisten bread.

3. Spoon into prepared baking dish. Bake 30 minutes or until stuffing is heated through and lightly browned.
Makes 8 servings

Potato Veg•All® Casserole

3/4 cup butter or margarine, divided
1 package (30 ounces) frozen country-style hash browns, thawed
1 can (15 ounces) VEG•ALL® Original Mixed Vegetables, drained
1 can (10-3/4 ounces) cream of celery soup
1 package (8 ounces) sour cream
1 cup (4 ounces) shredded Cheddar cheese
1 teaspoon salt
1 teaspoon pepper
2 cups corn flakes cereal, crushed

Preheat oven to 350°F. In 13×9-inch baking dish, heat 1/2 cup butter 5 to 6 minutes or until melted.

Spread hash browns over butter; top with Veg•All.

In medium mixing bowl, stir together soup, sour cream, cheese, salt and pepper; spread over Veg•All.

In small saucepan, melt remaining 1/4 cup butter. In medium bowl, mix cereal and melted butter; sprinkle over casserole. Bake 45 minutes.
Makes 10 to 12 servings

Cajun Dirty Rice

(pictured on page 44)

1/2 pound pork sausage, crumbled
1 small onion, finely chopped
1 stalk celery, finely chopped
1 small clove garlic, minced
2 cups chicken broth
1 tablespoon Cajun seasoning
2 cups MINUTE® White Rice, uncooked

Cook sausage in medium skillet over medium heat until evenly browned, stirring occasionally. Add onions, celery and garlic; cook and stir 5 minutes or until sausage is cooked through and vegetables are tender. Add broth to skillet with seasoning; stir. Bring to a boil. Stir in rice; cover. Remove from heat. Let stand 5 minutes. Fluff with fork.
Makes 6 servings

Tip: For a more authentic dish, reduce sausage to 1/4 pound and add 1/4 pound chopped chicken livers.

Bacon and Cheese Brunch Potatoes

(pictured on page 44)

3 medium russet potatoes (about 2 pounds), peeled and cut into 1-inch dice
1 cup chopped onion
1/2 teaspoon seasoned salt
4 slices crisply cooked bacon, crumbled
1 cup (4 ounces) shredded sharp cheddar cheese
1 tablespoon water or chicken broth

SLOW COOKER DIRECTIONS
1. Coat 4-quart slow cooker with cooking spray. Place half of potatoes in slow cooker. Sprinkle 1/2 of onion and seasoned salt over potatoes; top with 1/2 of bacon and cheese. Repeat layers, ending with cheese. Sprinkle water over top.

2. Cover and cook on LOW 6 hours or on HIGH 3-1/2 hours or until potatoes and onion are tender. Stir gently to mix and serve hot.
Makes 6 servings

Hush Puppies

(pictured below)

Vegetable oil for frying
1 cup CREAM OF WHEAT® Hot Cereal (Instant, 1-minute, 2-1/2-minute or 10-minute cook time), uncooked
1/3 cup milk
1 egg
1/4 cup minced onions
1 tablespoon honey
1/2 teaspoon salt

1. Preheat oil in deep fryer or heavy saucepan to 360°F. Combine remaining ingredients in medium bowl. Let stand 5 minutes.

2. Using two tablespoons, form batter into 1-inch balls and drop into hot oil. Cook 3 minutes or until brown and crispy. Remove with slotted spoon and drain on paper towels. Serve warm.

Makes 12 hush puppies

Tip: For a sweet treat, sprinkle powdered sugar over the hush puppies before serving.

Hush Puppies

Bacon-Cheese Grits

2 cups milk
1/2 cup quick-cooking grits
4 thick-cut bacon slices, chopped
1-1/2 cups (6 ounces) shredded sharp cheddar cheese *or* 6 slices American cheese, torn into bite-size pieces
2 tablespoons butter
1 teaspoon Worcestershire sauce
1/2 teaspoon salt
1/8 teaspoon cayenne pepper (optional)

1. Bring milk to a boil in large saucepan over medium-high heat. Slowly stir in grits. Return to a boil. Reduce heat. Cover; simmer 5 minutes, stirring frequently.

2. Meanwhile, heat large skillet over medium-high heat. Add bacon. Cook and stir until browned. Drain on paper towels.

3. Remove grits from heat. Stir in cheese, butter, Worcestershire sauce, salt and cayenne pepper, if desired. Cover; let stand 2 minutes or until cheese melts. Top each serving with bacon.

Makes 4 servings

Variation: For a thinner consistency, add 1/2 cup milk.

Zucchini Romano

5 medium zucchini or yellow squash, sliced 1/4-inch thick
1-1/3 cups *French's®* Cheddar or Original French Fried Onions
2/3 cup shredded Parmesan cheese
1/8 teaspoon ground nutmeg
2 tablespoons melted butter

1. Boil zucchini for 5 minutes until just tender. Drain well.

2. Heat French Fried Onions on a microwave-safe plate in microwave for 45 seconds.

3. Mix French Fried Onions, cheese and nutmeg in plastic bag. Crush onions with hands or rolling pin.

4. Layer 1/3 of the zucchini with 1/3 of the onion mixture in serving bowl. Drizzle with 1/3 of the butter. Repeat layers twice. *Makes 6 servings*

Winter Squash Risotto

Winter Squash Risotto

(pictured above)

2 tablespoons olive oil
1 small butternut or medium delicata squash,
    peeled and cut into 3/4- to 1-inch cubes
    (about 2 cups)
1 large shallot or small onion, finely chopped
1/2 teaspoon paprika
1/4 teaspoon salt
1/4 teaspoon dried thyme
1/4 teaspoon pepper
1 cup arborio rice
4 to 5 cups hot chicken broth
1/2 cup grated Parmesan or Romano cheese

1. Heat oil in large skillet over medium heat. Add squash; cook 3 minutes, stirring frequently. Add shallot; cook 3 to 4 minutes or until squash is almost tender. Stir in paprika, salt, thyme and pepper. Add rice; stir to coat with oil.

2. Reduce heat to low. Add 1/2 cup broth; cook over medium heat, stirring occasionally. When rice is almost dry, stir in another 1/2 cup broth. Continue to stir rice occasionally, adding 1/2 cup broth each time previous addition is absorbed. Rice is done when consistency is creamy and grains are tender with slight resistance. (Total cooking time will be 20 to 30 minutes.)

3. Stir in cheese and additional salt, if desired. Serve immediately. *Makes 4 to 6 servings*

Loaded Baked Potato Casserole

Loaded Baked Potato Casserole

(pictured above)

1 bag (32 ounces) frozen Southern-style hash
    brown potatoes, thawed (about 7-1/2 cups)
1 can (6 ounces) French fried onions
    (2-2/3 cups)
1 cup frozen peas, thawed
1 cup shredded Cheddar cheese (4 ounces)
4 slices bacon, cooked and crumbled
2 cans (10-3/4 ounces *each*) CAMPBELL'S®
    Condensed Cream of Celery Soup (Regular
    or 98% Fat Free)
1 cup milk

1. Stir the potatoes, **1-1/3 cups** of the onions, peas,
cheese and bacon in a 13×9-inch (3-quart) shallow
baking dish.

2. Stir the soup and milk in medium bowl. Pour the
soup mix over the potato mixture. Cover.

3. Bake at 350°F. for 30 minutes or until hot. Stir.

4. Sprinkle with the remaining onions. Bake for
5 minutes more or until onions are golden brown.
Makes 8 servings

Time-Saving Tip: To thaw the hash browns, cut
off one corner of bag, microwave on HIGH for
5 minutes.

Apples Roasted with Root Vegetables

3 cups peeled tart Michigan Apples*
2 cups carrots, peeled, cut into 3/4-inch thick
    rounds
1 medium onion, cut into wedges
1 pound small red skin potatoes, cut into
    quarters
2 large yams, peeled and cut into 3/4-inch cubes
2 cups parsnips, peeled and cut into 3/4-inch
    chunks
2 teaspoons extra-virgin olive oil
    Salt and pepper to taste

BALSAMIC THYME VINAIGRETTE
3 tablespoons white balsamic vinegar
3 tablespoons extra-virgin olive oil
1 teaspoon chopped fresh thyme
1/2 teaspoon chopped fresh parsley

*Suggested apple varieties: Jonathan, Empire, Braeburn and McIntosh.

1. Preheat oven to 425°F. Combine apples, carrots,
onion, red skin potatoes, yams and parsnips in
large bowl. Drizzle with olive oil; season with salt
and pepper and toss thoroughly to coat. Spread
vegetables evenly on large baking sheet. Bake
20 to 25 minutes until vegetables are tender and
beginning to caramelize. Remove from oven.

2. While vegetables are roasting, whisk together
vinaigrette ingredients. Set aside.

3. To serve, transfer vegetables to serving platter
and drizzle with Balsamic Thyme Vinaigrette.
Season with salt and freshly ground pepper. Serve
immediately.   *Makes 6 to 8 servings*

Favorite recipe from **Michigan Apple Committee**

helpful hint

*To roast vegetables, use a jelly-roll pan or
baking sheet with low sides. The vegetables
can be turned over without falling off the pan
and they can be spread out during roasting so
they brown instead of steam.*

Barley and Pear-Stuffed Acorn Squash

(pictured at bottom right)

    3 small acorn or carnival squash
    2 cups chicken or vegetable broth
  3/4 teaspoon salt, divided
    1 cup uncooked quick-cooking barley
    2 tablespoons butter
    1 small onion, chopped
    1 celery stalk, chopped
    1 large unpeeled ripe pear, diced
  1/4 teaspoon pepper
  1/2 cup chopped toasted hazelnuts
  1/4 cup maple syrup
  1/2 teaspoon cinnamon

1. Pierce each squash with knife tip in several places. Microwave on HIGH 12 to 14 minutes or until tender, turning once. (Do not overcook.) Let stand 5 minutes. Cut squash in half lengthwise; scoop out seeds. Arrange halves in large baking dish.

2. Meanwhile, bring broth and 1/2 teaspoon salt to a boil in large saucepan over high heat. Stir in barley; reduce heat to low. Cover; simmer 12 minutes or until barley is tender. Remove from heat; do not drain.

3. Preheat oven to 350°F.

4. Melt butter in large skillet over medium heat. Add onion, celery, remaining 1/4 teaspoon salt and pepper. Cook and stir 5 minutes. Add pear; cook 5 minutes. Stir in barley, hazelnuts, syrup and cinnamon.

5. Spoon barley mixture into squash. Cover with foil. Bake 15 to 20 minutes or until heated through.

Makes 6 servings

Tip: To toast hazelnuts, preheat oven to 325°F. Spread hazelnuts on baking sheet. Toast 5 to 7 minutes. Remove from oven. Place nuts in a kitchen towel and rub to easily remove skins. Coarsely chop.

helpful hint

The seeds from winter squash, such as acorn, can be separated from the pulp and toasted for 15 to 20 minutes in a 350°F oven for a crunchy treat. If desired, sprinkle the seeds with salt or chili powder.

Roasted Sweet Potato Spears with Pineapple Salsa

    1 can (8 ounces) unsweetened pineapple
        chunks with juice
  1/2 cup diced red bell pepper
  1/2 cup finely diced onion
1-1/2 tablespoons lemon juice
    2 teaspoons chopped flat Italian parsley
    2 medium NC sweet potatoes
      Cooking oil spray
      Salt, to taste
      Cayenne pepper (optional)

1. Pour pineapple chunks and juice into glass or plastic bowl (if chunks are large, cut in half). Stir in red bell pepper, onion, lemon juice and parsley. Add salt and chill.

2. Preheat oven to 375°F. Wash and dry sweet potatoes. Cut each potato lengthwise into 8 wedges. Spray a baking sheet (one with sides) lightly with cooking oil spray. Arrange potato wedges in a single layer on the sheet and place in the center of the oven.

3. Bake 15 minutes, turn wedges over and bake 15 more minutes or until fork tender and golden brown. Sprinkle lightly with salt and cayenne pepper, if desired. Transfer to platter and spoon salsa over wedges. Serve immediately.

Makes 4 servings

Favorite recipe from **North Carolina Sweet Potato Commission**

Barley and Pear-Stuffed Acorn Squash

Savory Bread Stuffing

(pictured at right)

3 tablespoons butter
1/2 cup chopped onion
1/2 cup chopped celery
1 cup chicken broth
1/2 cup unsweetened apple juice
4 cups (7 ounces) seasoned, cubed bread
    stuffing mix
3/4 cup diced unpeeled red apple
1/4 cup chopped pecans, toasted

1. Preheat oven to 350°F. Coat 8- to 9-inch baking dish with nonstick cooking spray.

2. Melt butter in large saucepan over medium heat. Add onion and celery. Cook 7 to 8 minutes or until vegetables are tender and lightly browned on edges, stirring frequently. Add broth and juice. Bring to a boil over high heat. Remove from heat. Stir in stuffing mix, apple and pecans; mix well. Transfer to prepared baking dish. Cover; bake 30 to 35 minutes or until heated through.   *Makes 12 servings*

Toasted Coconut-Pecan Sweet Potato Casserole

2 cans (15 ounces each) sweet potatoes
    in heavy syrup, drained
1/2 cup (1 stick) butter, softened
1 egg
1/4 to 1/2 cup packed light brown sugar
1/2 teaspoon vanilla extract
1/8 teaspoon salt
1/2 cup chopped pecans
1/4 cup flaked sweetened coconut
2 tablespoons golden raisins (optional)

1. Preheat oven to 325°F. Combine potatoes, butter, egg, sugar, vanilla extract and salt in food processor or blender; purée.

2. Coat 8-inch square baking dish with cooking spray; spoon potato mixture into dish. Sprinkle evenly with pecans, coconut and raisins, if desired. Bake 22 to 25 minutes or until coconut is lightly golden.   *Makes 4 servings*

Garlic Ranch Whipped Potatoes

3 pounds all-purpose potatoes, peeled, if
    desired, and cubed
1/2 cup WISH-BONE® Garlic Ranch Dressing
1/2 cup chopped green onions
1/2 teaspoon salt (optional)
1/2 teaspoon ground black pepper

1. In 3-quart saucepan, cover potatoes with water. Bring to a boil over high heat. Reduce heat to low and simmer uncovered 20 minutes or until potatoes are very tender; drain.

2. Return potatoes to saucepan. With electric mixer or potato masher, mash until smooth. Stir in remaining ingredients.   *Makes 6 servings*

Irish Potato Pancakes

2 slices uncooked bacon, cut into small pieces
1/4 cup finely chopped green onions
1 cup SIMPLY POTATOES® Shredded Hash
    Browns
1 cup SIMPLY POTATOES® Mashed Potatoes
1 cup all-purpose baking mix
1/2 cup shredded Cheddar cheese
1/2 cup milk
1 egg, lightly beaten

1. In 12-inch nonstick skillet cook bacon and onions until browned. Remove from skillet. Reserve 1 tablespoon bacon grease. Set aside bacon and onions.

2. Meanwhile, in large bowl, stir together Simply Potatoes®, baking mix, cheese, cooked bacon and onions. Stir in milk and egg just until moistened.

3. Heat bacon grease in skillet over medium heat. Spoon 4 generous 1/4 cups of potato mixture into skillet at a time. Flatten slightly into pancakes. Cook each pancake about 2 minutes on each side or until golden brown. Use additional vegetable oil in skillet, if needed.   *Makes 8 servings (2 pancakes each)*

Rice and Cranberry Pilaf

Green Beans with Caramelized Onions

1 tablespoon unsalted margarine
1 large sweet onion, peeled and cut into strips
1 tablespoon sugar
3/4 pound green beans, trimmed
    Vegetable oil spray
1 tablespoon MRS. DASH® Lemon Pepper
    Seasoning

1. Heat margarine in large skillet, add onion, sprinkle with sugar. Cook over low heat until onions are golden and tender, about 20 minutes.

2. Cook green beans in boiling water for 10 to 13 minutes or until tender. Drain and place in bowl.

3. Spray hot beans with vegetable oil spray and sprinkle with MRS. DASH® Lemon Pepper Seasoning Blend; toss.

4. Garnish with caramelized onions.

Makes 4 servings

Rice and Cranberry Pilaf

(pictured above)

1 cup chicken broth
1 cup white cranberry juice
2 cups MINUTE® White Rice, uncooked
1/4 cup dried cranberries
1/4 cup sliced almonds, toasted
1 teaspoon orange peel (optional)

Pour broth and juice into medium saucepan. Bring to a boil over medium-high heat. Stir in rice and cranberries; return to a boil. Cover; remove from heat. Let stand 5 minutes. Stir in almonds. Top with orange peel, if desired. *Makes 6 servings*

Tip: To toast almonds quickly, spread them in a single layer in heavy-bottomed skillet. Cook over medium heat 1 to 2 minutes, stirring frequently, until nuts are lightly browned. Remove from skillet immediately. Cool before using.

Chipotle Cheddar Polenta

2 cups milk
1-1/2 cups water
2 teaspoons minced garlic
1 bay leaf
2 teaspoons fresh thyme leaves, chopped
1-1/2 teaspoons salt
1/2 teaspoon ground black pepper
1 cup polenta or cornmeal
4 tablespoons unsalted butter
1/2 cup (2 ounces) SARGENTO® Bistro® Blends
    Shredded Chipotle Cheddar Cheese
2 tablespoons SARGENTO® Fancy Parmesan
    Shredded Cheese

1. In a large, heavy saucepan, combine milk, water, garlic, bay leaf, thyme, salt and pepper. Bring to a boil and slowly add the polenta, whisking constantly.

2. Reduce the heat to low and simmer, stirring often with a large wooden spoon, until the polenta thickens, about 5 minutes.

3. Add butter and stir until melted. Add the cheeses and stir well. Serve hot. *Makes 4 servings*

Broccoli Baked Potatoes

6 medium IDAHO® potatoes
3 stalks broccoli
1/4 cup milk
1 cup shredded Cheddar cheese, divided
1/8 teaspoon pepper

1. Scrub potatoes. Make shallow slits around the middle as if you were cutting the potatoes in half lengthwise. Bake in 350°F oven for approximately 60 minutes, depending on size.

2. Peel broccoli stems. Steam whole stalks just until tender and chop finely.

3. Carefully slice the potatoes in half and scoop the insides into a bowl with the broccoli. Add the milk, 3/4 cup cheese and pepper. Mash together until the mixture is pale green with dark-green flecks.

4. Heap mixture into potato skins. Sprinkle with remaining cheese. Return to oven to heat thoroughly (about 15 minutes).

Makes 12 servings

Asparagus Parmesan Au Gratin

2 cups *French's*® French Fried Onions
1-1/2 pounds fresh asparagus, trimmed and peeled if thick
1 (10-3/4-ounce) can CAMPBELL'S® Cream of Celery Soup
1/2 cup half 'n' half cream or milk
1/4 cup grated Parmesan cheese
1 tablespoon Dijon mustard

1. Crush French Fried Onions in plastic bag with hands or rolling pin.

2. Cook asparagus in boiling water for 3 minutes. Drain well.

3. Mix soup, cream, Parmesan cheese and mustard. Pour half the sauce into greased 1-1/2 quart baking dish. Arrange asparagus on top of sauce. Spoon remaining sauce over asparagus.

4. Bake at 400°F for 20 minutes or until hot. Top with crushed onions. Bake 5 minutes until golden and crispy.

Makes 6 to 8 servings

Scalloped Potato-Onion Bake

(pictured below)

1 can (10-3/4 ounces) CAMPBELL'S® Condensed Cream of Celery Soup (Regular *or* 98% Fat Free)
1/2 cup milk
Dash ground black pepper
4 medium potatoes (about 1 1/4 pounds), thinly sliced
1 small onion, thinly sliced (about 1/4 cup)
1 tablespoon butter, cut into pieces
Paprika

1. Stir the soup, milk and black pepper with a whisk or fork in a small bowl. Layer half of the potatoes, half of the onion and half of the soup mixture in a 1-1/2-quart casserole. Repeat the layers. Place the butter over the soup mixture. Sprinkle with the paprika. Cover the dish with foil.

2. Bake at 400°F. for 1 hour. Uncover and bake for 15 minutes more or until the potatoes are fork-tender.

Makes 6 servings

Scalloped Potato-Onion Bake

Stovetop Macaroni and Cheese

(pictured at right)

1 tablespoon salt
12 ounces elbow macaroni, uncooked
1 (12-ounce) can evaporated milk
1/4 cup CREAM OF WHEAT® Hot Cereal (Instant, 1-minute, 2-1/2-minute or 10-minute cook time), uncooked
2 eggs
1 teaspoon Dijon mustard
1/2 teaspoon TRAPPEY'S® Red Devil™ Cayenne Pepper Sauce
1/2 teaspoon salt
8 ounces Cheddar cheese, shredded
1/2 cup milk

1. Bring large pot of water to a boil. Stir in salt. Add macaroni. Stir, then cook 8 minutes or until tender. Drain and return pasta to pot.

2. While pasta is cooking, whisk evaporated milk, Cream of Wheat, eggs, mustard, pepper sauce and salt in medium bowl.

3. Add mixture to cooked pasta. Cook and stir over medium-low heat until mixture thickens. Gradually stir in cheese, adding more as it melts. Add 1/2 cup milk; stir until creamy. Serve warm.

Makes 6 servings

Tip: To add some extra crunch to this old favorite, combine 1/4 cup fresh bread crumbs with 1/4 cup Cream of Wheat. Melt 1 tablespoon butter in small saucepan over medium heat. Add Cream of Wheat mixture; cook and stir until mixture is golden brown. Sprinkle on top of each serving.

Mozzarella Zucchini Skillet

2 tablespoons vegetable oil
5 medium zucchini, sliced (about 7-1/2 cups)
1 medium onion, chopped (about 1/2 cup)
1/4 teaspoon garlic powder *or* 2 garlic cloves, minced
1-1/2 cups PREGO® Traditional Pasta Sauce
1/2 cup shredded mozzarella *or* Cheddar cheese

1. Heat the oil in a 12-inch skillet over medium-high heat. Add the zucchini, onion and garlic powder and cook until the vegetables are tender-crisp.

2. Stir in the sauce and heat through. Sprinkle with the cheese. Cover and cook until the cheese melts.

Makes 7 servings

Fire-Roasted Chili Mashed Potatoes

2-1/2 pounds potatoes
1/2 cup (1 stick) butter, cubed
2 tablespoons ORTEGA® Taco Seasoning Mix
1/2 to 3/4 cup heavy cream, warmed
1 can (4 ounces) ORTEGA® Diced Green Chiles
Salt and black pepper, to taste

Thoroughly wash, clean, peel and dice potatoes. Place in large pot of salted water and bring to a boil. Reduce heat to low. Simmer 12 to 15 minutes or until potatoes are fork-tender. Drain well. Return to pot and add butter. Mash with hand-held masher. Add seasoning mix and enough warm cream to reach desired smoothness. Fold in chiles and salt and pepper to taste.

Makes 6 servings

Spinach Spoonbread

1 package frozen onions in cream sauce
1 (10-ounce) package frozen chopped spinach
1 (8-ounce) package corn muffin mix
1 cup CABOT® Sour Cream
1/2 cup grated CABOT® Cheddar (about 2 ounces)
2 large eggs, lightly beaten
1/4 teaspoon salt

1. Preheat oven to 350°F. Butter 1-1/2-quart baking dish or coat with nonstick cooking spray and set aside.

2. Prepare onions according to package directions. Cook spinach according to package directions and drain well.

3. In large bowl, combine onions and spinach with remaining ingredients, mixing thoroughly. Transfer mixture to prepared dish.

4. Bake for 30 to 35 minutes.

Makes 4 servings

helpful hint

Spoonbread is a cornmeal-based bread with a pudding-like texture. It is usually served as a side dish and must be eaten with a spoon or fork.

Skillet Succotash

Skillet Succotash

(pictured above)

1 tablespoon vegetable oil
1 cup diced onion
1 cup diced green bell pepper
1 cup diced celery
1 teaspoon paprika
1-1/2 cups corn
1-1/2 cups frozen baby lima beans
1 cup diced canned tomatoes with juices
2 teaspoons dried parsley flakes *or* 2 tablespoons
    minced fresh parsley
1/2 teaspoon salt
1/2 teaspoon pepper

1. Heat oil in large skillet over medium heat. Add onion, bell pepper and celery. Cook and stir about 5 minutes or until onion is translucent and pepper and celery are crisp-tender. Stir in paprika.

2. Add corn, lima beans and tomatoes. Reduce heat. Cover. Simmer about 20 minutes or until lima beans are tender. (Add water by tablespoonful, if needed, during cooking.) Stir in parsley, salt and pepper.

Makes 4 servings

Tip: For additional flavor, add 1 garlic clove, minced, and 1 bay leaf with the onion, pepper and celery. Remove and discard the bay leaf before serving.

Mexican Corn Casserole

(pictured at bottom right)

Vegetable cooking spray
1 can (10-3/4 ounces) CAMPBELL'S® Condensed
  Cheddar Cheese Soup
1 cup PACE® Chunky Salsa
1 bag (16 ounces) frozen whole kernel corn,
  thawed (about 4 cups)
1 cup coarsely crushed tortilla chips

1. Spray a 2-quart casserole with the cooking spray. Stir the soup, salsa and corn into the prepared dish. Sprinkle the tortilla chips over the corn mixture.

2. Bake at 350°F. oven for 30 minutes or until hot and bubbly. Serve immediately.   *Makes 6 servings*

Twice-Baked Idaho Potato

4 IDAHO® potatoes (10 to 11 ounces each)
2/3 cup Monterey Jack cheese, shredded
1/2 cup crumbled blue cheese
1/3 cup heavy cream
1/4 cup sour cream
3 tablespoons bacon, cooked and crumbled
  (3 to 4 slices)
2 tablespoons butter, softened
2 tablespoons green onions, thinly sliced
1/4 to 1/2 teaspoon salt
1/8 teaspoon ground nutmeg

1. Heat conventional oven to 425°F. Pierce tops of potatoes with fork several times. (Do not wrap in aluminum foil.) Bake potatoes on oven rack 60 to 70 minutes or until tender when pierced. (When using a convection oven, bake at 375°F for 55 minutes.) Remove from oven; cool 10 to 15 minutes.

2. Meanwhile, in large bowl, combine all remaining ingredients. Cut a thin slice off top of each potato. Using a teaspoon, scoop out center of each, leaving the shell. Add potato centers to cheese mixture. Using fork, break up potatoes and mix until well blended. Spoon mixture into potato shells. Transfer to baking sheet.

3. Position potatoes under broiler so that tops are 5 inches from heat source. Broil 4 to 6 minutes or until tops are golden brown. Turn off heat; close oven door and leave potatoes in oven for an additional 7 to 10 minutes.   *Makes 4 servings*

Moroccan Couscous

1/4 cup I CAN'T BELIEVE IT'S NOT BUTTER!®
  Mediterranean Blend spread
1 small onion, chopped
1 medium carrot, grated
1/8 teaspoon curry powder
2 cups chicken broth
1/2 cup raisins
1/2 teaspoon salt
1-1/2 cups couscous
1/2 cup toasted sliced almonds

In 2-quart saucepan, melt I CAN'T BELIEVE IT'S NOT BUTTER!® Mediterranean Blend spread over medium-high heat and cook onion and carrot, stirring occasionally, 4 minutes or until tender. Stir in curry powder and cook, stirring frequently, 1 minute. Stir in broth, raisins and salt. Bring to a boil over high heat. Remove from heat and stir in couscous. Cover and let stand 5 minutes. Stir in almonds and fluff with fork.   *Makes 4 servings*

Mexican Corn Casserole

Kettle Cooked Baked Beans With
Smoked Sausage

Grilled Ratatouille

(pictured on page 44)

> 1-1/4 cups LAWRY'S® Herb & Garlic Marinade With
> Lemon Juice
> 3 medium tomatoes, halved
> 1 medium zucchini, halved lengthwise
> 1 medium yellow squash, halved lengthwise
> 1 medium eggplant (about 1-1/2 pounds), cut
> into 1/4-inch thick slices
> 1 large red onion, cut into 1/2-inch thick slices
> 4 ounces Parmigiano-Reggiano cheese, shaved

1. In 13×9-inch glass baking dish, combine LAWRY'S® Herb & Garlic Marinade With Lemon Juice with vegetables. Cover and marinate 30 minutes.

2. Remove vegetables from Marinade, reserving Marinade. Grill vegetables, turning occasionally and brushing frequently with reserved Marinade, 12 minutes or until tender; coarsely chop. Top with cheese. Serve, if desired, with hot cooked rice.
Makes 7 cups

Note: Also terrific with LAWRY'S® Italian Garlic Steak Marinade With Roasted Garlic & Olive Oil.

Tip: For easier grilling, skewer onions.

Kettle Cooked Baked Beans With Smoked Sausage

(pictured above)

> 1 package (3 ounces) fully cooked bacon,
> chopped
> 1 pound smoked sausage, sliced diagonally
> 1 medium onion, chopped (about 1/2 cup)
> 2 cans (31 ounces each) VAN CAMP'S® Pork
> and Beans
> 1 can (6 ounces) HUNT'S® Tomato Paste
> 1/2 cup HUNT'S® Ketchup
> 1/4 cup packed brown sugar
> 2 tablespoons GULDEN'S® Spicy Brown Mustard

1. Combine bacon, sausage, onion, beans, tomato paste, ketchup, sugar and mustard in **CROCK-POT®** slow cooker. Stir to blend.

2. Cook on LOW for 4 to 6 hours or on HIGH for 2 to 3 hours. Stir before serving. *Makes 8 servings*

Apple and Almond Rice Pilaf

> 1 (6.7-ounce) box mushroom, whole grain and
> wild rice mix
> 1 medium Red Delicious apple, peeled and diced
> 1/2 cup slivered almonds, toasted
> 1/2 cup finely chopped red, yellow or orange bell
> pepper
> 2 tablespoons finely chopped red onion
> 1/8 teaspoon crushed red pepper flakes

1. In large saucepan, cook rice mix according to package directions.

2. Stir in apple, almonds, bell pepper, onion and pepper flakes. Cover. Let stand 5 minutes before serving. *Makes 8 servings*

Easy Cauliflower & Broccoli Au Gratin

    1 pound large cauliflower florets
    1 pound large broccoli florets
1/2 cup water
    4 ounces (1/2 of 8-ounce package)
        PHILADELPHIA® Cream Cheese, cubed
1/4 cup milk
1/2 cup BREAKSTONE'S® or KNUDSEN® Sour
        Cream
1-1/2 cups KRAFT® Shredded Sharp Cheddar Cheese
   10 RITZ® Crackers, crushed
    3 tablespoon KRAFT® 100% Grated Parmesan
        Cheese

PLACE cauliflower and broccoli in 2-quart microwaveable dish. Add water; cover. Microwave on high (100%) 8 to 10 minutes or until vegetables are tender; drain. Set aside.

MICROWAVE cream cheese and milk in 2-cup microwaveable measuring cup or medium bowl 1 minute or until cream cheese is melted and mixture is well blended when stirred. Add sour cream; mix well. Pour over vegetables; sprinkle with Cheddar cheese. Microwave 2 minutes or until cheese is melted.

MIX cracker crumbs and Parmesan cheese. Sprinkle over vegetables.

Makes 10 servings, about 3/4 cup each.

Sweet Potato Fries

        Nonstick cooking spray
1/4 teaspoon salt (kosher or sea salt preferred)
1/4 teaspoon pepper
1/4 teaspoon cayenne pepper
    1 large sweet potato (about 1/2 pound)
    2 teaspoons olive oil

1. Preheat oven to 350°F. Lightly coat baking sheet with cooking spray.

2. Mix together salt and peppers in small bowl.

3. Peel sweet potato. Cut lengthwise into long spears. Toss with oil.

4. Place spears on baking sheet, leaving room between each spear. Sprinkle spears with salt mixture. Bake for 45 minutes or until lightly browned. *Makes 2 servings*

Creamy Corn and Vegetable Orzo

(pictured below)

    2 tablespoons butter
    4 medium green onions, sliced (about 1/2 cup)
    2 cups frozen whole kernel corn
    1 package (10 ounces) frozen vegetable
        (chopped broccoli, peas, sliced carrots or
        cut green beans)
1/2 of a 16 ounce package rice-shaped pasta
        (orzo), cooked and drained
    1 can (10-3/4 ounces) CAMPBELL'S® Condensed
        Cream of Celery Soup (Regular *or* 98% Fat
        Free)
1/2 cup water

1. Heat the butter in a 12-inch skillet over medium heat. Add the green onions and cook until tender. Add the corn, vegetable and pasta. Cook and stir for 3 minutes.

2. Stir the soup and water into the skillet. Cook and stir for 5 minutes or until mixture is hot and bubbling. Serve immediately.   *Makes 6 servings*

Creamy Corn and Vegetable Orzo

Rice Verde

(pictured at right)

1 cup uncooked white rice
1 cup ORTEGA® Salsa Verde
4 ounces frozen spinach, thawed
1/2 teaspoon salt

Cook rice according to package directions; leave in saucepan.

Pour salsa into food processor. Add spinach. Pulse several times until spinach is thoroughly chopped and mixture is well combined.

Add salsa mixture and salt to saucepan with rice. Heat over medium heat, stirring until well mixed. Serve warm or at room temperature.

Makes 4 servings

Unstuffed Baked Potato Casserole

4 baking potatoes
1 can (10-3/4 ounces) CAMPBELL'S® Condensed Cream of Mushroom Soup (Regular, 98% Fat Free *or* 25% Less Sodium)
1/2 cup milk
2 cups frozen chopped broccoli, thawed
1 cup shredded Cheddar cheese (4 ounces)

1. Bake the potatoes in a 400°F. oven for 45 minutes or until the potatoes are fork-tender. Cut the potatoes lengthwise into quarters.

2. Arrange the potato pieces in a 13×9×2-inch shallow baking dish. Stir the soup, milk, broccoli and **1/2 cup** of the cheese in a medium bowl. Pour the soup mixture over the potatoes. Cover the dish with foil.

3. Bake at 400°F. for 30 minutes or until hot and bubbly. Top with remaining cheese.

Makes 8 servings

Wild Rice, Mushroom and Cranberry Dressing

3 cups water
1 teaspoon salt, divided
1 cup wild rice
1 tablespoon olive oil
1 cup chopped shiitake or button mushrooms
1 small red onion, finely chopped
1 celery stalk, finely chopped
1/2 cup dried sweetened cranberries
1/2 cup chopped toasted pecans (optional)
1/2 teaspoon minced fresh sage *or* 1/8 teaspoon dried sage
1/8 teaspoon pepper

1. Preheat oven to 325°F. Grease 8-inch square baking dish. Bring water and 1/2 teaspoon salt to a boil in medium saucepan. Stir in wild rice. Cover; reduce heat to low. Cook 45 minutes or until tender. Drain well.

2. Heat oil in large skillet over medium heat. Add mushrooms, onion and celery. Cook and stir 7 to 10 minutes or until tender. Stir in wild rice, cranberries, pecans, if desired, remaining 1/2 teaspoon salt, sage and pepper.

3. Spoon mixture into prepared baking dish. Bake 20 minutes or until heated through.

Makes 8 servings

Tip: To toast pecans, spread in single layer in heavy-bottomed skillet. Cook over medium heat 1 to 2 minutes, stirring frequently, until nuts are lightly browned. Remove from skillet immediately. Cool before using.

helpful hint

Wild rice is actually not a type of rice but a long-grain marsh grass that has a chewy texture and nutty flavor. It requires more time to cook than regular rice. Perfectly cooked wild rice consists of tender chewy grains that are butterflied, well rounded and plump.

The Mashed Potato

Prepare mashed potatoes for a multitude of uses. Add additional ingredients to boost the flavor or use leftover potatoes in new ways for quick, simple and delicious side dishes.

Perfect Potatoes

• Choose starchy potatoes such as russets or Idahoes for fluffy mashed potatoes.

• To keep raw cut potatoes from turning brown, place them in a bowl of water with a little lemon juice or vinegar, but do not allow the potatoes to soak too long in the water.

• If the potatoes have started to turn brown, simmer them in milk to whiten them.

• To keep potatoes white for a long time after cooking, add a few teaspoons of lemon juice to the cooking water.

• To test potatoes for doneness without breaking up the flesh, use a cake tester or bamboo skewer.

• For better flavor, boil potatoes with their skins on. The potatoes will hold their shape better and absorb less water. They will peel easily after being cooked.

• For the fluffiest potatoes, mash potatoes with a potato masher or press through a food mill. If using an electric mixer, do not overbeat and avoid using a food processor because the starch in the potatoes creates a gummy texture.

• To prevent lumps, always warm the milk before adding it to the potatoes.

Tasty Additions

Mashed potatoes are the classic comfort food. They taste great with nearly everything. For a change of pace, customize the basic recipe with a few new ingredients. The possibilities are endless.

• Stir in cheddar cheese, prepared horseradish or even wasabi paste or roasted garlic.

• Substitute buttermilk for milk or cream. It gives a tangy, sour cream flavor with less calories and fat than cream.

• To heighten the flavor, add chopped fresh herbs like snipped chives or rosemary, grated lemon peel or crumbled bacon to the hot mashed potatoes.

• Chicken or vegetable broth enhances the flavor of bland mashed potatoes. Either replace the milk with broth or use part broth and part milk or cream.

• To boost the flavor of mashed potatoes, steam them instead of boiling them.

• Mix potatoes with sweet potatoes, yams, parsnips, rutabagas, turnips, celery root, carrots, onions or cauliflower. Cook and mash the potatoes and vegetables together for delicious side dishes.

Mashed Potato Dish Makeovers

• Create a new side dish with leftover mashed potatoes. Place them in a small buttered baking dish and top with a mixture of buttered breadcrumbs or crackers and shredded cheese. Bake at 375°F until warmed through and top is browned, about 30 minutes.

• Recycle mashed potatoes as a decorative yet tasty touch to baked casseroles. Add a lightly beaten egg to the mashed potatoes, spoon into a piping bag and pipe over the top of the dish before baking.

- Use leftover mashed potatoes to thicken soups, stews and sauces.

- Refrigerate leftover potatoes and the potato cooking water to use in making great yeast breads or even delicious pancakes the next day.

Roasted Vegetables

Roasting is an easy and flavorful way to prepare vegetables. Roasting intensifies and concentrates the flavor, resulting in a slightly sweeter taste.

Roasting Tips

- Use shallow rimmed baking sheets.

- Toss the raw vegetables in olive oil with fresh or dried herbs, coarse salt and pepper.

- Don't overcrowd the vegetables. Spreading them apart in a single layer allows them to brown instead of steam. They brown on the surfaces that come in contact with the pan.

- Cut vegetables into similar sizes for even doneness. To roast vegetables quickly, cut them into 1/2-inch pieces. Roast at 450°F until browned at the edges, about 10 to 25 minutes (depending on the vegetable), turning once during roasting.

- Turn the vegetables occasionally during roasting to get them browned on all sides and to keep them moist.

- After the vegetables are roasted, toss with chopped fresh herbs, such as parsley, cilantro or dill.

- Sprinkle vegetables with grated Parmesan cheese for 10 to 15 minutes before the end of roasting.

- Roast soft-fleshed vegetables like tomatoes at a lower temperature (325°F to 375°F) for a longer time for a denser texture.

- To test the doneness of roasted vegetables, insert a toothpick, the tip of a knife or a wooden skewer into the center of the largest vegetable. Or, remove a piece of vegetable and cut with a fork.

- To add a garlic flavor to roasted vegetables, place unpeeled cloves of garlic on the baking sheet and roast for 10 to 15 minutes. Remove and peel the garlic cloves. Then chop and combine the garlic with the roasted vegetables when they are done.

- Roasted garlic adds a sweet and wonderful flavor to a variety of dishes. It softens and caramelizes as it roasts. Simply put the head of garlic on a piece of foil, cut off about 1/4 inch of the top to expose the cloves, drizzle with olive oil and wrap in foil. Roast at 350°F about 1 hour or until soft. To use, cool enough to handle and squeeze the pulp from each clove.

- Roasting times for vegetables depend on the type and size of the vegetable. Here is a list of approximate roasting times:

- **Long roasting vegetables** *(30 to 60 minutes):* Acorn squash, beets, butternut squash, carrots, parsnips, potatoes and sweet potatoes.

- **Medium roasting vegetables** *(20 to 30 minutes):* Bell peppers, broccoli, cauliflower, eggplant, fennel, onions, summer squash and zucchini.

- **Quick roasting vegetables** *(10 to 15 minutes):* Asparagus, corn, mushrooms and tomatoes.

Soups

Twice-Baked Potato Soup
(pictured at left)

6 large baking potatoes, scrubbed and pricked with a fork
2 tablespoons butter
1 small sweet onion, finely chopped (about 1/2 cup)
5 cups SWANSON® Chicken Broth (Regular, Natural Goodness™ *or* Certified Organic)
1/4 cup light cream
1 tablespoon chopped fresh chives
Potato Toppers

1. Heat the oven to 425°F. Arrange the potatoes on a rack and bake for 30 minutes or until tender. Place the potatoes in a bowl with a lid and let steam. Remove the skin and mash pulp.

2. Heat the butter in a 3-quart saucepan. Add the onion and cook until tender. Add the broth and **5 cups** of the potato pulp.

3. Place **1/3** of the broth mixture into an electric blender or food processor container. Cover and blend until smooth. Place in a medium bowl. Repeat the blending process with the remaining broth mixture. Return all of the puréed mixture into the saucepan. Stir in the cream and chives and cook for 5 minutes more. Season to taste.

4. Place **1/4 cup** of the remaining pulp mixture in each of 8 serving bowls. Divide the broth mixture among the bowls. Serve with one or more Potato Toppers.   *Makes 8 servings*

Potato Toppers: Cooked crumbled bacon, shredded Cheddar cheese **and/or** sour cream.

Time-Saving Tip: Microwave the potatoes on HIGH for 10 to 12 minutes or until fork-tender.

Clockwise from top left: *Twice-Baked Potato Soup, Double Corn Chowder (p. 84), Chipotle Chili (p. 73), Italian Stew Bread Bowls (p. 86)*

Spicy Squash & Chicken Soup

(pictured at right)

> 1 tablespoon vegetable oil
> 1 small onion, finely chopped
> 1 stalk celery, finely chopped
> 1 small delicata or butternut squash, cut
>   into 1-inch cubes (2 cups)
> 2 cups chicken broth
> 1 can (14-1/2 ounces) diced tomatoes
> 1 cup chopped cooked chicken
> 1/2 teaspoon ground ginger
> 1/4 teaspoon salt
> 1/8 teaspoon ground cumin
> 1/8 teaspoon pepper
> 2 teaspoons fresh lime juice
> 1 tablespoon minced fresh cilantro (optional)

1. Heat oil in large saucepan over medium heat. Add onion and celery; cook and stir 5 minutes or just until tender. Stir in squash, broth, tomatoes, chicken, ginger, salt, cumin and pepper; mix well.

2. Cover and cook over low heat 30 minutes or until squash is tender. Stir in lime juice. Sprinkle with cilantro. *Makes 4 servings*

Note: For extra-spicy soup, use diced tomatoes with chiles.

Chicken Tortilla and Rice Soup

> 2 cups MINUTE® White Rice, uncooked
> 5 cups low-sodium chicken broth
> 1 cup carrots, peeled and sliced thin
> 1 can (10-1/2 ounces) diced tomatoes with
>   green chiles
> 1 cup (6 ounces) cooked chicken breast, cubed
> 1 tablespoon lime juice (optional)
> 20 baked tortilla chips (about 1 cup), slightly
>   crushed
> 1/2 cup shredded low-fat Mexican cheese blend
> 1/4 cup chopped fresh cilantro
> 1 avocado, diced (optional)

Prepare rice according to package directions. Bring broth to a boil in medium pot. Reduce heat and add carrots, tomatoes with chiles and chicken; simmer 10 minutes. Stir in rice; add lime juice, if desired. Divide equally into 6 serving bowls and top with tortilla chips, cheese, cilantro and avocado, if desired. *Makes 6 servings*

Tip: To dice an avocado, insert a utility knife into the stem end. Slice in half lengthwise to the pit, turning the avocado while slicing. Remove the knife blade and twist the halves in opposite directions to pull apart. Press the knife blade into the pit, twisting the knife gently to pull the pit away from the avocado. Discard the pit. Cut the avocado flesh in a crisscross fashion to dice it, then run a spoon underneath to scoop out the avocado pieces.

Creamy Cauliflower Bisque

> 1 pound frozen cauliflower florets
> 1 pound baking potatoes, peeled and cut into
>   1-inch cubes
> 2 cans (14-1/2 ounces each) chicken broth
> 1 cup chopped yellow onion
> 1/2 teaspoon dried thyme
> 1/4 teaspoon garlic powder
> 1/8 teaspoon cayenne pepper
> 1 cup evaporated milk
> 2 tablespoons butter
> 1/2 teaspoon salt
> 1/4 teaspoon pepper
> 1 cup (4 ounces) shredded sharp cheddar cheese
> 1/4 cup finely chopped fresh parsley
> 1/4 cup finely chopped green onions

SLOW COOKER DIRECTIONS

1. Combine cauliflower, potatoes, broth, onion, thyme, garlic powder and cayenne pepper in 4-quart slow cooker. Cover and cook on LOW 8 hours or on HIGH 4 hours.

2. Working in batches, process soup in blender or food processor until smooth. Return to slow cooker. Add milk, butter, salt and pepper. Cook, uncovered, on HIGH 30 minutes or until heated through.

3. Ladle into bowls. Top each serving with cheese, parsley and green onions.

Makes 8 to 10 servings

---

helpful hint

"Bisque" is a fancy word for a thick, rich soup. It usually includes milk or cream and a main ingredient that is blended until smooth.

Cincinnati Chili

(pictured at right)

1-1/2 pounds ground beef
2 large onions, chopped (about 2 cups)
1/4 teaspoon garlic powder *or* 2 cloves garlic, minced
2 teaspoons chili powder
1/4 teaspoon ground cinnamon
Dash ground cloves
4 cups CAMPBELL'S® Tomato Juice
2 cans (about 15 ounces *each*) kidney beans, drained
Hot cooked spaghetti, shredded cheese and chopped onion

1. Cook the beef, onions and garlic powder in 2 batches in a 6-quart saucepot over medium-high heat until the beef is well browned, stirring frequently to break up meat. Pour off any fat.

2. Add the chili powder, cinnamon and cloves. Cook and stir for 2 minutes. Add the tomato juice. Heat to a boil. Reduce the heat to low. Cover and cook for 30 minutes.

3. Stir in the beans. Cover and cook for 15 minutes, stirring occasionally. Serve over spaghetti topped with shredded cheese and onion.

Makes 8 servings

Have Your Way with Cincinnati Chili: Serve it with just pasta (two-way) or add your choice of toppings: cheese, beans, onions or all three (five-way).

Bacon and Potato Chowder

6 slices bacon, cut into small pieces
1 cup chopped carrots
1 package SIMPLY POTATOES® Diced Potatoes with Onions
1/4 cup all-purpose flour
1 can (14-1/2 ounces) chicken broth
1/2 cup water
1 cup milk
Salt and black pepper, to taste

1. Cook bacon in 3-quart saucepan over medium heat until crisp; drain grease. Add carrots. Continue cooking 2 minutes or until crisp tender. Stir in Simply Potatoes® and flour.

2. Slowly stir in broth and water. Continue cooking, stirring constantly, until mixture comes to a boil and starts to thicken. Reduce heat to medium-low, cook 15 to 20 minutes, stirring occasionally, until potatoes are tender. Stir in milk. Continue cooking 2 to 3 minutes or until thoroughly heated (do not boil). Season with salt and pepper.

Makes 6 servings

Ravioli Minestrone

1 package (7 ounces) refrigerated three-cheese ravioli
2 teaspoons olive oil
2 carrots, peeled and chopped
1 stalk celery, chopped
1 medium onion, chopped
2 garlic cloves, minced
6 cups water
1 can (15 ounces) chickpeas, rinsed and drained
1 can (14-1/2 ounces) diced tomatoes
3 tablespoons tomato paste
1 teaspoon dried basil
1 teaspoon dried oregano
3/4 teaspoon salt
3/4 teaspoon pepper
1 medium zucchini, cut in half lengthwise and sliced (about 2 cups)
1 package (10 ounces) baby spinach

1. Cook ravioli according to package directions. Drain; keep warm.

2. Meanwhile, heat oil in Dutch oven over medium-high heat. Add carrots, celery, onion and garlic; cook, stirring occasionally, about 5 minutes or until vegetables are softened.

3. Stir in water, chickpeas, tomatoes, tomato paste, basil, oregano, salt and pepper. Bring to a boil; reduce heat and simmer 15 minutes or until vegetables are tender. Add zucchini; cook 5 minutes. Stir in spinach; cook 2 minutes or just until spinach wilts. Stir in ravioli.

Makes 8 servings

helpful hint

Use a large pot with lots of water to properly cook pasta. Too little water and a too small pan cause the pasta to clump and stick together.

Cincinnati Chili

Smoky Navy Bean Soup

(pictured below)

2 tablespoons olive oil
4 ounces Canadian bacon or ham, diced
1 cup diced onion
1 large carrot, thinly sliced
1 stalk celery, thinly sliced
3 cups water
6 ounces red potatoes, diced
2 bay leaves
1/4 teaspoon dried tarragon
1 can (15 ounces) navy beans, rinsed and drained
1-1/2 teaspoons liquid smoke
1/2 teaspoon salt
1/2 teaspoon pepper

1. Heat oil in Dutch oven over medium-high heat. Add bacon; cook and stir 2 minutes or until brown. Transfer to plate.

2. Add onion, carrot and celery to Dutch oven; cook and stir 4 minutes or until onion is translucent. Add water; bring to a boil over high heat. Add potatoes, bay leaves and tarragon; return to a boil. Reduce heat; simmer, covered, 20 minutes or until potatoes are tender. Remove from heat.

Smoky Navy Bean Soup

3. Stir in navy beans, bacon, liquid smoke, salt and pepper. Remove and discard bay leaves; let stand 10 minutes before serving.

Makes 4 to 6 servings

Italian Wedding Soup

1 tablespoon olive oil
1 pound bulk Italian sausage* (hot or sweet)
1/2 cup chopped onion
1/2 cup chopped carrot
1 teaspoon Italian seasoning
7-1/2 cups chicken broth
3 cups packed roughly chopped kale
1 cup uncooked ditalini or other small shaped pasta
Grated Parmesan cheese

*If bulk sausage is not available, use sausage links and remove the casings.

1. Heat oil in Dutch oven or large saucepan over medium-high heat. Add sausage, onion, carrot and Italian seasoning; cook and stir about 4 minutes or until sausage is cooked through. Drain fat.

2. Stir in broth and kale; bring to a boil over high heat. Stir in pasta. Reduce heat to medium-low; simmer, partially covered, about 9 minutes or until pasta is tender. Sprinkle with Parmesan.

Makes 6 servings

Chunky Potato Soup

3 slices BOB EVANS® Bacon, cut into 1/2-inch pieces
1 small leek, white part only, diced
1 package (20 ounces) BOB EVANS® Diced Seasoned Home Fries
2 cans (14-1/2 ounces each) chicken broth
2 cups whole milk
1 cup frozen corn, thawed
1 teaspoon parsley flakes

In large saucepan over medium heat, cook bacon until crisp. Remove and set aside. In bacon drippings, saute leek until softened, about 3 minutes. Add home fries and chicken broth. Cover and bring to boil, reduce heat and simmer until potatoes are tender, about 15 minutes. Lightly mash with a potato masher. Add milk, corn, parsley and reserved bacon. Heat until hot, about 5 minutes. Refrigerate leftovers. *Makes 4 to 5 servings*

Easy As Pie Pumpkin Soup

Easy As Pie Pumpkin Soup

(pictured above)

2 tablespoons butter

2 large onions, sliced (about 2 cups)

2 cups SWANSON® Chicken Broth (Regular,
   Natural Goodness™ *or* Certified Organic)

1 cup heavy cream

1 can (30 ounces) pumpkin pie mix (3-1/4 cups)

1. Heat the butter in a 10-inch skillet over medium heat. Add the onions and cook until tender.

2. Spoon **half** of the onion mixture in an electric blender container. Add **half** of the broth, cream and pumpkin. Cover and blend until smooth. Pour into a 3-quart saucepan. Repeat with the remaining onion, broth, cream and pumpkin.

3. Heat the soup over medium heat until hot.

Makes 6 servings

Chipotle Chili

(pictured on page 66)

1 jar (16 ounces) PACE® Chunky Salsa

1 cup water

2 tablespoons chili powder

1 teaspoon ground chipotle chile pepper

1 large onion, chopped (about 1 cup)

2 pounds beef for stew, cut into 1/2-inch pieces

1 can (about 15 ounces) red kidney beans, rinsed
   and drained
   Shredded Cheddar cheese (optional)
   Sour cream (optional)

1. Stir the salsa, water, chili powder, chipotle powder, onion, beef and beans in a 3-1/2-quart slow cooker.

2. Cover and cook on LOW for 8 to 9 hours* or until the beef is fork-tender. Serve with the cheese and sour cream, if desired. *Makes 8 servings*

*Or on HIGH for 4 to 5 hours

Ham, Potato & Cabbage Soup

(pictured at right)

- 1 tablespoon vegetable oil
- 1 large sweet onion, chopped (about 2 cups)
- 1 clove garlic, minced
- 6 cups SWANSON® Chicken Broth (Regular, Natural Goodness™ *or* Certified Organic)
- 1/4 teaspoon ground black pepper
- 3 cups shredded cabbage
- 1 large potato, diced (about 2 cups)
- 1/2 of an 8-ounce cooked ham steak, cut into 2-inch-long strips (about 1 cup)
- 2 tablespoons chopped fresh parsley
- 1 teaspoon caraway seed (optional)

1. Heat the oil in a 6-quart saucepot over medium-high heat. Add the onion and garlic and cook for 3 minutes or until tender.

2. Stir in the broth, black pepper, cabbage, potato and ham. Heat to a boil. Reduce the heat to medium-low. Cover and cook for 20 minutes or until the potato is tender.

3. Stir in the parsley and caraway seed, if desired.
Makes 6 servings

Kitchen Tip: A small head of cabbage, about 1 pound, will be enough for the amount of cabbage needed for this soup.

Country Turkey and Veggie Soup with Cream

- 2 tablespoons butter, divided
- 8 ounces sliced mushrooms
- 1/2 cup chopped onion
- 1/2 cup thinly sliced celery
- 1 medium carrot, thinly sliced
- 1 medium red bell pepper, chopped
- 1/2 teaspoon dried thyme
- 4 cups (32 ounces) chicken or turkey broth
- 4 ounces uncooked egg noodles
- 2 cups chopped cooked turkey
- 1 cup half-and-half cream
- 1/2 cup frozen peas, thawed
- 3/4 teaspoon salt

1. Melt 1 tablespoon butter in large saucepan over medium-high heat. Add mushrooms and onion; cook and stir 4 minutes or until onion is translucent. Add celery, carrot, bell pepper and thyme; cook and stir 5 minutes or until soft.

2. Add broth, noodles and turkey. Cover; cook 20 minutes. Stir in cream, peas, remaining 1 tablespoon butter and salt. Cook until heated through.
Makes 6 to 8 servings

Italian Skillet Roasted Vegetable Soup

- 1 tablespoon olive oil
- 1 medium red, yellow or orange bell pepper, chopped
- 1 garlic clove, minced
- 2 cups water
- 1 can (14-1/2 ounces) fire-roasted or diced tomatoes
- 1 medium zucchini, thinly sliced
- 1/8 teaspoon crushed red pepper flakes
- 1 can (15 ounces) navy beans, rinsed and drained
- 3 to 4 tablespoons chopped fresh basil
- 1 tablespoon balsamic vinegar
- 3/4 teaspoon salt

1. Heat oil in Dutch oven over medium-high heat. Add pepper; cook and stir 4 minutes or until edges are browned. Add garlic; cook and stir 15 seconds. Add water, tomatoes, zucchini and pepper flakes. Bring to a boil over high heat. Reduce heat; simmer, covered, 20 minutes.

2. Add beans, basil, vinegar and salt. Remove from heat. Let stand, covered, 10 minutes before serving.
Makes 4 servings

helpful hint

A Dutch oven is a large pot or kettle with a tight lid so the steam cannot escape, often used in cooking soups and stews. For stovetop cooking, use a slightly larger pot than necessary, such as a Dutch oven, to avoid spills as you stir.

Ham, Potato & Cabbage Soup

Roasted Corn and Chicken Soup

(pictured at right)

4 tablespoons olive oil, divided
1 can (15 ounces) yellow corn, drained
1 can (15 ounces) white corn, drained
1 onion, diced
3 tablespoons ORTEGA® Diced Green Chiles
1/2 of (1-1/2- to 2-pound) cooked rotisserie
    chicken, bones removed and meat shredded
1 packet (1.25 ounces) ORTEGA® Taco
    Seasoning Mix
4 cups chicken broth
4 ORTEGA® Yellow Corn Taco Shells, crumbled

Heat 2 tablespoons olive oil over medium heat in large skillet until hot. Add corn. Cook and stir until brown, about 8 minutes; stir often to prevent corn from burning. Add remaining 2 tablespoons olive oil, onion and chiles. Cook and stir 3 minutes longer.

Transfer mixture to large pot. Stir in shredded chicken. Add seasoning mix and toss to combine. Stir in chicken broth and bring to a boil. Reduce heat to low. Simmer 15 minutes. Serve with crumbled taco shells.   *Makes 8 servings*

Note: To make sure the canned corn is well drained, press excess water out with a paper towel.

Manhattan Clam & Potato Chowder

2 large IDAHO® Potatoes, peeled and diced
1 (14-1/2-ounce) can stewed tomatoes, not
    drained and chopped
1 (8-ounce) bottle clam juice
1/4 cup thinly sliced celery
1 medium carrot, peeled and chopped
1 small onion, chopped
1/2 teaspoon dried whole thyme
1 (6-1/2-ounce) can minced clams, not drained

1. Combine potatoes, tomatoes, clam juice, celery, carrot, onion and thyme in a deep 3-quart microwave-safe casserole dish.

2. Cover with microwaveable plastic wrap and microwave on HIGH 15 to 18 minutes, or until potatoes are tender, stirring every 5 minutes.

3. Stir in clams; cover and microwave on HIGH 2 to 3 minutes, or until thoroughly heated.
            Makes 4 servings

Italian Sausage Soup

SAUSAGE MEATBALLS
    1 pound mild Italian sausage, casings removed
1/2 cup plain dry bread crumbs
1/4 cup grated Parmesan cheese
1/4 cup milk
    1 egg
1/2 teaspoon dried basil
1/2 teaspoon pepper
1/4 teaspoon garlic salt

SOUP
    4 cups chicken broth
    1 tablespoon tomato paste
    1 garlic clove, minced
1/4 teaspoon crushed red pepper flakes
1/2 cup uncooked miniature shell pasta*
    1 bag (10 ounces) baby spinach
    Grated Parmesan cheese

Or use other tiny pasta, such as ditalini (miniature tubes) or farfallini (miniature bowties).

SLOW COOKER DIRECTIONS
1. Combine all meatball ingredients in large bowl. Form into marble-size balls.

2. Combine broth, tomato paste, garlic and red pepper flakes in 4-quart slow cooker. Add meatballs. Cover and cook on LOW 5 to 6 hours.

3. Add pasta; cook on LOW 30 minutes or until pasta is tender. Stir in spinach. Ladle into bowls; sprinkle with cheese. Serve immediately.
            Makes 4 to 6 servings

helpful hint

Slow cookers should be at least halfway but no more than three-quarters full for efficient and safe operation.

Beef, Lentil and Onion Soup

(pictured at right)

Nonstick cooking spray
3/4 pound beef for stew (1-inch pieces)
2 cups chopped carrots
1 cup sliced celery
1 cup uncooked lentils
2 teaspoons dried thyme
1/4 teaspoon pepper
1/8 teaspoon salt
3-1/4 cups water
1 can (10-1/2 ounces) condensed French onion soup, undiluted

SLOW COOKER DIRECTIONS

1. Spray large skillet with cooking spray. Heat skillet over medium-high heat. Add beef; cook until browned on all sides.

2. Place carrots, celery and lentils in 4-quart slow cooker. Top with beef. Sprinkle with thyme, pepper and salt. Pour water and soup over mixture. Cover and cook on LOW 7 to 8 hours or HIGH 3-1/2 to 4 hours or until meat and lentils are tender.

Makes 4 servings

Italian Split Pea Soup

1 pound Italian turkey sausage
1 medium onion, diced
2 carrots, diced
1 stalk celery, diced
2 garlic cloves, minced
6 cups chicken broth
2 cans (14-1/2 ounces each) Italian-style diced tomatoes
1 pound dried split peas (2 cups)
1/2 teaspoon salt
1/2 teaspoon pepper

SLOW COOKER DIRECTIONS

1. Heat large nonstick skillet over medium heat. Remove sausage from casings; crumble sausage into skillet. Brown sausage 7 to 8 minutes, stirring to break up meat.

2. Add onion, carrots, celery and garlic to skillet. Cook 5 minutes, stirring occasionally, until vegetables are tender.

3. Transfer mixture to 4- or 5-quart slow cooker. Stir in broth, tomatoes, peas, salt and pepper. Cover and cook on LOW 8 hours or until peas are tender.

Makes 8 servings

Carrot Soup

2 teaspoons butter
1/3 cup chopped onion
1 tablespoon chopped gingerroot
1 pound baby carrots
1/2 teaspoon salt
1/4 teaspoon pepper
3 cups vegetable broth
1/4 cup whipping cream
1/4 cup orange juice
Pinch ground nutmeg
4 tablespoons sour cream

1. Melt butter in large saucepan over high heat. Add onion and gingerroot; cook and stir about 1 minute or until ginger is fragrant. Stir in carrots, salt and pepper; cook and stir 2 minutes.

2. Stir in broth; bring to a boil. Reduce heat to medium-low; cover and simmer 30 minutes or until carrots are tender.

3. Working in batches, process mixture in blender until smooth. Return to saucepan and stir in cream, orange juice and nutmeg; heat through. Thin soup with additional broth, if necessary. Top each serving with dollop of sour cream.   *Makes 4 servings*

Ham and Broccoli Potato Soup

1 can (14 ounces each) chicken broth
2 cups SIMPLY POTATOES® Diced Potatoes with Onion
1-1/2 cups chopped fully cooked ham
2 cups small broccoli florets
1-1/2 cups half and half
1 cup CRYSTAL FARMS® Shredded Sharp Cheddar cheese
3 ounces cream cheese, softened, cut into small pieces
1/2 teaspoon cayenne pepper sauce

1. In 2-quart saucepan, combine chicken broth, Simply Potatoes® and ham. Bring to boil. Reduce heat to medium-low. Cook uncovered on low, stirring occasionally, 20 minutes. Add broccoli and half and half. Continue cooking 10 to 15 minutes or until Simply Potatoes® are tender.

2. Stir in cheddar cheese, cream cheese and cayenne pepper sauce. Cook until cheese is melted.

Makes 4 servings

Winter Squash Soup

(pictured at right)

5-1/4 cups SWANSON® Chicken Broth (Regular,
    Natural Goodness™ *or* Certified Organic)
1/4 cup packed brown sugar
2 tablespoons minced fresh ginger
1 cinnamon stick
1 butternut squash (about 1-3/4 pounds), peeled,
    seeded and cut into 1×1-1/2-inch pieces
    (about 4 cups)
1 large acorn squash, peeled, seeded and cut
    into 1×1-1/2-inch pieces (about 3-1/2 cups)
1 large sweet onion, coarsely chopped (about
    1-1/2 cups)

1. Place the broth, brown sugar, ginger, cinnamon
stick, squash and onion in a 6-quart slow cooker.
Cover and cook on LOW for 7 to 8 hours* or until
the squash is tender.

2. Remove the cinnamon stick. Place **1/3** of the
squash mixture into an electric blender or food
processor container. Cover and blend until smooth.
Pour the mixture into a large bowl. Repeat the
blending process twice more with the remaining
squash mixture. Return all of the puréed mixture to
a 3-quart saucepan. Cook over medium heat until
the mixture is hot. Serve with a sprinkle of ground
cinnamon, if desired.   *Makes 8 servings*

Or on HIGH for 4 to 5 hours

Creamy Winter Squash Soup: Stir in 1/2 cup
half-and-half when reheating the soup in step 2.

Hearty Vegetable Stew

1 tablespoon olive oil
1 cup chopped onion
3/4 cup chopped carrots
3 garlic cloves, minced
4 cups coarsely chopped green cabbage
3-1/2 cups coarsely chopped red potatoes (about
    3 medium)
1 teaspoon dried rosemary
1 teaspoon salt
1/2 teaspoon pepper
4 cups vegetable broth
1 can (15 ounces) great northern beans, rinsed
    and drained
1 can (14-1/2 ounces) diced tomatoes
    Grated Parmesan cheese

1. Heat oil in large saucepan over high heat. Add
onion and carrots; cook and stir 3 minutes. Add
garlic; cook and stir 1 minute.

2. Add cabbage, potatoes, rosemary, salt and
pepper; cook 1 minute. Stir in broth, beans and
tomatoes; bring to a boil. Reduce heat to medium-
low; simmer about 15 minutes or until potatoes are
tender. Sprinkle with cheese.

Makes 6 to 8 servings

Chocolate Chili

2 tablespoons olive oil
1 onion, diced
1 teaspoon POLANER® Chopped Garlic
2 pounds lean ground beef
1 can (4 ounces) ORTEGA® Diced Green Chiles
1 packet (1.25 ounces) ORTEGA® Taco
    Seasoning Mix
1 can (28 ounces) diced tomatoes
1 jar (16 ounces) ORTEGA® Thick & Chunky
    Salsa
2 cups water
1/2 cup semisweet chocolate chips
1/2 cup slivered almonds
1 teaspoon ground cinnamon
1 can (15 ounces) pinto beans, drained

Heat oil over medium heat in large pot until hot.
Add onion and garlic. Cook and stir until onions
are tender, about 3 minutes. Add beef, chiles and
seasoning mix. Cook and stir about 5 minutes or
until meat is browned. Stir in tomatoes, salsa, water,
chocolate chips, almonds and cinnamon. Bring to a
boil. Reduce heat to low. Simmer 45 minutes, stirring
every 15 minutes. Add beans; heat 15 minutes
longer or until beans are heated through.

Makes 8 servings

Serving Suggestion: Garnish with crumbled taco
shells, shredded Cheddar cheese, cilantro and
diced tomatoes.

helpful hint

*If you chop more onion than a recipe calls for,
freeze the extra in a resealable freezer bag for
later use. Use it as you would fresh onion; it
will thaw in a matter of seconds as it cooks.*

3. Drain porcini mushrooms, reserving liquid. Chop mushrooms; add mushrooms and reserved liquid to saucepan. Bring to a boil over high heat. Reduce heat; simmer 10 minutes. Stir in cream and pepper. Simmer 5 minutes or until heated through. Serve immediately. *Makes 6 to 8 servings*

Broccoli Cream Soup with Green Onions

1 tablespoon olive oil
2 cups chopped onions
1 pound fresh or frozen broccoli florets or spears
1 can (14-1/2 ounces) chicken broth
6 tablespoons cream cheese
1 cup milk
1/8 teaspoon cayenne pepper
3/4 teaspoon salt
1/3 cup finely chopped green onions

1. Heat oil in Dutch oven over medium-high heat. Add onions; cook 4 minutes or until translucent, stirring frequently. Add broccoli and broth; bring to a boil over high heat. Reduce heat; simmer, covered, 10 minutes or until broccoli is tender.

2. Working in batches, process mixture in blender until smooth. Return puréed soup to Dutch oven over medium heat. Whisk in cream cheese until melted. Stir in milk, cayenne pepper and salt. Cook 2 minutes or until heated through. Top each serving with green onions. *Makes 4 servings*

Italian Mushroom Soup

Italian Mushroom Soup

(pictured above)

1-1/2 cups boiling water
1/2 cup dried porcini mushrooms (about 1/2 ounce)
1 tablespoon olive oil
2 cups chopped onions
8 ounces sliced crimini or button mushrooms
2 garlic cloves, minced
1/4 teaspoon dried thyme
1/4 cup all-purpose flour
4 cups chicken or vegetable broth
1/2 cup whipping cream
1/2 teaspoon pepper

1. Combine boiling water and porcini mushrooms in small bowl; let stand 15 to 20 minutes or until mushrooms are tender.

2. Meanwhile, heat oil in large saucepan over medium heat. Add onions; cook 5 minutes or until translucent, stirring occasionally. Add crimini mushrooms, garlic and thyme; cook 8 minutes, stirring occasionally. Add flour; cook and stir 1 minute. Stir in broth.

Hearty Harvest Soup

1/2 pound Italian pork sausage links, casings removed
1 medium onion, chopped (about 1/2 cup)
2 cans (14 ounces each) chicken broth
1 can (14.5 ounces) HUNT'S® Diced Tomatoes with Roasted Garlic, undrained
1 can (15 ounces) cannellini beans, drained, rinsed
1 package (9 ounces) baby spinach

1. Brown sausage and onions in large saucepan over medium-high heat, stirring frequently to crumble sausage; drain.

2. Add broth, tomatoes with liquid, and the beans; mix well. Cook 5 minutes, stirring occasionally

3. Stir in spinach; cover saucepan with lid. Cook 5 minutes, or just until spinach is wilted, stirring occasionally. *Makes 6 servings*

Deep Bayou Chowder

(pictured below)

2 tablespoons olive oil
1-1/2 cups chopped onions
1 large green bell pepper, chopped
1 large carrot, chopped
8 ounces red potatoes, diced
1 cup frozen corn
1 cup water
1/2 teaspoon dried thyme
2 cups milk
2 tablespoons chopped parsley
1-1/2 teaspoons seafood seasoning
3/4 teaspoon salt

1. Heat oil in Dutch oven over medium-high heat. Add onions, pepper and carrot; cook and stir 4 minutes or until onions are translucent.

2. Add potatoes, corn, water and thyme; bring to a boil over high heat. Reduce heat; cover and simmer 15 minutes or until potatoes are tender. Stir in milk, parsley, seasoning and salt. Cook 5 minutes more.

Makes 4 servings

Souped-Up Soup

1 can (10 ounces) condensed tomato soup, plus 1-1/2 cans water
1 carrot, peeled and sliced (1/3 cup)
1/4 cup elbow macaroni
1/4 cup chopped celery
1/4 cup diced zucchini
1/2 teaspoon Italian seasoning
1/2 cup croutons
2 tablespoons grated Parmesan cheese

1. Stir soup and water in medium saucepan over medium heat. Add carrot, elbow macaroni, celery, zucchini and Italian seasoning. Bring to a boil. Reduce heat; simmer 10 minutes or until macaroni is cooked and vegetables are tender.

2. Top with croutons and Parmesan cheese.

Makes 3 to 4 servings

Serving Tip: For a school lunchtime treat, pack heated soup in a thermos. Be sure to include croutons and Parmesan cheese in snack-size resealable food storage bags. Kids can top their soup just before eating.

Deep Bayou Chowder

Moroccan Chicken Soup

(pictured at right)

4 cups SWANSON® Chicken Broth (Regular,
   Natural Goodness™ *or* Certified Organic)
3 cloves garlic, minced
2 tablespoons honey
2 teaspoons ground cumin
1/2 teaspoon ground cinnamon
1 can (about 14.5 ounces) diced tomatoes,
   undrained
1 large green pepper, cut into 2-inch-long strips
   (about 2 cups)
1 medium onion, chopped (1 cup)
1/2 cup raisins
8 skinless, boneless chicken thighs (about
   1 pound), cut up
   Hot cooked orzo (optional)

1. Stir the broth, garlic, honey, cumin, cinnamon,
tomatoes, green pepper, onion and raisins in a
3-1/2- to 6-quart slow cooker. Add the chicken.

2. Cover and cook on LOW for 8 hours* or until the
chicken is cooked through.

3. Divide the soup among **8** serving bowls. Place
about **1/2 cup** orzo centered on top of **each** of the
serving bowls.   *Makes 8 servings*

*Or on HIGH for 4 hours

Double Corn Chowder

(pictured on page 66)

2 small celery stalks, trimmed and chopped
6 ounces Canadian bacon, chopped
1 small onion or 1 large shallot, chopped
1 serrano chile or jalapeño pepper,* cored,
   seeded and minced
1 cup frozen corn, thawed
1 cup canned hominy
1/4 teaspoon salt
1/4 teaspoon dried thyme
1/4 teaspoon pepper
1 cup chicken broth
1 tablespoon all-purpose flour
1-1/2 cups milk, divided

*Hot peppers can sting and irritate the skin, so wear rubber gloves
when handling peppers and do not touch your eyes.*

SLOW COOKER DIRECTIONS
1. Combine celery, Canadian bacon, onion, chile,
corn, hominy, salt, thyme and pepper in 4-quart
slow cooker. Add broth. Cover and cook on LOW
5 to 6 hours or on HIGH 3 to 3-1/2 hours.

2. Stir together flour and 2 tablespoons milk in small
bowl. Stir into corn mixture. Add remaining milk.
Cover; cook on LOW 20 minutes.
                    Makes 4 servings

Variation: For a richer chowder, use 3/4 cup milk
and 3/4 cup half-and-half cream.

Louisiana Gumbo

2 cups MINUTE® White Rice, uncooked
2 tablespoons butter
2 tablespoons all-purpose flour
1/2 cup chopped onion
1/2 cup chopped celery
1/2 cup chopped green bell pepper
1 clove garlic, minced
1 package (14 ounces) smoked turkey sausage,
   sliced
1 can (14-1/2 ounces) diced tomatoes
1 can (13-3/4 ounces) condensed chicken broth
1 package (10 ounces) frozen sliced okra,*
   thawed
1 tablespoon Cajun seasoning
1/4 teaspoon dried thyme
1/2 pound shrimp, peeled, deveined
   Salt and black pepper, to taste

*Or substitute 1 package (10 ounces) frozen cut green beans.

Prepare rice according to package directions. Melt
butter in large skillet over medium-high heat. Stir
in flour; cook and stir until light golden brown,
about 5 minutes. Add onions, celery, bell pepper
and garlic; cook 2 to 3 minutes or until tender.
Stir in sausage, tomatoes, broth, okra, seasoning
and thyme; cover. Simmer 5 minutes, stirring
occasionally. Add shrimp; cook 5 minutes or until
shrimp are pink. Season with salt and pepper to
taste. Serve with rice.   *Makes 6 servings*

helpful hint

*Cook rice and pasta separately and
add it to the soup when ready to serve. This
prevents the rice and pasta from overcooking
and making the soup cloudy.*

Summer's Best Gazpacho

(pictured at right)

3 cups tomato juice
2-1/2 cups finely diced tomatoes (2 large)
1 cup finely diced yellow or red bell pepper
  (1 small)
1 cup finely diced unpeeled cucumber
1/2 cup chunky salsa
1 tablespoon olive oil
1 garlic clove, minced
1 ripe avocado, diced
1/4 cup finely chopped cilantro or basil

Combine all ingredients except avocado and cilantro in large bowl. Mix well. Cover. Chill at least 1 hour or up to 24 hours before serving. Just before serving, stir in avocado and cilantro. *Makes 4 servings*

Italian Stew Bread Bowls

(pictured on page 66)

4 round sourdough loaves (8 ounces each)
1/4 cup butter, melted
2 tablespoons olive oil, divided
1 cup chopped onion
1 medium green bell pepper, chopped
8 ounces eggplant, stemmed and cut into
  1/2-inch cubes
4 ounces whole mushrooms, quartered
1 can (14-1/2 ounces) stewed tomatoes
1 cup water
2 tablespoons tomato paste
1 teaspoon dried oregano
1/4 teaspoon dried rosemary
1/8 teaspoon crushed red pepper flakes
1 can (15 ounces) dark kidney beans, rinsed
  and drained
3/4 teaspoon salt
1/4 cup chopped fresh basil
4 slices provolone cheese, whole or cut into
  narrow strips

1. Preheat oven to 350°F. Cut 1/2-inch lid off bread loaves. Remove bread from interior, leaving 1/2-inch-thick bowl. (Reserve extra bread for another use.) Brush inside of bowls and lids with melted butter. Place directly on oven rack, buttered side up. Bake about 15 minutes or until crisp. Set aside.

2. Heat 1 tablespoon oil in Dutch oven over medium-high heat. Add onion and bell pepper. Cook and stir 4 minutes or until onion is translucent. Add eggplant, mushrooms, tomatoes, water, tomato paste, oregano, rosemary and pepper flakes. Bring to a boil. Reduce heat, cover tightly and simmer 25 minutes.

3. Add beans and salt. Cook, uncovered, 15 minutes or until thickened slightly. Remove from heat; stir in basil and remaining 1 tablespoon oil.

4. Place 1 bread bowl on each plate. Place bread lid alongside. Ladle soup into bread bowls. Top each with 1 slice of cheese. Let stand 2 minutes to allow cheese to melt slightly before serving.

Makes 4 servings

Tip: This Italian Stew freezes well.

Lentil Soup with Polish Sausage

1 pound USA lentils, rinsed
5 cups water
2 (16-ounce) cans tomatoes
2 bay leaves
1/2 tablespoon salt
1/4 teaspoon pepper
1 pound polish sausage
8 slices bacon, cut up
1 cup carrots, chopped
1 cup celery, chopped
1 medium onion, chopped

In a large saucepan, combine lentils, water, tomatoes, bay leaves, salt and pepper. Bring to a boil. Reduce heat and add polish sausage. Cover and simmer 15 minutes. Meanwhile, in a large skillet over high heat, fry the bacon pieces until slightly limp. Spoon all but about 1 tablespoon of the fat from the skillet. Add the carrots, celery and onion to the bacon and cook over medium heat for 15 minutes, stirring occasionally. Add the mixture to the lentils and continue cooking for 30 minutes. Slice sausage into serving size portions.

Makes 8 to 10 servings

Favorite recipe from **USA Dry Pea & Lentil Council**

Summer's Best Gazpacho

Make a Big Batch

Let soup be your answer to quick and easy meals. Most soups reheat well, making them convenient for on-the-go schedules.

- Make a double batch of soup to eat throughout the week, or donate half to your church's freezer for easy take-in meals.

- Send kids to school with hot soup in insulated travel containers. Add garnishes in separate bags on the side.

The Big Chill

- To maintain the best flavor and ensure food safety, be sure to cool soup quickly before storing in the refrigerator or freezer.

- The easiest way to cool soup fast is to ladle the soup into small shallow containers. Let the containers sit on the counter, uncovered, until the soup cools to room temperature.

- Or, put the pot of soup in a bowl of ice water, stirring occasionally, until the soup reaches room temperature.

- To quickly cool smaller amounts of soup (less than 4 cups), put the uncovered soup pot in the refrigerator. Let cool before covering the pot.

The Big Freeze

- Freeze soup in individual heat-and-serve freezerproof containers for no-fuss meals that can be reheated in the microwave.

- Leave about half an inch at the top of the freezer containers to allow for expansion.

- The smaller the container, the quicker the soup will freeze and defrost.

- Defrost soup in the same container in the refrigerator. Serve soup as soon as possible after defrosting it.

- To save freezer space, store soup in resealable food storage bags stacked in the freezer like pages in a book. Be sure to label each bag with its contents.

- Puréed soup separates after defrosting. It can be whisked back together while warming.

Soup Solutions

Try these many easy fixes when preparing homemade soup.

- Improve the flavor of many soups by making them a day ahead and refrigerating overnight, allowing the flavors to blend.

- To remove extra fat from soups, refrigerate overnight to allow any fat to solidify. The solid fat is then easy to skim off with a spoon.

- To make a soup less salty, add a slice or two of raw peeled potato at the end of the cooking time. Cook for 10 to 15 minutes and remove before serving.

- Add a teaspoon of vinegar or brown sugar or both during the last 15 minutes of cooking to lessen a salty taste.

- Instant coffee granules or a browning and seasoning sauce will darken the color and heighten the flavor of many soups.

- Add a little beef bouillon to heighten the flavor of a flat or flavorless soup.

- Finely chop vegetables and meat if you want them to cook faster.

- To prevent curdling, stir sour cream or yogurt into the hot soup or stew. Then, reduce the heat to low and cook only until the mixture is warmed through.

- Pasta and noodles can easily become soggy in long-cooking soup mixtures. To keep pasta from becoming soggy, cook it separately and add to the soup just before serving.

- Instead of noodles, cut stacks of wonton wrappers into strips. Drop them into the hot soup just before serving.

- To easily thicken soups and retain all the flavor, remove and purée some of the vegetables in a food processor or blender and stir the mixture back into the soup.

- To thicken chili, simply stir in a small amount of cornmeal.

- A slow cooker is ideal for preparing soup. Start a recipe before work and come home to a warm, comforting meal that's ready to eat!

- Use leftover vegetables from dinner in a soup the following night. Combine the vegetables with canned broth and purée in a blender. After heating, stir in a little cream or even buttermilk for a creamy, tasty soup.

Blending Hot Liquids

- Soups often call for blending hot broth and cooked vegetables. A blender works the best, but immersion blenders and food processors are also great for this task. When using a blender to process hot liquids, proceed with CAUTION!

- Since the hot steam from the soup gets trapped between the liquid and the lid, the blender contents can create a volcano spattering hot soup everywhere. The solution is to blend in batches, filling the container no more than half full. Blend on low speed, leaving the small cap slightly opened. Covering the container with a towel will also help to avoid a mess.

Serve it Up

- When making soup for parties, serve the soup in mugs instead of bowls. Mugs make it not only easy to serve but also much easier to eat.

- Some herbs lose their flavor and aroma when cooked for more than 15 minutes. Taste the soup at the end of the cooking time and add a pinch or more herbs, if necessary.

- Stir in 1 tablespoon of butter or up to 1/4 cup whipping cream just before serving for a rich taste and texture.

- For a more substantial meal, serve thick and hearty soups over rice, noodles, mashed potatoes or in bread bowls.

- Garnishing a soup can take it from ordinary to spectacular. Use ingredients that will complement the flavors and textures of the soup.

- Add garnishes at the last minute before serving soup.

Popular Garnishes

- Fresh chopped herbs such as snipped chives, sliced green onions, chopped parsley or cilantro.

- Crostini (thin toasts) floated over the soup and topped with grated cheese.

- Oyster crackers, tortilla strips or garlic croutons.

- Toasted sliced almonds or chopped pecans.

- Grated or cubed cheeses.

- Diced tomato, avocado, cucumber or bell pepper.

- Crispy crumbled bacon or diced ham.

- A dollop of sour cream or yogurt dusted with regular or smoked paprika.

Sandwiches

Cheesy Havana Shrimp Panini

(pictured at left)

3/4 cup plus 2 tablespoons LAWRY'S® Havana Garlic & Lime
　　Marinade With Lime Juice, divided
1-1/2 pounds uncooked medium shrimp, peeled, deveined and
　　tails removed
1 tablespoon vegetable oil
1-1/2 cups shredded Monterey Jack cheese (about 6 ounces)
1/2 cup HELLMANN'S® or BEST FOODS® Real Mayonnaise
1/4 cup finely chopped red onion
1/4 cup chopped fresh cilantro
12 slices crusty country white bread
2 tablespoons SHEDD'S® SPREAD COUNTRY CROCK®
　　Spread, melted

1. In large resealable plastic bag, pour 3/4 cup LAWRY'S®
Havana Garlic & Lime Marinade With Lime Juice over
shrimp; turn to coat. Close bag and marinate in refrigerator
30 minutes.

2. Remove shrimp from Marinade, discarding Marinade. In
12-inch nonstick skillet, heat oil over medium-high heat and
cook shrimp, stirring occasionally, until shrimp turn pink.
Drain; cool slightly, then coarsely chop.

3. Meanwhile, in large bowl, combine next 4 ingredients with
remaining 2 tablespoons Marinade. Add shrimp and toss
gently. On 6 bread slices, evenly spoon shrimp mixture, then
top with remaining bread slice; brush outsides of sandwiches
with Spread.

4. In panini grill, cook sandwiches 4 minutes or until golden
brown.　　　　　　　　　　　　　　　　*Makes 6 servings*

Clockwise from top left: *Cheesy Havana
Shrimp Panini, Roast Beef Wrappers (p. 102),
Slow-Cooked Kielbasa in a Bun (p. 105), Pressed
Party Sandwich (p. 106)*

Hawaiian Chicken Sandwich

(pictured at right)

> 1 can (8 ounces) DOLE® Pineapple Slices
> 1/2 teaspoon dried oregano leaves, crushed
> 1/4 teaspoon garlic powder
> 4 skinless, boneless, small chicken breast halves
> 1/2 cup light prepared Thousand Island salad dressing
> 1/4 teaspoon ground red pepper (optional)
> 4 whole grain or whole wheat sandwich rolls
> Red or green bell pepper, sliced into rings

• Drain pineapple; reserve juice.

• Combine reserved juice, oregano and garlic powder in medium bowl. Pour 1/4 cup into shallow non-metallic dish. Add chicken breasts to dish; turn to coat both sides with marinade. Cover; marinate 15 minutes in refrigerator.

• Add pineapple slices to bowl; turn to coat sides.

• Grill or broil chicken 8 minutes, brushing occasionally with reserved marinade; turn over. Add pineapple slices to grill; continue cooking 8 to 10 minutes or until chicken is no longer pink in center and pineapple is golden brown. Discard any remaining marinade.

• Combine dressing and red pepper. Spread on bottom halves of rolls. Top with chicken, bell pepper rings, pineapple slices and top halves of rolls. *Makes 4 servings*

Bratwurst & Grilled-Onion Hoagies

> 1 tablespoon butter or margarine
> 1 large onion, thinly sliced, separated into rings
> 1/2 teaspoon paprika
> 1/4 teaspoon salt
> 1/4 teaspoon freshly ground black pepper
> 1 package JENNIE-O TURKEY STORE® Lean Turkey Bratwurst
> 1/2 cup beer, non-alcoholic beer or water
> 2 teaspoons olive or vegetable oil
> 5 hoagie or submarine sandwich rolls, split, lightly toasted
> Spicy brown mustard (optional)

Melt butter in large skillet over medium-high heat. Add onion rings; cook 3 minutes or until wilted, stirring occasionally. Sprinkle with paprika, salt and pepper. Reduce heat to medium-low; cook 15 to 20 minutes or until golden brown and tender, stirring occasionally. Meanwhile, combine bratwurst and beer or water in large saucepan. Cover and simmer 10 minutes. Pour off and discard liquid. Add oil to pan; brown bratwurst on all sides, about 6 minutes. Serve in rolls topped with onions and mustard, if desired. *Makes 5 servings*

Weeknight Waffle-Wiches

> 1 can (12 fluid ounces) NESTLÉ® CARNATION® Evaporated Milk, divided
> 1 package (8 ounces) shredded cheddar cheese, divided
> 3 cups plus 1 teaspoon all-purpose baking mix (such as BISQUICK®), divided
> 3/4 cup water
> 1 large egg, beaten
> 3 tablespoons prepared yellow mustard
> 12 slices turkey bacon, cooked, divided
> 6 slices thinly-sliced deli ham (about 4 ounces), divided

COMBINE *3/4 cup* evaporated milk, *1-1/2 cups* cheese and 1 teaspoon baking mix in small saucepan. Cook over medium heat, stirring constantly, until cheese is melted and sauce has slightly thickened to a creamy consistency. Remove from heat; cover.

WHISK together remaining evaporated milk, water, remaining *1/2 cup* cheese, egg and mustard in medium bowl. Stir remaining 3 cups baking mix into milk mixture until well blended.

PREHEAT Belgian waffle maker* according to manufacturer's directions. Pour about *1-1/4 cups* batter onto waffle maker. (This amount is enough for a square or round waffle maker.) Cook according to manufacturer's directions. Repeat with remaining batter. Keep cooked waffles warm in oven.

TO ASSEMBLE
SPREAD *2 tablespoons* cheese sauce evenly over one side of 6 waffle squares. Place *2 slices* of bacon and *1 slice* of ham on cheese sauce on each. Top with second waffle to make waffle-wiches.
Makes 6 Belgian-style waffle sandwiches

Can also be cooked in a standard waffle maker (makes about 18 standard-sized waffles).

Tip: Waffles can be made ahead and frozen.

Sautéed Onion & Bacon Cheeseburger Deluxe

(pictured at right)

4 slices bacon, chopped
1 medium onion, sliced
1/2 cup shredded Mexican blend cheese (about 2 ounces)
1/2 cup LAWRY'S® Steak & Chop Marinade With Garlic & Cracked Black Pepper
1/4 teaspoon LAWRY'S® Seasoned Salt
1/4 teaspoon LAWRY'S® Seasoned Pepper
1 pound ground beef
4 hamburger buns, toasted if desired
1/4 cup HELLMANN'S® or BEST FOODS® Real Mayonnaise

1. In 10-inch nonstick skillet, cook bacon over medium heat, stirring occasionally, 5 minutes or until crisp. Remove bacon and drain on paper towels; reserve 1 tablespoon drippings.

2. In reserved drippings, cook onion over medium heat, stirring occasionally until tender. Remove skillet from heat. Stir in bacon, cheese and 2 tablespoons LAWRY'S® Steak & Chop Marinade With Garlic & Cracked Black Pepper; set aside.

3. In medium bowl, combine LAWRY'S® Seasoned Salt, Seasoned Pepper and ground beef; shape into 4 patties.

4. Grill or broil hamburgers, turning once and brushing with remaining Marinade, to desired doneness. Evenly spread buns with Mayonnaise, then top with burgers, bacon mixture, and, if desired, lettuce and tomato. *Makes 4 servings*

Tip: Serve with grilled fries! Microwave all-purpose potatoes until tender, then cut into wedges and toss with LAWRY'S® Seasoned Salt, Garlic Salt and/or Seasoned Pepper and olive oil. Grill, turning once, until golden and tender.

Easy Meatball Parm Heroes

2 cups PREGO® Traditional Italian Sauce
16 (1 ounce *each*) frozen cooked meatballs
4 long hard rolls, split
1 cup shredded mozzarella cheese (4 ounces)
Grated Parmesan cheese

1. Heat the sauce and meatballs in a 3-quart saucepan over medium-high heat to a boil. Reduce the heat to low. Cook for 20 minutes or until the meatballs are heated through, stirring occasionally.

2. Divide the meatballs and sauce among the rolls. Sprinkle with the mozzarella and Parmesan cheeses. *Makes 4 sandwiches*

Meaty Chili Dogs

1 pound ground beef
1/4 pound Italian sausage, casings removed
1 large onion, chopped
2 medium stalks celery, diced
2 fresh jalapeño peppers,* seeded and chopped
2 garlic cloves, minced
1 teaspoon sugar
1 teaspoon chili powder
1/2 teaspoon salt
1/2 teaspoon ground cumin
1/2 teaspoon dried thyme
1/8 teaspoon pepper
1 can (28 ounces) tomatoes, chopped
1 can (15 ounces) pinto beans, rinsed and drained
1 can (12 ounces) tomato juice
1 cup water
1/4 cup ketchup
8 frankfurters
8 frankfurter buns, split and toasted

Jalapeño peppers can sting and irritate the skin, so wear rubber gloves when handling peppers and do not touch your eyes.

1. Cook beef, sausage, onion, celery, jalapeño peppers and garlic in 5-quart Dutch oven over medium heat until meat is cooked through and onion is tender, stirring to break up meat. Drain fat.

2. Stir in sugar, chili powder, salt, cumin, thyme and pepper. Add tomatoes, beans, tomato juice, water and ketchup. Bring to a boil over high heat. Reduce heat to low; simmer, uncovered, 30 minutes, stirring occasionally.

3. Arrange frankfurters on grill rack directly above medium-hot coals. Grill, uncovered, 5 to 8 minutes or until heated through, turning often. Place frankfurters in buns. Spoon about 1/4 cup chili over each. *Makes 8 servings*

Sautéed Onion & Bacon
Cheeseburger Deluxe

Quick Breakfast Sandwich

Cheese Steak Pockets

1 tablespoon vegetable oil
1 medium onion, sliced
1 package (14 ounces) frozen beef *or* chicken
    sandwich steaks, separated into 8 portions
1 can (10-3/4 ounces) CAMPBELL'S® Condensed
    Cheddar Cheese Soup
1 jar (about 4-1/2 ounces) sliced mushrooms,
    drained
4 pita breads (6-inch), cut in half

1. Heat the oil in a 10-inch skillet over medium-high heat. Add the onion. Cook and stir until the onion is tender.

2. Add the sandwich steaks and cook until they're browned. Pour off any fat.

3. Add the soup and mushrooms. Reduce the heat to low. Cook and stir until the mixture is hot and bubbling.

4. Divide and spoon the meat mixture into the pita halves. *Makes 8 sandwiches*

Kitchen Tip: For a little bit of crunch in this sandwich, heat the whole pitas in a 400°F. oven for 2 minutes before cutting them in half and filling with the steak mixture.

Quick Breakfast Sandwich

(pictured above)

2 turkey breakfast sausage patties
3 eggs
    Salt and pepper
2 teaspoons butter
2 slices cheddar cheese
2 whole wheat English muffins, split and toasted

1. Cook sausage according to package directions; set aside and keep warm.

2. Beat eggs, salt and pepper in small bowl. Melt butter in small skillet over low heat. Pour eggs into skillet; cook and stir gently until just set.

3. Place cheese on bottom halves of English muffins; top with sausage and scrambled eggs. Serve immediately. *Makes 2 sandwiches*

Tip: Turkey sausage breakfast patties may vary in size. If patties are small, use two patties for each sandwich.

Chicken Salsa Pockets

1 can (10-3/4 ounces) CAMPBELL'S®
    Condensed Cream of Chicken Soup
    (Regular *or* 98% Fat Free)
1/2 cup PACE® Chunky Salsa
2 cups cooked chicken, cut into strips
1/2 cup shredded Cheddar cheese
3 pita breads (6-inch), cut in half, forming
    2 pockets
    Green leaf lettuce leaves

1. Stir the soup, salsa and chicken in a 2-quart saucepan. Cook and stir over medium heat until hot. Stir in the cheese. Cook until the cheese melts.

2. Line the pita halves with lettuce. Spoon about 1/3 cup chicken mixture into each pita half.
Makes 6 sandwiches

Easy Substitution Tip: Substitute 2 cans (4.5 ounces each) SWANSON® Premium Chunk Chicken breast, drained, for the cooked chicken.

Stuffed Focaccia Sandwich

(pictured below)

1 container (about 5 ounces) soft cheese with garlic and herbs
1 (10-inch) round herb or onion focaccia, cut in half horizontally
1/2 cup thinly sliced red onion
1/2 cup coarsely chopped pimiento-stuffed green olives, drained
1/4 cup sliced mild banana pepper
4 ounces thinly sliced deli hard salami
6 ounces thinly sliced oven-roasted turkey breast
1 package (2/3 ounce) fresh basil, stems removed

1. Spread soft cheese over cut sides of focaccia. Layer bottom half evenly with remaining ingredients. Cover sandwich with top half of focaccia; press down firmly.

2. Cut sandwich into 4 equal pieces. Serve immediately or wrap individually in plastic wrap and refrigerate until serving time.

Makes 4 sandwiches

Tip: This sandwich is great for make-ahead lunches or picnics.

Creamy Roast Beef Sandwiches

1 cup sliced onions, separated into rings
1 tablespoon butter or margarine
6 ounces (3/4 of 8-ounce package) PHILADELPHIA® Cream Cheese, cubed
1/2 cup milk
1 tablespoon KRAFT® Prepared Horseradish
6 pita breads, cut in half
1 pound shaved deli roast beef
2 medium tomatoes, chopped
2 cups shredded lettuce

COOK and stir onions in butter in medium skillet on medium heat until tender. Add cream cheese and milk; stir. Reduce heat to low; cook until cream cheese is completely melted and mixture is well blended, stirring occasionally. Stir in horseradish.

FILL pita pockets evenly with meat, tomatoes and lettuce.

DRIZZLE with the horseradish sauce.

Makes 6 servings, 2 filled pita halves each.

Stuffed Focaccia Sandwich

Grilled Muffuletta

(pictured at right)

4 round hard rolls, split
2 tablespoons vinaigrette salad dressing
1/3 cup olive salad or tapenade
6 ounces thinly sliced Genoa salami
6 ounces thinly sliced ham
6 ounces thinly sliced provolone cheese
Olive oil

1. Brush insides of rolls with salad dressing. Layer half of olive salad, salami, ham, cheese and remaining olive salad on roll bottoms; close sandwiches with roll tops. Brush outsides of sandwiches lightly with oil.

2. Heat large grill pan or nonstick skillet over medium heat. Add sandwiches; press down lightly with spatula or weigh down with small plate. Cook sandwiches 4 to 5 minutes per side or until cheese melts and sandwiches are golden brown.

Makes 4 sandwiches

Chicken Enchilada Roll-Ups

1-1/2 pounds boneless skinless chicken breasts
1/2 cup plus 2 tablespoons all-purpose flour, divided
1/2 teaspoon salt
2 tablespoons butter
1 cup chicken broth
1 small onion, diced
1/4 to 1/2 cup canned jalapeño peppers,* sliced
1/2 teaspoon dried oregano
2 tablespoons whipping cream or milk
6 (7- to 8-inch) flour tortillas
6 thin slices American cheese or American cheese with jalapeño peppers

*Jalapeño peppers can sting and irritate the skin, so wear rubber gloves when handling peppers and do not touch your eyes.

SLOW COOKER DIRECTIONS
1. Cut each chicken breast lengthwise into 2 or 3 strips. Combine 1/2 cup flour and salt in resealable food storage bag. Add chicken strips and shake to coat with flour mixture. Melt butter in large skillet over medium heat. Brown chicken strips in batches, 2 to 3 minutes per side. Place chicken into 4-quart slow cooker.

2. Add chicken broth to skillet and scrape up any browned bits. Pour broth mixture into slow cooker. Add onion, jalapeño peppers and oregano. Cover and cook on LOW 7 to 8 hours or on HIGH 3 to 4 hours.

3. *Turn slow cooker to HIGH.* Blend remaining 2 tablespoons flour and cream in small bowl until smooth. Stir into chicken mixture. Cook, uncovered, on HIGH 15 minutes or until thickened. Spoon chicken mixture onto center of flour tortillas. Top with 1 cheese slice. Fold up tortillas and serve.

Makes 6 servings

Serving Suggestion: This rich creamy chicken mixture can also be served over hot cooked rice.

The Heartland

1 pound JENNIE-O TURKEY STORE® Deli Homestyle Honey Cured Turkey Breast, thinly sliced
8 slices whole grain bread
8 ounces Gouda cheese, thinly sliced
4 thin slices red onion, separated into rings
4 leaves of lettuce

CRANBERRY MAYO
1/4 cup cranberry relish (chopped, if too coarse)
1/4 cup mayonnaise
1 tablespoon Dijon mustard

Spread cranberry mayo on each slice of bread. On 4 slices, layer JENNIE-O TURKEY STORE® Homestyle Honey Cured Turkey Breast, Gouda cheese, red onion and leaf lettuce, dividing evenly for each sandwich. Top with remaining bread slices and cut into halves or quarters.

Makes 4 servings

Havarti & Onion Sandwiches

1-1/2 teaspoons olive oil
1/3 cup thinly sliced red onion
4 slices pumpernickel bread
6 ounces dill havarti cheese, cut into slices
1/2 cup prepared coleslaw

1. Heat oil in large skillet over medium heat. Add onion; cook and stir 5 minutes or until tender. Layer 2 bread slices with onion, cheese and coleslaw; top with remaining 2 bread slices.

2. Heat same skillet over medium heat. Add sandwiches; press down with spatula or weigh down with small plate. Cook 4 to 5 minutes on each side or until cheese melts and sandwiches are browned.

Makes 2 sandwiches

Southwestern Omelet Wrap

(pictured at right)

> 2 teaspoons cornstarch
> 1 tablespoon water
> 1 egg
>   Nonstick cooking spray
> 3 tablespoons canned refried beans, warmed
> 1/2 cup finely shredded romaine or iceberg lettuce
> 1/4 cup (1 ounce) shredded Monterey Jack or cheddar cheese
> 2 tablespoons chunky salsa
> 1 tablespoon bacon bits

1. To make omelet, dissolve cornstarch in water in small bowl. Add egg; whisk until blended.

2. Spray large nonstick skillet lightly with cooking spray; heat over medium-high heat. Add egg mixture, tilting skillet to cover bottom of skillet. Cook 1 to 2 minutes or until set. Turn omelet over; cook 30 seconds. Turn out onto cutting board, browned side down.

3. To make wrap, spread beans to edge of omelet. Sprinkle evenly with lettuce, cheese, salsa and bacon bits.

4. Gently roll up, sealing with refried beans. Serve immediately.   *Makes 1 serving*

Firecracker Burgers

> 1-1/2 pounds ground beef chuck
> 4 sesame seed sandwich rolls, split, toasted
> 1 cup watercress *or* mixed spring greens

SEASONING:
> 1 tablespoon curry powder
> 1 tablespoon Caribbean jerk seasoning
> 1 teaspoon salt

SAUCE:
> 1/2 cup mayonnaise
> 1/4 cup plain yogurt
> 1 tablespoon fresh lime juice
> 2 teaspoons grated lime peel
> 1/4 teaspoon salt

1. Combine ground beef and seasoning ingredients in large bowl, mixing lightly but thoroughly. Shape into four 3/4-inch thick patties. Place patties on grid over medium, ash-covered coals. Grill, uncovered, 13 to 15 minutes (over medium heat on preheated gas grill, covered, 13 to 14 minutes) until instant-read thermometer inserted horizontally into center registers 160°F, turning occasionally.

2. Meanwhile combine sauce ingredients in small bowl; set aside.

3. Spread sauce on cut sides of rolls. Place one burger on bottom half of each roll; top evenly with watercress. Close sandwiches.   *Makes 4 servings*

Favorite recipe courtesy of **The Beef Checkoff**

Pear Gorgonzola Melts

> 4 ounces creamy Gorgonzola cheese (do not use crumbled blue cheese)
> 8 slices walnut raisin bread
> 2 pears, cored and sliced
> 1/2 cup fresh spinach leaves
>   Butter, melted

1. Spread cheese evenly on 4 bread slices; layer with pears and spinach. Top with remaining bread slices. Brush outsides of sandwiches with butter.

2. Heat large nonstick skillet over medium heat. Add sandwiches; cook 4 to 5 minutes per side or until cheese melts and sandwiches are golden brown.
            Makes 4 sandwiches

Spicy Barbecued Chicken Pitas

> 2 cups chicken, cooked and shredded or chopped
> 3/4 cup (3 ounces) SARGENTO® Bistro® Blends Shredded Chipotle Cheddar Cheese
> 1/4 cup barbecue sauce
> 2 pita pocket bread rounds, preferably whole wheat
> 4 lettuce leaves
> 4 slices tomato

1. Combine chicken, cheese and barbecue sauce.

2. Cut pita bread in half crosswise; open into pockets. Fill pockets with lettuce, tomato and chicken mixture.   *Makes 2 pitas*

Grilled Reubens with Coleslaw

(pictured at right)

2 cups sauerkraut
1/4 cup (1/2 stick) butter, softened
8 slices rye or marble rye bread
12 ounces thinly-sliced deli corned beef or pastrami
4 slices Swiss cheese
1/4 to 1/2 cup prepared Thousand Island dressing
2 cups deli coleslaw
4 kosher garlic pickle spears

1. Preheat indoor grill or large grill pan. Drain sauerkraut well on paper towels.

2. Spread butter evenly over one side of each slice of bread. Turn 4 bread slices over; top with equal amounts corned beef, sauerkraut and cheese. Top with remaining 4 bread slices, butter side up.

3. Place sandwiches on grill; grill 4 minutes or just until cheese begins to melt.

4. Place on serving platter. Remove the bread slice touching the meat and spread 1 to 2 tablespoons of the dressing evenly over each sandwich. Serve with coleslaw and pickles. *Makes 4 servings*

Note: Stack sandwich ingredients in the order given to prevent sogginess.

Toasted Turkey & Swiss on Rye

1-1/2 tablespoons Dijon-style mustard
1-1/2 tablespoons salad dressing
1/2 teaspoon dried tarragon leaves
8 slices marbled rye bread
2 (5-ounce) cans HORMEL® chunk turkey, drained and flaked
4 (1-ounce) slices Swiss cheese
2 tablespoons butter or margarine, melted

In small bowl, combine mustard, salad dressing, and tarragon. Spread 4 bread slices with mustard mixture. Top with chunk turkey and sliced Swiss cheese. Cover with remaining bread slices. Brush both sides of each sandwich with melted butter. In large skillet, grill sandwiches until golden brown and cheese is melted. *Makes 4 servings*

Sweet & Tasty Hawaiian Sandwich

1/2 cup pineapple preserves
1 tablespoon Dijon mustard
1 round loaf (16 ounces) Hawaiian bread
8 ounces brick cheese, thinly sliced
8 ounces thinly sliced deli ham
Olive oil
Pimiento stuffed green olives (optional)

1. Combine preserves and mustard in small bowl. Cut bread in half horizontally. Pull out and discard center from bread top, leaving 1-inch shell. Spread preserves mixture on bottom half of bread. Layer with cheese, ham and top half of bread. Brush outsides of sandwich lightly with oil.

2. Heat large nonstick skillet over medium heat. Add sandwich; press down lightly with spatula. Cook sandwich 4 to 5 minutes per side or until cheese melts and sandwich is golden brown. Cut into wedges; garnish with olives.
Makes 4 to 6 servings

Roast Beef Wrappers

(pictured on page 90)

1/2 cup whipped cream cheese
2 tablespoons mayonnaise
1 to 2 teaspoons prepared horseradish
Salt and pepper
4 (8-inch) flour tortillas
4 green leaf lettuce leaves
1/2 red onion, thinly sliced
1/2 pound deli sliced roast beef
1 tomato, thinly sliced

1. Combine cream cheese, mayonnaise, horseradish, salt and pepper in small bowl; mix well. Wrap tortillas in paper towels. Microwave on HIGH 20 seconds to soften slightly.

2. Divide cream cheese mixture evenly between tortillas. Spread, leaving 1-inch border. Divide lettuce, onion, roast beef and tomato between tortillas.

3. Roll up tortillas; wrap in plastic wrap. Refrigerate 30 minutes. Cut in half to serve.
Makes 4 sandwiches

Panini with Fresh Mozzarella and Basil

Panini with Fresh Mozzarella and Basil

(pictured above)

1/2 cup prepared vinaigrette
1 loaf (16 ounces) Italian bread, cut in half lengthwise
6 ounces fresh mozzarella cheese, cut into 12 slices
8 ounces thinly sliced oven-roasted deli turkey
12 to 16 fresh whole basil leaves
1 large tomato, thinly sliced
1/2 cup thinly sliced red onion
1/8 teaspoon crushed red pepper flakes

1. Preheat indoor grill. Spoon vinaigrette evenly over both cut sides of bread.

2. Arrange cheese evenly over bottom half of bread; top with turkey, basil, tomato and onion. Sprinkle with red pepper flakes. Cover with top half of bread; press down firmly. Cut into 4 sandwiches.

3. Place sandwiches on grill; close lid. Cook 5 to 7 minutes or until cheese melts.

Makes 4 servings

Tuna Nicoise Sandwiches

2 tablespoons mayonnaise
2 tablespoons Dijon-style mustard
1 can (6 ounces) low-sodium chunk white tuna packed in water, drained
1 sliced green onion, sliced (about 2 tablespoons)
1 tablespoon pitted, chopped Kalamata olives
1 tablespoon drained capers
4 slices PEPPERIDGE FARM® Whole Grain 100% Whole Wheat Bread
Red leaf lettuce leaves

1. Stir the mayonnaise and mustard in a medium bowl. Stir in the tuna, onion, olives and capers.

2. Divide the tuna mixture between **2** bread slices. Top with the lettuce and remaining bread slices.

Makes 2 sandwiches

Super-Sloppy Sloppy Joes with Broccoli Slaw

1-1/2 pounds ground beef (95% lean)
1/2 cup chopped onion
1/4 teaspoon pepper
1/2 cup canned black beans, rinsed, drained
1/2 cup frozen corn
1/2 cup ketchup
1/2 cup prepared barbecue sauce
6 whole wheat sandwich buns, toasted

BROCCOLI SLAW:
1/4 cup prepared ranch dressing
1 tablespoon Dijon-style mustard
2 cups packaged broccoli slaw

1. Brown ground beef with onion in large nonstick skillet over medium heat 8 to 10 minutes or until beef is not pink, breaking up into 3/4-inch crumbles. Season with pepper. Stir in beans, corn, ketchup and barbecue sauce. Cook 3 to 5 minutes or until heated through, stirring occasionally.

2. Meanwhile, prepare Broccoli Slaw. Combine dressing and mustard in medium bowl. Add broccoli slaw; toss to coat.

3. Place about 2/3 cup beef mixture on bottom half of each bun; top with 1/4 cup Broccoli Slaw. Close sandwiches. *Makes 6 servings*

Favorite recipe courtesy of **The Beef Checkoff**

Italian Beef Wraps

(pictured below)

1/2 pound thin lean beef strips*
1/4 teaspoon black pepper
    Nonstick cooking spray
1 large yellow onion, halved, sliced
1 medium green bell pepper, thinly sliced
1 medium red bell pepper, thinly sliced
1 packet Italian salad dressing and recipe mix
1-1/4 cups water
1 cup MINUTE® Brown Rice, uncooked
4 (8-inch) flour tortillas, warmed
    Light sour cream (optional)

Purchase beef strips already cut for stir-fry.

Season meat with pepper. Spray large nonstick skillet with nonstick cooking spray. Add meat; cook 5 minutes or until cooked through. Remove meat from skillet; cover to keep warm. Add onions, bell peppers, salad dressing mix and water to skillet. Bring to a boil. Stir in rice; cover. Reduce heat to medium-low; simmer 5 minutes. Remove from heat. Add meat mixture; stir. Let stand, covered, 5 minutes. Spoon meat mixture evenly onto tortillas and top with sour cream, if desired; roll up.

Makes 4 servings

Slow-Cooked Kielbasa in a Bun

(pictured on page 90)

1 pound kielbasa sausage, cut into
    4 (4- to 5-inch) pieces
1 large onion, thinly sliced
1 large green bell pepper, cut into strips
1/4 teaspoon salt
1/4 teaspoon dried thyme
1/4 teaspoon pepper
1/2 cup chicken broth
4 hoagie rolls, split

SLOW COOKER DIRECTIONS

1. Brown sausage 3 to 4 minutes in large skillet over medium-high heat. Place sausage in 4-quart slow cooker. Add onion, bell pepper, salt, thyme and pepper. Stir in broth.

2. Cover and cook on LOW 7 to 8 hours.

3. Serve sausage in rolls; top with onion and bell pepper.

Makes 4 servings

Tip: For zesty flavor, top sandwiches with pickled peppers and a dollop of mustard.

Italian Beef Wrap

Shredded Apricot Pork Sandwiches

(pictured below)

2 medium onions, thinly sliced
1 cup apricot preserves
1/2 cup packed dark brown sugar
1/2 cup barbecue sauce
1/4 cup cider vinegar
2 tablespoons Worcestershire sauce
1/2 teaspoon crushed red pepper flakes
1 (4-pound) boneless pork top loin roast, trimmed
2 tablespoons cornstarch
1 tablespoon grated gingerroot
1 teaspoon salt
1 teaspoon pepper
1/4 cup cold water
10 to 12 sesame or onion rolls, toasted

SLOW COOKER DIRECTIONS

1. Combine onions, preserves, brown sugar, barbecue sauce, vinegar, Worcestershire sauce and pepper flakes in small bowl. Place pork roast in 5-quart slow cooker. Pour apricot mixture over roast. Cover and cook on LOW 8 to 9 hours.

Shredded Apricot Pork Sandwich

2. Transfer pork to cutting board; cool slightly. Shred pork into coarse shreds using 2 forks. Let cooking liquid stand 5 minutes to allow fat to rise. Skim fat.

3. *Turn slow cooker to HIGH.* Blend cornstarch, gingerroot, salt, pepper and water in small bowl until smooth. Whisk cornstarch mixture into cooking liquid. Cook, uncovered, on HIGH 15 to 30 minutes or until thickened. Return shredded pork to slow cooker; mix well. Serve on toasted buns.

Makes 10 to 12 sandwiches

Variation: A 4-pound pork shoulder roast, cut into pieces and trimmed, can be substituted for pork loin roast.

Pressed Party Sandwich

(pictured on page 90)

1 (12-inch) unsliced loaf hearty peasant bread or sourdough bread
1-1/2 cups fresh basil leaves
6 ounces thinly sliced smoked provolone or mozzarella cheese (about 9 slices)
3 plum tomatoes, sliced
1 red onion, thinly sliced*
2 roasted red bell peppers
2 to 3 tablespoons extra-virgin olive oil
1 tablespoon balsamic vinegar
1/4 teaspoon salt
1/4 teaspoon pepper

*To reduce the onion's strong flavor, place slices in sieve or colander; rinse with cold water. Shake slices and pat dry.

1. Cut bread in half lengthwise. Place halves cut side up on work surface. Gently pull out some of interior, leaving at least 1-1/2-inch bread shell.

2. Layer basil, cheese, tomatoes, onion and roasted peppers on bottom half of loaf; drizzle with oil and vinegar. Sprinkle with salt and pepper; top with remaining loaf half.

3. Wrap sandwich tightly in plastic wrap; place on baking sheet. Top with another baking sheet. Place canned goods or heavy pots and pans on top of baking sheet. Refrigerate sandwich several hours or overnight.

4. To serve, remove weights and plastic wrap from sandwich. Cut sandwich into 1-inch-thick slices; arrange on serving platter. *Makes 12 slices*

Pressed Makes the Best

Pressing is a must to ensure the best grilled ham and cheese, toasted panini or Cuban sandwich.

• Cook and press sandwiches in a wide range of electric countertop grills for toasty outsides and melted insides.

• If you don't have an electric grill, put a plate over the sandwich in the skillet and press down while toasting one side. Turn the sandwich over and repeat the procedure on the opposite side.

• Or, use two heavy skillets. Place a buttered sandwich in a dry skillet over medium heat. Place the second skillet on top of the sandwich, pressing down slightly. Turn the sandwich halfway through cooking.

Grilled Variations

Take a simple grilled cheese in new and delicious directions.

• Replace the sliced American cheese with a different type of cheese such as Monterey Jack, Muenster or Swiss, or use several different types in the same sandwich.

• Add crispy bacon slices, thin avocado slices or jalapeño slices between the cheese slices before grilling.

• Create an open-face classic. Layer slices of cheddar over a slice of crusty bread, top with thinly sliced tomatoes and sprinkle with dried herb seasoning. Broil until bubbly and melted.

• For a new twist on an old favorite, grill your PB&J. Add raisins or sliced bananas for a warm and tasty sandwich.

Sandwiches to Go

Build travel-ready, first-class sandwiches for tasty meals away from home.

• Most sandwiches can be made ahead of time and kept for at least one day. Wrap sandwiches airtight in plastic wrap and refrigerate.

• To keep lunch box sandwiches from becoming boring, select a variety of breads such as pita bread, bagels, croissants, soft rolls or flavored tortillas.

• Leftovers make divine sandwiches. Use meat loaf, roast chicken, turkey or ham and even grilled vegetables from last night's dinner for sandwich fillings.

• Sandwiches with fillings like lean meat, cheese or peanut butter can be made in advance and frozen for up to two weeks. Remove the frozen sandwich from the freezer in the morning and it will be thawed by lunchtime.

• Avoid freezing sandwiches that include mayonnaise or fresh vegetables. These items separate or become mushy during thawing.

Prevent Soggy Sandwiches

• Spread softened butter or cream cheese on the bread to form a barrier from the wet ingredients.

• Pack veggies like lettuce, tomatoes and pickles in separate containers and put them on the sandwich just before eating.

• Tuck moist ingredients like mustard and ketchup, pickle relish or other condiments between cheese or meat slices instead of putting them directly on the bread.

• Package tuna, chicken or egg salad in separate containers. Spread on the bread just before eating.

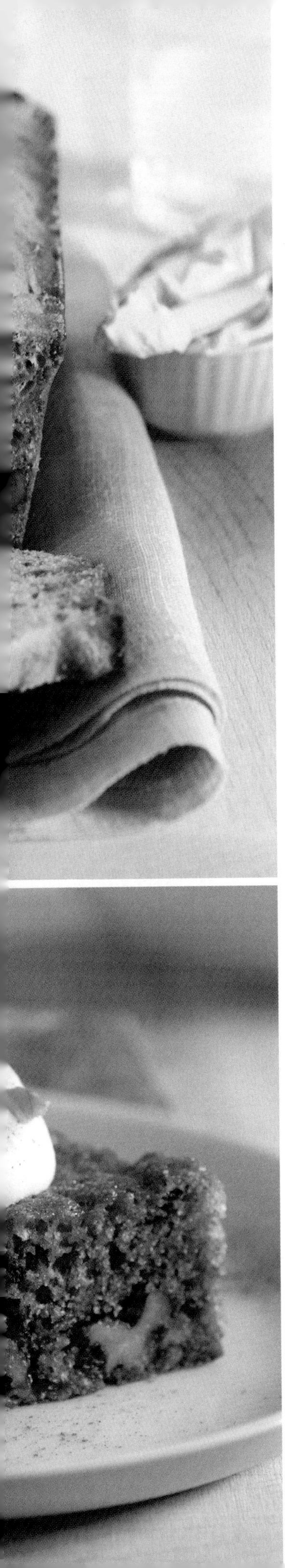

Breads

Pumpkin Apple Streusel Muffins
(pictured at left)

MUFFINS
- 2-1/2 cups all-purpose flour
- 2 cups granulated sugar
- 1 tablespoon pumpkin pie spice
- 1 teaspoon baking soda
- 1/2 teaspoon salt
- 1-1/4 cups LIBBY'S® 100% Pure Pumpkin
- 2 large eggs
- 1/4 cup vegetable oil
- 2 cups peeled, cored and finely chopped apples (2 small)

STREUSEL TOPPING
- 1/4 cup granulated sugar
- 2 tablespoons all-purpose flour
- 1/2 teaspoon ground cinnamon
- 2 tablespoons butter or margarine

FOR MUFFINS

PREHEAT oven to 350°F. Grease or paper-line 24 muffin cups.

COMBINE flour, sugar, pumpkin pie spice, baking soda and salt in large bowl. Combine pumpkin, eggs and vegetable oil in medium bowl; mix well. Stir into flour mixture just until moistened. Stir in apples. Spoon batter into prepared muffin cups, filling 3/4 full.

FOR STREUSEL TOPPING

COMBINE sugar, flour and cinnamon in medium bowl. Cut in butter with pastry blender or two knives until mixture is crumbly. Sprinkle over muffin batter.

BAKE for 30 to 35 minutes or until wooden pick inserted in centers comes out clean. Cool in pans for 5 minutes; remove to wire racks to cool slightly. *Makes 24 muffins*

Clockwise from top left: *Cinnamon Streusel Muffin Tops (p. 115), Banana Date Bread (p. 120), Nutty Toffee Coffee Cake (p. 118), Pumpkin Apple Streusel Muffins*

Cinnamon Walnut Coffee Cake

(pictured at right)

3/4 cup chopped walnuts
1 teaspoon ground cinnamon
1-1/4 cups sugar
1 cup (2 sticks) butter, softened
2 eggs
1 cup sour cream
1-1/3 cups all-purpose flour
1/3 cup CREAM OF WHEAT® Cinnamon Swirl
    Instant Hot Cereal, uncooked
1-1/2 teaspoons baking powder
1/2 teaspoon baking soda
1 teaspoon vanilla extract

1. Coat Bundt® pan with nonstick cooking spray. Sprinkle lightly with flour; shake out any excess. Combine walnuts and cinnamon in small bowl; set aside.

2. Cream sugar, butter and eggs in mixing bowl with electric mixer at medium speed. Add sour cream; blend well. Add flour, Cream of Wheat, baking powder and baking soda; mix well. Stir in vanilla. Sprinkle half of walnut mixture into bottom of prepared Bundt pan. Evenly spread half of batter over mixture. Sprinkle remaining walnut mixture over batter. Top with remaining batter, spreading evenly in Bundt pan.

3. Set oven to 350°F (do not preheat); place Bundt pan in cold oven. Bake 45 minutes, or until toothpick inserted into center comes out clean. Remove from oven; let stand 5 minutes. Place serving plate over Bundt pan and turn pan over carefully onto plate; remove pan. Serve cake warm or cool.   *Makes 12 to 16 servings*

Tip: If you do not have a Bundt® pan, you can bake this cake in regular square or round cake pans. Divide the batter between two 8- or 9-inch pans, and sprinkle each with one-half of walnut mixture. Bake 25 to 30 minutes.

helpful hint

Baking powder is perishable, so store it in a cool, dry place. If you think it may have lost its power, combine a teaspoon with a little hot water. If it bubbles vigorously, it's fine to use.

Apricot-Filled Blueberry Biscuits

1 package (12 ounces) frozen blueberries,
    unthawed *or* 2-1/2 cups fresh blueberries
2-1/4 cups all-purpose baking mix
2/3 cup milk
2 tablespoons sugar
1 teaspoon ground cinnamon
1/2 cup apricot jam
    Whipped cream (optional)

Preheat oven to 450°F. Reserve 1/2 cup blueberries for garnish. In large bowl combine baking mix, milk, sugar, cinnamon and remaining 2 cups blueberries. Stir just until soft dough forms. Turn dough onto surface dusted with baking mix; knead 5 times. Roll 1/2 inch thick; cut dough with 3-inch heart or other shaped cookie cutter. Place on ungreased cookie sheet. Gently reroll and cut out scraps; place on cookie sheet. Bake until golden brown, 8 to 10 minutes. To serve, slice biscuits horizontally in half. Spread apricot jam on bottom halves; cover with tops. Serve with reserved blueberries and whipped cream, if desired.   *Makes 8 servings*

Favorite recipe from **U.S. Highbush Blueberry Council**

Calico Veg•All® Cornbread

1 box (8-1/2 ounces) cornbread mix
1 can (15 ounces) VEG•ALL® Original Mixed
    Vegetables, drained
1 cup grated Cheddar cheese
1/2 cup chopped onion
1/3 cup milk
1 egg, slightly beaten

Preheat oven to 400°F.

In large mixing bowl, combine ingredients.

Spoon into lightly greased 8-inch square pan.

Bake 25 minutes.

Cool 5 minutes before cutting.

Makes 6 to 8 servings

Note: Leftover chopped, cooked ham or sausage can be added.

Pineapple Spice Scones

Pineapple Spice Scones

(pictured above)

- 2-1/4 cups all-purpose flour
- 1/3 cup plus 1 tablespoon sugar, divided
- 2-1/4 teaspoons baking powder
- 1/2 teaspoon baking soda
- 1/4 teaspoon salt
- 1/2 cup butter or margarine, softened
- 1 can (8 ounces) DOLE® Crushed Pineapple, undrained
- 1 teaspoon vanilla extract
  Milk or cream
- 3 tablespoons almonds, finely chopped
- 1/2 teaspoon ground cinnamon

• Combine flour, 1/3 cup sugar, baking powder, baking soda and salt in mixing bowl. Stir to combine. Cut in butter with pastry blender until mixture resembles coarse crumbs. Make well in center. Stir in undrained pineapple and vanilla until dry ingredients are just moistened and forms ball.

• Knead dough gently 10 to 12 times on lightly floured surface. Pat dough to 1/2-inch thickness. Cut with floured 2-1/2-inch biscuit cutter.

• Place on baking sheet, sprayed with nonstick vegetable cooking spray. Brush tops with milk or cream.

• Combine almonds, remaining 1 tablespoon sugar and cinnamon. Sprinkle evenly over tops of scones. Bake at 400°F., 12 to 15 minutes. Serve warm.

Makes 12 scones

Banana Walnut Muffins

- 1/2 cup (1 stick) butter, softened
- 1/3 cup granulated sugar
- 1/3 cup firmly packed light brown sugar
- 2 large ripe bananas, mashed
- 2 large eggs
- 1 teaspoon vanilla extract
- 2-1/4 cups all-purpose flour
- 2 teaspoons baking powder
- 1/2 teaspoon baking soda
- 1/4 teaspoon salt
- 1/2 cup buttermilk
- 3/4 cup chopped walnuts, divided
- 1 cup "M&M's"® Semi-Sweet Chocolate Mini Baking Bits, divided
  Chocolate Glaze (recipe follows)

Preheat oven to 350°F. Lightly grease 18 (2-3/4-inch) muffin cups or line with paper or foil liners; set aside. In large bowl cream butter and sugars until light and fluffy; beat in bananas, eggs and vanilla. In medium bowl combine flour, baking powder, baking soda and salt. Alternately add one-third flour mixture and half of buttermilk to creamed mixture, ending with flour mixture. Stir in 1/2 cup walnuts. Divide batter evenly among prepared muffin cups. Sprinkle with 3/4 cup "M&M's"® Semi-Sweet Chocolate Mini Baking Bits. Bake 20 to 25 minutes or until toothpick inserted in centers comes out clean. Cool completely on wire racks. Prepare Chocolate Glaze. Drizzle over muffins; sprinkle with remaining 1/4 cup walnuts and remaining 1/4 cup "M&M's"® Semi-Sweet Chocolate Mini Baking Bits. Store in tightly covered container.   *Makes 18 muffins*

Chocolate Glaze

- 1 cup powdered sugar
- 1 tablespoon plus 1 teaspoon unsweetened cocoa powder
- 1 tablespoon plus 1 teaspoon water
- 3/4 teaspoon vanilla extract

In medium bowl combine powdered sugar and cocoa powder. Stir in water and vanilla; mix well.

---

helpful hint

Can't eat all the bananas you bought? Freeze them to use later in banana bread. Peel and store them in a freezer bag or freeze whole and unpeeled. They will keep for several months.

Dried Cherry-Almond Bread

(pictured at bottom right)

1-POUND LOAF

   3/4 cup milk
     1 tablespoon butter or margarine
     1 large egg
   3/4 teaspoon salt
     2 cups bread flour
   1/3 cup dried tart red cherries or dried cranberries
   1/4 cup slivered almonds, toasted*
     1 tablespoon sugar
 1-1/2 teaspoons FLEISCHMANN'S® Bread Machine Yeast

1-1/2-POUND LOAF

     1 cup plus 2 tablespoons milk
     1 tablespoon butter or margarine
     1 large egg
     1 teaspoon salt
     3 cups bread flour
   1/2 cup dried tart red cherries or dried cranberries
   1/3 cup slivered almonds, toasted*
     4 teaspoons sugar
     2 teaspoons FLEISCHMANN'S® Bread Machine Yeast

Toasting nuts brings out their full flavor and helps keep them crisp in breads. To toast nuts, spread the chopped nuts in a shallow baking pan large enough to accommodate a single layer. Bake the nuts at 350°F for 5 to 15 minutes or until lightly toasted, stirring several times and checking often. Be sure to cool the nuts before adding to the bread machine.

BREAD MACHINE DIRECTIONS

Use the 1-pound recipe if your machine pan holds 10 cups or less of water. Add ingredients to bread machine pan in the order suggested by manufacturer, adding dried tart red cherries and almonds with flour. Recommended cycle: Basic/white bread cycle; light or medium/normal crust color setting. *Do not use delay cycle.*

Makes 1 loaf (8 or 12 slices)

helpful hint

Bread machine yeast and rapid-rise yeast are especially formulated for the bread machine. They become active more quickly and can be mixed with other dry ingredients instead of dissolved first in liquid.

Marathon Muffins

 2-1/2 cups all-purpose flour
     2 cups uncooked quick oats
     1 cup raisins
 2-1/2 teaspoons baking soda
   1/2 teaspoon salt
     1 cup wheat germ
     1 cup buttermilk
     1 cup honey
   2/3 cup orange juice concentrate
   1/2 cup (1 stick) butter, melted and cooled
     2 eggs, beaten

1. Preheat oven to 375°F. Grease 16 standard (2-1/2-inch) muffin cups.

2. Combine flour, oats, raisins, baking soda and salt in large bowl. Stir together wheat germ, buttermilk, honey, orange juice concentrate, butter and eggs in separate medium bowl. Make a well in the center of the flour mixture; add wheat germ mixture. Stir until just blended. Mixture may be slightly lumpy.

3. Spoon batter into prepared muffin cups, filling two-thirds full. Bake 25 minutes or until toothpick inserted into centers comes out clean. Cool 5 minutes in pans. Remove from pans to wire racks.

Makes 16 muffins

Dried Cherry-Almond Bread

Cherry Orange Poppy Seed Muffins

Cherry Orange Poppy Seed Muffins

(pictured above)

2 cups all-purpose flour
3/4 cup granulated sugar
1 tablespoon baking powder
1 tablespoon poppy seeds
1/4 teaspoon salt
1 cup milk
1/4 cup (1/2 stick) butter, melted
1 egg, lightly beaten
1/2 cup dried tart cherries
3 tablespoons grated orange peel

Combine flour, sugar, baking powder, poppy seeds and salt in large mixing bowl. Add milk, melted butter and egg, stirring just until dry ingredients are moistened. Gently stir in cherries and orange peel. Fill paper-lined muffin cups three-fourths full.

Bake in preheated 400°F oven 18 to 22 minutes or until wooden pick inserted in centers comes out clean. Let cool in pan 5 minutes. Remove from pan and serve warm or let cool completely.

Makes 12 muffins

Favorite recipe from **Cherry Marketing Institute**

Honey Pumpkin Muffins

1/4 cup butter or margarine, softened
3/4 cup honey
1 egg
1 cup solid-pack pumpkin
1-1/2 cups all-purpose flour
1-1/2 teaspoons baking powder
1 teaspoon baking soda
1/4 teaspoon salt
1 cup chopped toasted walnuts

Using electric mixer, beat butter until light; gradually add honey, beating until light and creamy. Beat in egg and pumpkin.

In medium bowl, combine flour, baking powder, baking soda and salt. Gradually add to butter mixture, mixing until blended; stir in walnuts. Spoon batter into 12 greased or paper-lined 2-1/2-inch muffin cups. Bake at 350°F for 25 to 30 minutes or until toothpick inserted in center comes out clean. Remove muffins from pan; cool on wire rack.

Makes 12 muffins

Favorite recipe from **National Honey Board**

Apple and Yogurt Coffee Cake

1/2 cup butter, at room temperature
1/2 cup granulated sugar
1/4 cup brown sugar
1/2 teaspoon vanilla
2 eggs
2 cups unbleached all-purpose flour
1 teaspoon ground cinnamon
3/4 teaspoon baking powder
3/4 teaspoon baking soda
1/4 teaspoon ground nutmeg
3 medium apples, peeled, cored and coarsely chopped
1 cup raisins
1/2 cup chopped walnuts
1 cup vanilla STONYFIELD FARM® Yogurt

TOPPING
1/4 cup brown sugar
2 tablespoons unbleached all-purpose flour
1/2 teaspoon ground cinnamon
2 tablespoons chopped walnuts

Preheat the oven to 325°F. Lightly grease a 9×13 pan. In a large bowl, cream together the butter and sugars. Add the vanilla and eggs and beat together. In another bowl, sift together the flour, cinnamon, baking powder, soda and nutmeg. Add apples, raisins and walnuts and toss lightly to coat.

Add the flour mixture to the butter mixture and mix thoroughly. Gently fold in the yogurt until evenly mixed. Pour the batter into the baking pan.

To make the topping, mix together the brown sugar, flour, cinnamon and walnuts. Sprinkle the topping over the batter. Bake the coffee cake for 40 to 50 minutes or until a toothpick inserted into the center comes out clean. Cool for 10 minutes on a wire rack before serving.   *Makes 14 servings*

Cinnamon Streusel Muffin Tops

(pictured on page 108)

1-2/3 cups (10-ounce package) HERSHEY'S Cinnamon Chips, divided
2 tablespoons butter or margarine
3 cups all-purpose flour, divided
1 cup sugar
1 cup chopped nuts
1-1/2 teaspoons baking powder
1/2 teaspoon baking soda
1/2 teaspoon ground cinnamon
1/4 teaspoon salt
2/3 cup milk
1/4 cup vegetable oil
1 egg, slightly beaten

1. Heat oven to 375°F. Lightly grease cookie sheet or line with parchment paper.

2. Place 2/3 cup cinnamon chips and butter in medium microwave-safe bowl. Microwave at medium (50%) 30 seconds; stir. If necessary, microwave at medium an additional 10 seconds at a time, stirring after each heating, until chips are melted and mixture is smooth when stirred. Add 3/4 cup flour; blend until mixture forms crumbs. Set aside.

3. Stir together remaining 2-1/4 cups flour, remaining chips, sugar, nuts, baking powder, baking soda, cinnamon and salt in large mixing bowl. Stir together milk, oil and egg; add all at once to flour mixture. Stir until just moistened (batter should be lumpy).

4. Spoon batter in 2-tablespoon size mounds 2 inches apart on prepared cookie sheet. Sprinkle reserved crumb mixture evenly over muffin tops. Bake 10 to 12 minutes or until golden brown. Cool slightly; remove from cookie sheet. Serve warm.

Makes about 20 muffin tops

Mini Pumpkin Cranberry Breads

(pictured at right)

 3 cups all-purpose flour
 1 tablespoon plus 2 teaspoons pumpkin pie spice
 2 teaspoons baking soda
 1-1/2 teaspoons salt
 3 cups granulated sugar
 1 can (15 ounces) LIBBY'S® 100% Pure Pumpkin
 4 large eggs
 1 cup vegetable oil
 1/2 cup orange juice or water
 1 cup sweetened dried, fresh or frozen
   cranberries

PREHEAT oven to 350°F. Grease and flour five or six 5×3-inch mini disposable or meatloaf pans.

COMBINE flour, pumpkin pie spice, baking soda and salt in large bowl. Combine sugar, pumpkin, eggs, oil and orange juice in large mixer bowl; beat just until blended. Add pumpkin mixture to flour mixture; stir just until moistened. Fold in cranberries. Spoon batter into prepared loaf pans.

BAKE for 50 to 55 minutes or until wooden pick inserted into center comes out clean. Cool in pans on wire racks for 10 minutes; remove to wire racks to cool completely. *Makes 5 or 6 mini loaves*

Peanut Butter Apple Muffins

 2 cups flour, sifted
 4 teaspoons baking powder
 3/4 teaspoon salt
 3/4 teaspoon cinnamon, divided
 1/4 teaspoon nutmeg
 1/4 cup peanut oil
 1/4 cup peanut butter
 1/4 cup plus 2 tablespoons sugar, divided
 1 egg
 1 cup milk
 3/4 cup chopped apple

Sift flour with baking powder, salt, 1/2 teaspoon cinnamon and nutmeg. Set aside. Cream oil and peanut butter with 1/4 cup sugar, beating until light and fluffy. Add egg; beat well. Stir in milk and chopped apple. Add flour mixture; stir just enough to moisten dry ingredients. Fill greased muffin tins 2/3 full and sprinkle top of batter with 2 tablespoons sugar mixed with 1/4 teaspoon cinnamon. Bake at 400°F for 20 to 25 minutes. *Makes 15 muffins*

Favorite recipe from **Peanut Advisory Board**

Banana Coffeecake

STREUSEL
 1/2 cup chopped pecans
 1/3 cup firmly packed brown sugar
 1 teaspoon ground cinnamon
 1 teaspoon ground nutmeg
CAKE
 1 package DUNCAN HINES® Moist Deluxe®
   Banana Supreme Cake Mix
 1 package (4-serving size) vanilla-flavor instant
   pudding and pie filling mix
 4 eggs
 1 cup ripe mashed bananas
 1/3 cup vegetable oil
 1/4 cup water
   Confectioners' sugar

1. Preheat oven to 350°F. Grease and flour 10-inch bundt pan or tube pan.

2. For streusel, combine pecans, brown sugar, cinnamon and nutmeg in small bowl. Stir until blended. Set aside.

3. For cake, combine cake mix, pudding mix, eggs, bananas, oil and water in large bowl. Beat at medium speed with electric mixer for 2 minutes. Pour half of batter into prepared pan. Sprinkle streusel over batter. Spread remaining batter over streusel. Swirl with knife in figure-eight pattern. Bake at 350°F for 55 to 60 minutes or until toothpick inserted in center comes out clean. Cool in pan 25 minutes. Invert onto cooling rack. Cool completely. Dust with confectioners' sugar.
Makes 12 to 16 servings

Note: Coffeecake can be made using two greased and floured 8-1/2×4-1/2-inch loaf pans. Pour batter into prepared pans. Sprinkle streusel on top and press mixture lightly with fork. Bake at 350°F for 45 to 50 minutes or until toothpick inserted in center comes out clean.

Tip: A quick powdered sugar glaze can be used to dress up any coffeecake or quick bread and give it a professional look. Be sure to wait until the bread has cooled slightly before adding the glaze, or it will be absorbed into the bread.

Mini Pumpkin Cranberry Bread

Banana-Chocolate Chip Bread

(pictured at right)

1-POUND LOAF
> 1/3 cup milk
> 1/3 cup mashed very ripe banana
> 1 large egg
> 1 tablespoon butter or margarine
> 3/4 teaspoon salt
> 2 cups bread flour
> 1/4 cup semisweet chocolate pieces
> 1-1/2 teaspoons FLEISCHMANN'S® Bread
>   Machine Yeast

1-1/2-POUND LOAF
> 1/2 cup milk
> 1/2 cup mashed very ripe banana
> 1 large egg
> 1 tablespoon butter or margarine
> 1 teaspoon salt
> 3 cups bread flour
> 1/3 cup semisweet chocolate pieces
> 2 teaspoons FLEISCHMANN'S® Bread
>   Machine Yeast

BREAD MACHINE DIRECTIONS
Use the 1-pound recipe if your machine pan holds 10 cups or less of water. Add ingredients to bread machine pan in the order suggested by manufacturer, adding mashed banana with milk, and semisweet chocolate pieces with flour. Recommended cycle: Basic/white bread cycle; medium/normal or light crust color setting. *Do not use delay cycle.*   *Makes 1 loaf (8 or 12 slices)*

Note: How this bread turns out depends on your machine. Some machines will make a smooth chocolate-colored bread. Others will leave bits of chocolate chips, and still others will give a marbled loaf.

Harvest Minis

> 1 cup all-purpose flour
> 1-1/2 teaspoons sugar
> 1-1/2 teaspoons baking powder
> 1/4 teaspoon salt
> 1/4 teaspoon pepper
> 1/2 cup milk
> 1 egg
> 2 tablespoons vegetable oil
> 2/3 cup frozen mixed diced vegetables, such as
>   carrots, corn, green beans and peas
> 1/2 cup shredded cheddar cheese

1. Preheat oven to 400°F. Grease 18 miniature (1-3/4-inch) muffin cups.

2. Combine flour, sugar, baking powder, salt and pepper in medium bowl. Combine milk, egg and oil in small bowl until blended; stir into flour mixture just until moistened. Stir in vegetables and cheese.

3. Spoon batter evenly into prepared muffin cups. Bake 15 to 20 minutes or until golden brown. Cool in pan on wire rack 5 minutes; remove from pan. Serve warm or let cool completely.
Makes 18 miniature muffins

Nutty Toffee Coffee Cake

(pictured on page 108)

> 1-1/3 cups (8-ounce package) HEATH®
>   BITS 'O BRICKLE® Toffee Bits, divided
> 1/3 cup plus 3/4 cup packed light brown sugar,
>   divided
> 2-1/4 cups all-purpose flour, divided
> 9 tablespoons butter or margarine, softened
>   and divided
> 3/4 cup granulated sugar
> 2 teaspoons baking powder
> 1/2 teaspoon ground cinnamon
> 1/4 teaspoon salt
> 1-1/4 cups milk
> 1 egg
> 1 teaspoon vanilla extract
> 3/4 cup chopped nuts

1. Heat oven to 350°F. Grease and flour 13×9×2-inch baking pan. Stir together 1/2 cup toffee bits, 1/3 cup brown sugar, 1/4 cup flour and 3 tablespoons butter. Stir until crumbly; set aside.

2. Combine remaining 2 cups flour, granulated sugar, remaining 3/4 cup brown sugar, remaining 6 tablespoons butter, baking powder, cinnamon and salt in large mixer bowl; mix until well blended. Gradually add milk, egg and vanilla, beating until thoroughly blended. Stir in remaining toffee bits and nuts. Spread batter in prepared pan.

3. Sprinkle reserved crumb topping over batter. Bake 30 to 35 minutes or until wooden pick inserted in center comes out clean. Serve warm or cool.
Makes 12 to 16 servings

Orange-Raisin Bran Muffins

Orange-Raisin Bran Muffins

(pictured above)

MAZOLA PURE® Cooking Spray
1/3 cup boiling water
1 cup natural high-fiber bran cereal shreds
1/2 cup orange juice
1/2 cup KARO® Light or Dark Corn Syrup
1/4 cup sugar
1/4 cup MAZOLA® Oil
1 egg
1/2 cup raisins
1 cup flour
1 teaspoon baking soda
1/4 teaspoon salt

1. Preheat oven to 400°F. Spray 12 (2-1/2-inch) muffin pan cups with cooking spray. In large bowl pour boiling water over cereal; let stand 2 minutes. Stir in orange juice, corn syrup, sugar, oil, egg and raisins.

2. In medium bowl combine flour, baking soda and salt. Stir flour mixture into cereal mixture until well blended. Spoon into prepared muffin pan cups.

3. Bake 15 to 20 minutes or until lightly browned and firm to touch. Cool in pan on wire rack 5 minutes; remove from pan.   *Makes 12 muffins*

Light and Cheesy Drop Biscuits

2 cups all-purpose flour
2 teaspoons baking powder
3/4 teaspoon salt
1/4 teaspoon baking soda
2-1/2 tablespoons shortening
1 cup buttermilk
1/4 cup finely shredded Cheddar cheese
1-1/2 teaspoons dried parsley (optional)

Combine flour, baking powder, salt and baking soda. Cut in shortening. Add buttermilk, cheese and parsley. Stir until flour is just moist. Drop by heaping tablespoons onto pan coated with nonstick spray. Bake at 400°F for 12 to 15 minutes.

Makes 15 biscuits

Favorite recipe from **North Dakota Wheat Commission**

Banana Date Bread

(pictured on page 108)

2 cups flour
1-1/2 teaspoons baking powder
1/4 teaspoon salt
2 eggs
2/3 cup KARO® Light or Dark Corn Syrup
1/2 cup MAZOLA® Oil
1 cup mashed ripe bananas (about 2 medium)
1 cup chopped dates
1 cup chopped walnuts

1. Preheat oven to 375°F. Grease and flour 9×5×3-inch loaf pan. In medium bowl combine flour, baking powder and salt.

2. In large bowl with mixer at medium speed, beat eggs, corn syrup and oil until blended. Beat in bananas. Gradually stir in flour mixture just until moistened. Stir in dates and walnuts. Pour into prepared pan.

3. Bake 60 to 70 minutes or until toothpick inserted into center comes out clean. Cool in pan 10 minutes. Remove from pan; cool on wire rack.

Makes 1 loaf or 12 servings

Toffee Scones Mix

(pictured at bottom right)

3-1/4 cups all-purpose flour
1/2 cup sugar
1 tablespoon plus 1 teaspoon baking powder
1/4 teaspoon salt
1-1/3 cups (8-ounce package) HEATH®
BITS 'O BRICKLE® Toffee Bits
1/2 cup toasted chopped walnuts*
Baking Instructions (recipe follows)

To toast walnuts: Heat oven to 350°F. Spread walnuts in thin layer in shallow baking pan. Bake 8 to 10 minutes, stirring occasionally. Cool.

1. Stir together flour, sugar, baking powder, salt, toffee bits and walnuts. Place in 1-quart heavy-duty resealable plastic food storage bag. Press out air; seal.

2. Place toffee baking mix bag in decorative gift bag or container. Attach baking directions.

BAKING INSTRUCTIONS
1. Heat oven to 375°F. Lightly grease 2 baking sheets.

2. Empty contents of toffee baking mix into large bowl. Stir 2 cups (1 pint) whipping cream into mixture, stirring just until ingredients are moistened.

3. Turn mixture out onto lightly floured surface. Knead gently until soft dough forms (about 2 minutes). Divide dough into three equal balls. One ball at a time, flatten into 7-inch circle; cut into 8 triangles. Transfer triangles to prepared baking sheets, spacing 2 inches apart. Brush with melted butter and sprinkle with sugar.

4. Bake 15 to 20 minutes or until lightly browned. Serve warm or cool.   *Makes 2 dozen scones*

helpful hint

Create an unforgettable gift for friends and family by giving them a homemade gift container filled with ingredients to make delicious scones. Since most of the ingredients are premeasured in the container, recipe preparation is easier and more fun.

Carrot and Raisin Muffins

2 cups all-purpose flour
1 tablespoon baking powder
1/2 teaspoon ground allspice (optional)
1/4 teaspoon salt
3/4 cup firmly packed dark brown sugar
1/2 cup SHEDD'S® Spread Country Crock® Spread
2 eggs
1 cup milk
1 cup raisins
1 carrot, shredded (about 3/4 cup)

Preheat oven to 375°F. Grease 12-cup muffin pan or line with paper cupcake liners; set aside.

In large bowl, combine flour, baking powder, allspice and salt; set aside.

In another large bowl, with electric mixer, beat sugar and SHEDD'S® Spread Country Crock Spread on medium-high speed until light and fluffy, about 5 minutes. Beat in eggs, scraping sides occasionally, until blended. Alternately beat in flour mixture and milk until blended. Stir in raisins and carrot. Evenly spoon batter into prepared pan.

Bake 18 minutes or until toothpick inserted in centers comes out clean. On wire rack, cool 10 minutes; remove from pan and cool completely.
Makes 12 muffins

Toffee Scones

Focaccia

(pictured at right)

- 1 cup water
- 1 tablespoon olive oil, plus additional for brushing
- 1 teaspoon salt
- 1 tablespoon sugar
- 3 cups bread flour
- 2-1/4 teaspoons (1 packet) RED STAR® Active Dry Yeast or QUICK•RISE™ Yeast or Bread Machine Yeast
-       Suggested toppings: sun-dried tomatoes, roasted bell pepper slices, sautéed onion rings, fresh and dried herbs in any combination, grated hard cheese

BREAD MACHINE METHOD

Place room temperature ingredients except toppings in pan in order listed. Select dough cycle. Check dough consistency after 5 minutes of kneading, making adjustments if necessary.

HAND-HELD MIXER METHOD

Combine yeast, 1 cup flour, sugar and salt. Combine water and 1 tablespoon oil; heat mixture to 120° to 130°F. Combine dry and liquid mixtures in mixing bowl on low speed. Beat 2 to 3 minutes on medium speed. By hand, stir in enough remaining flour to make a firm dough. Knead on floured surface 5 to 7 minutes or until smooth and elastic. Add additional flour, if necessary.

STAND MIXER METHOD

Combine yeast, 1 cup flour, sugar and salt. Combine water and 1 tablespoon oil; heat mixture to 120° to 130°F. Combine dry and liquid mixtures in mixing bowl with paddle or beaters for 4 minutes on medium speed. Gradually add remaining flour and knead with dough hook 5 to 7 minutes or until smooth and elastic. Add additional flour, if necessary.

FOOD PROCESSOR METHOD

In 2-cup measure, heat 1/4 cup water to 110° to 115°F; keep remaining 3/4 cup water cold. Add yeast; set aside. Insert dough blade in work bowl; add bread flour, sugar and salt. Pulse to combine. Add cold water and olive oil to yeast mixture; stir to combine. With machine running, add liquid mixture through feed tube in a steady stream only as fast as flour will absorb it. Open lid to check dough consistency. If dough is stiff and somewhat dry, add 1 teaspoon water; if soft and sticky, add 1 tablespoon flour. Close lid and process for 10 seconds. Check dough consistency again, making additional adjustments if necessary.

RISING, SHAPING AND BAKING

Place dough in lightly oiled bowl and turn to grease top. Cover; let rise until dough tests ripe.* Turn dough onto lightly floured surface; punch down to remove air bubbles. On lightly floured surface, shape dough into a ball. Place on greased baking sheet. Flatten to 14-inch circle. With knife, cut circle in dough about 1 inch from edge, cutting almost through to baking sheet. Pierce center with fork. Cover; let rise about 15 minutes. Brush with oil and sprinkle with desired toppings. Bake in preheated 375°F oven 25 to 30 minutes or until golden brown. Remove from baking sheet to cool. Serve warm or at room temperature.   *Makes 1 (14-inch) loaf*

*Place two fingers into the risen dough up to the second knuckle, then remove them. If the indentations remain the dough is ripe and ready to punch down.

Baker's Note: When flattening dough into a circle, if the dough does not stretch easily, let it rest a couple of minutes, then press it out. Repeat if necessary.

Grandma's® Molasses Banana Bread

- 1 cup whole wheat flour
- 3/4 cup all-purpose flour
- 2 teaspoons baking soda
- 1/2 teaspoon salt
- 1/2 cup butter, softened
- 3 large mashed bananas
- 1 cup GRANDMA'S® Molasses
- 1 egg
- 1/2 cup chopped walnuts

Heat oven to 350°F. In medium bowl, combine flours, baking soda and salt; set aside. Cream butter in large bowl. Beat in bananas, molasses and egg. Stir in walnuts. Mix in dry ingredients just until blended. Pour mixture into greased and floured 9×5-inch loaf pan. Bake 50 to 60 minutes. Cool on wire rack.

Makes 1 loaf

Yeast Bread Hints

Treat yourself to fresh-from-the-oven home-baked bread and rolls.

- Make the most of your time by making two breads from one dough recipe. Bake buttery rolls for dinner and use the same dough for super cinnamon buns for breakfast the next day.

- Almost any loaf recipe can be shaped into rolls.

- Breads containing eggs tend to brown more quickly than other breads. Watch the bread during the last 10 minutes of baking. If the bread is getting too brown, loosely cover with aluminum foil, shiny side up.

- To prevent bread from sweating and having a soggy crust, remove the bread from the pan as soon as it is done and let it cool on a wire rack.

Bread Machine Basics

For homemade bread enthusiasts, a bread machine is a versatile tool to make dough for all types of breads.

- Be sure to follow the manufacturer's directions. The ingredients must be added in a specific order.

- Until you become an expert, do not use a regular yeast bread recipe in a bread machine.

- If you are using the delayed cycle, do not use fresh ingredients such as milk, eggs and cheese so you avoid the risk of food poisoning.

Yeast Bread Washes

Washes produce crusts of varying colors and textures. Gently brush one of the following over the dough just before baking.

- **Water Wash:** For a crunchier crust, lightly brush or mist the top of the bread with water.

- **Egg Wash:** For a shiny, deep golden brown crust, make a wash with a whole egg beaten with a tablespoon of water.

- **Egg White Wash:** For a shiny, light golden crust, beat an egg white with 2 teaspoons of water.

- **Egg Yolk Wash:** For a very golden crust, beat an egg yolk with 2 teaspoons of water.

- **Milk Wash:** For a soft, less shiny, deep golden brown crust, brush the dough with milk.

- **Butter:** For a soft, richer-tasting crust, brush melted butter over the bread dough before or after baking.

Quick Breads

Quick breads include sweet and savory breads, biscuits, muffins and scones —all using either eggs, baking powder or baking soda as leavening instead of yeast.

- To prepare the most tender quick breads, avoid overmixing. Leave a few lumps or patches of flour in the batter.

- Since dried fruits such as raisins or dried apricots absorb moisture, plump the dried fruit in boiling water before adding it to the batter. The plumped fruit will help retain moisture in the baked bread.

- When baking muffins, fill any cups not filled with batter halfway full of water. The water not only keeps the pan from warping, but adds moisture to the oven, enlarging the muffins and allowing for even baking.

Sprinkles & Brush-ons

- To dress up bread or rolls and add more flavor, sprinkle unbaked dough with one of the following: seeds (such as sesame, poppy or sunflower), coarse salt, dehydrated minced garlic or onions, grated cheese or chopped nuts.

- Brush an egg wash over the dough first to make sure the sprinkles stick to the dough.

- For yeast doughs, add sprinkles after forming yeast bread loaves or rolls but before they begin the final rise.

- For quick breads, sprinkle toppings over biscuit dough or muffins just before baking.

- Try some of the following savory or sweet flavor combinations:

- **Peppercorn-Cheese Sprinkle:** Mix grated Parmesan cheese and cracked black pepper.

- **Multi-Seeds Sprinkle:** Mix equal amounts of several types of seeds such as sesame, poppy, sunflower or caraway.

- **Cinnamon-Sugar Sprinkle:** Mix regular or coarse (raw or sanding) sugar with ground cinnamon for a delicious sprinkle over muffins or sweet rolls.

- **Herb Brush-On:** Combine melted butter with dried rosemary, oregano and basil. Brush over biscuits or yeast roll dough before the last rise.

- **Garlic Brush-On:** Combine melted butter with garlic powder and coarse salt.

- **Streusel:** Add additional flavor to a basic coffeecake or muffin recipe by topping with streusel—a combination of flour, sugar, butter, various spices and sometimes chopped nuts.

When are They Done?

- **Biscuits** are done when the tops and bottoms of the biscuits are browned. For crispy biscuits browned on all sides, place them at least 1 inch apart on the baking sheet. For soft-sided biscuits, place them closer together, about 1/2 inch apart.

- **Muffins and Quick Breads** are done when a toothpick inserted near the center comes out clean and the edges start to shrink from the sides of the pan.

- **Yeast Breads** are done when the bread starts to pull away from the sides of the pan, the top and bottom are brown and the bread sounds hollow when tapped.

Freeze for Later

- **Biscuits:** Freeze unbaked cut biscuits immediately in a single layer. Once frozen, transfer the biscuits to a resealable freezer food storage bag. When ready to bake, do not thaw. Place the frozen biscuits on a baking sheet and double the baking time.

- **Muffins:** Keep a batch of unbaked muffins in the freezer for breakfast or an afternoon snack. There's no need to thaw them. Spoon the batter into paper-lined muffin cups, then place in the freezer. Once frozen, the individual cups can be transferred to a resealable freezer food storage bag. To bake, put the cups into a muffin pan. Bake at 300°F until they rise, then increase the temperature to 425°F to finish baking (about another 10 to 15 minutes).

- **Yeast Bread Dough:** Unbaked yeast bread dough can be frozen before baking either before or after it has been shaped. For best results, use specially developed recipes for freezer dough.

Main Dishes

Amazin' Crab Rice Cakes

(pictured at left)

1 cup chicken broth
1 cup MINUTE® White Rice, uncooked
2 eggs
2 cans (6 ounces each) crabmeat, drained, flaked*
2 tablespoons seafood seasoning
1/4 cup (1/2 stick) butter or margarine
Fresh lemon wedges (optional)

Or substitute 12 ounces canned salmon.

Bring broth to a boil in small saucepan. Stir in rice; cover. Remove from heat; let stand 5 minutes. Fluff with fork. Beat eggs lightly in medium bowl. Add rice, crabmeat and seasoning; mix well. Refrigerate 5 minutes. Shape into 8 patties. Melt butter in large skillet over medium heat. Add patties; cook 5 minutes on each side or until golden brown and heated through. Serve with lemon, if desired.

Makes 4 servings

Tip: To serve as appetizers, make patties bite-sized.

Clockwise from top left: *Amazin' Crab Rice Cakes, Cauliflower Mac & Gouda (p. 128), Marmalade-Glazed Ham Steak (p. 157), Chicken, Hummus and Vegetable Wraps (p. 156)*

Spanish Chicken and Rice

(pictured at right)

1 tablespoon olive oil
1 pound boneless skinless chicken breasts, diced
1 medium onion, chopped
1 medium red bell pepper, chopped
1 cup chicken broth
1 can (15 ounces) Spanish-style diced tomatoes, undrained
1 cup frozen peas
1 teaspoon garlic powder
1 teaspoon turmeric (optional)
2 cups MINUTE® White Rice, uncooked

Heat oil in large skillet over medium-high heat. Cook chicken, onions and bell peppers until chicken is browned, stirring occasionally. Add broth, tomatoes, peas, garlic powder and turmeric, if desired; bring to a boil. Stir in rice. Reduce heat to low; cover. Cook 5 minutes or until rice is tender.

Makes 4 servings

Tip: To make Easy Paella with Shrimp, add 1/2 pound peeled and deveined medium shrimp at the same time as the broth.

Autumn Beef and Cider Stew

2 slices bacon, cut into 1/2-inch pieces
2 pounds beef for stew, cut into 1 to 1-1/2-inch pieces
1 teaspoon salt
1/2 teaspoon pepper
1 can (10-1/2 ounces) condensed French onion soup
1 cup apple cider
1 pound sweet potatoes, peeled, cut into 1-inch pieces (about 3 cups)
1/3 cup sweetened dried cranberries

1. Cook bacon in stockpot over medium heat until crisp; remove with slotted spoon to paper-towel-lined plate. Brown 1/2 of beef in bacon drippings over medium heat; remove from stockpot. Repeat with remaining beef; season with salt and pepper.

2. Return beef and bacon to stockpot. Add soup and cider; bring to a boil. Reduce heat; cover tightly and simmer 1-3/4 hours.

3. Add sweet potatoes and cranberries to stockpot; bring to a boil. Reduce heat; continue simmering, covered, 20 to 30 minutes or until beef and potatoes are fork-tender. *Makes 4 to 6 servings*

Favorite recipe courtesy of **The Beef Checkoff**

Cauliflower Mac & Gouda

(pictured on page 126)

1 package (about 16 ounces) uncooked bowtie pasta
4 cups milk
2 garlic cloves, peeled and smashed
1/4 cup (1/2 stick) plus 3 tablespoons butter, divided
5 tablespoons all-purpose flour
1 pound Gouda cheese, shredded
1 teaspoon ground mustard
1/8 teaspoon smoked paprika or paprika
Salt and pepper
1 head cauliflower, cored and cut into florets
1 cup panko bread crumbs

1. Cook pasta according to package directions until almost tender. Drain pasta, reserving pasta water; keep warm. Return water to a boil.

2. Bring milk and garlic to a boil in small saucepan. Reduce heat; keep warm. Discard garlic.

3. Melt 1/4 cup butter in large saucepan over medium heat; whisk in flour. Cook 1 minute, whisking constantly. Gradually add milk, whisking after each addition. Bring to a boil. Reduce heat; cook and stir 10 minutes or until thickened. Remove from heat.

4. Add cheese, mustard and paprika to sauce mixture; whisk occasionally until melted. Season with salt and pepper. Keep warm.

5. Preheat broiler. Add cauliflower to boiling pasta water. Cook 3 to 5 minutes or just until tender; drain. Toss pasta and cauliflower with sauce mixture. Spoon pasta mixture into 10 to 12 ramekins or 13×9-inch baking dish.

6. Melt remaining 3 tablespoons butter in small saucepan over medium heat. Add panko; stir just until moistened. Remove from heat. Sprinkle panko mixture over pasta mixture. Broil 2 minutes or until golden brown. *Makes 6 to 8 servings*

Asian Pork Ribs with Spicy Noodles

(pictured at right)

1 can (14-1/2 ounces) beef broth
1/2 cup water
1/4 cup rice wine vinegar
1 ounce (2-inch piece) gingerroot, peeled and grated
1 cup (about 1 ounce) dried sliced shiitake mushrooms
1/4 teaspoon crushed red pepper flakes
1 tablespoon Chinese 5-spice powder
1 teaspoon ground ginger
1 teaspoon chili powder
1 tablespoon dark sesame oil
2 full racks pork back ribs (about 4 pounds total)
3/4 cup hoisin sauce, divided
1 pound (16 ounces) thin spaghetti, cooked according to package directions
1/4 cup thinly sliced green onions
1/4 cup chopped fresh cilantro

SLOW COOKER DIRECTIONS

1. Stir together broth, water, vinegar, grated gingerroot, mushrooms and red pepper flakes in 6-quart slow cooker.

2. Stir together 5-spice powder, ground ginger, chili powder and sesame oil to form a paste. Cut rib racks in half; blot dry with paper towels. Rub all surfaces with spice paste; brush tops with half of hoisin sauce.

3. Place ribs in slow cooker with broth mixture (do not stir). Cover and cook on LOW 8 to 10 hours or on HIGH 5 to 6 hours or until meat is tender when pierced with fork. Remove ribs to platter; brush lightly with remaining hoisin sauce. Keep warm. Skim off any fat from cooking liquid.

4. Place warm spaghetti in shallow bowls. Ladle some hot cooking liquid over spaghetti; sprinkle with green onions and cilantro. Slice ribs; serve over pasta. *Makes 4 servings*

helpful hint

To control the degree of spicy heat in a recipe, it's always better to start with too little crushed red pepper flakes since you can always add more. Keep in mind that leftover spicy food often tastes even hotter the next day.

Chili Dog Casserole

1 package SIMPLY POTATOES® Homestyle Slices
2 cans (15 ounces each) chili (no beans)
1 package (16 ounces) jumbo hot dogs, cut into 1-inch pieces
1 package (1 pound 3 ounces) refrigerated large flaky layer biscuits
2 cups (8 ounces) CRYSTAL FARMS® Shredded Cheddar cheese

1. Heat oven to 350°F. Spray 13×9-inch glass baking dish with nonstick cooking spray. Spread Simply Potatoes® in thin layer in bottom of baking dish. Top evenly with *one* can chili. Cover with aluminum foil; bake 30 minutes.

2. Uncover; top Simply Potatoes® with hot dogs and remaining chili. Separate biscuits; place over chili. Sprinkle with cheese. Continue baking, uncovered, 15 to 18 minutes or until biscuits are golden brown. *Makes 8 servings*

Italian Five-Cheese Chicken Roll-Ups

1 cup KRAFT® Finely Shredded Italian* Five Cheese Blend, divided
2 ounces (1/4 of 8-ounce package) PHILADELPHIA® Cream Cheese, softened
1/4 cup finely chopped green bell peppers
1/2 teaspoon dried oregano leaves
1/4 teaspoon garlic salt
4 small boneless, skinless chicken breast halves (1 pound), pounded to 1/4-inch thickness
1 cup spaghetti sauce

Made with quality cheeses crafted in the USA.

PREHEAT oven to 400°F. Mix 1/2 cup of the shredded cheese, the cream cheese, peppers, oregano and garlic salt until well blended. Shape into 4 logs. Place 1 log on one of the short ends of each chicken breast; press into chicken lightly. Roll up each chicken breast tightly, tucking in ends of chicken around filling to completely enclose filling.

PLACE, seam-sides down, in 13×9-inch baking dish sprayed with cooking spray. Spoon spaghetti sauce evenly over chicken; cover with foil.

BAKE 30 minutes or until chicken is cooked through (170°F). Remove foil; sprinkle chicken with remaining 1/2 cup shredded cheese. Bake an additional 3 to 5 minutes or until cheese is melted. *Makes 4 servings*

Asian Pork Ribs with Spicy Noodles

Orange-Cranberry Turkey Slice

Orange-Cranberry Turkey Slices

(pictured above)

1 pound turkey breast slices or cutlets
Salt and black pepper
2 tablespoons margarine
1 cup fresh cranberries*
1/3 cup orange juice
2 tablespoons packed brown sugar
1/4 cup raisins
2 tablespoons chopped green onion
2 tablespoons frozen orange juice concentrate

If fresh cranberries are not available, omit brown sugar, reduce orange juice to 2 tablespoons and substitute 1/4 cup canned whole cranberry sauce for 1 cup fresh cranberries.

1. Season turkey slices with salt and pepper. Brown turkey slices in margarine in skillet 2 to 3 minutes per side. Remove to platter; keep warm.

2. Add cranberries, orange juice and brown sugar to skillet; cook 5 minutes or until cranberries pop.

3. Stir in raisins, green onion and orange juice concentrate; heat through.

4. Serve sauce over warm turkey slices.

Makes 6 servings

Favorite recipe from **National Turkey Federation**

Magic Grilled Pork Tenderloin

2 pork tenderloins (about 1 pound each)
3 tablespoons CHEF PAUL PRUDHOMME'S PORK AND VEAL MAGIC®
1/2 cup orange marmalade
2 tablespoons Creole or Dijon mustard
1 tablespoon prepared horseradish
Vegetable oil, for brushing

Season the tenderloins evenly with the PORK AND VEAL MAGIC.

Combine the remaining ingredients and stir well. Set aside.

Preheat a charcoal or gas grill to medium-high heat. Brush the grill top lightly with vegetable oil. Place the tenderloins on the grill. Grill on one side about 5 minutes, adjusting the tenderloins to create a crosshatch pattern.

Turn the tenderloins and repeat the process on the other side. Continue to grill, turning several times, until a meat thermometer reads at least 155°F in the center of the meat, (about 30 minutes, but this varies depending on the size).

Brush the tenderloins with the glaze and turn quickly until the glaze is cooked, about 2 minutes. Remove from heat and serve.

Makes 6 to 8 servings

Slow Cooker Mustard Spiced Brats

1 package (19 ounces) BOB EVANS® Original or Beer Brats
1 small onion, finely diced, about 1/2 cup
1/2 cup spicy brown mustard
1/4 cup horseradish
1/4 cup malt vinegar
2 tablespoons brown sugar
1 tablespoon cornstarch
6 buns

In nonstick skillet over medium heat, brown brats, then transfer to crock pot. Add onion. In small bowl, combine mustard, horseradish, vinegar, brown sugar and cornstarch. Pour over brats. Cover and cook on low 4 to 6 hours or until brats are fully cooked. Place brats into buns. Stir mustard sauce and serve with brats. *Makes 5 servings*

Note: Recipe can be doubled. Just use 2 packages of brats and same amounts for the sauce.

Grande Beef Empanada

1 pound ground beef
1/4 cup raisins, chopped
1/4 cup chili sauce
1 teaspoon ground cumin
1/4 teaspoon salt
1/4 teaspoon pepper
1 refrigerated pie crust (1/2 of 15-ounce package)
Water

TOPPINGS
Salsa con queso, prepared salsa, chopped fresh cilantro

1. Heat oven to 400°F. Cook ground beef in large nonstick skillet over medium heat 8 to 10 minutes, breaking into small crumbles and stirring occasionally. Pour off drippings.

2. Stir in raisins, chili sauce, cumin, salt and pepper. Cook and stir 1 minute. Remove from heat.

3. Unfold pie crust; place on baking sheet. Spoon beef mixture evenly over 1/2 of dough, leaving 1-1/2-inch border around edge. Moisten edge of dough with water; fold pastry over filling. Press edges of dough together with fork to seal. Prick center of dough with fork once or twice to form steam vents.

4. Bake in 400°F oven 16 to 18 minutes or until pastry is golden brown. Serve with toppings, if desired.   *Makes 4 servings*

Beef Empanada Appetizers: Increase refrigerated pie crusts to 3 or 1-1/2 (15-ounce) packages. Prepare ground beef filling as above. Roll out each pie crust to a 14-inch circle on a lightly floured surface. Cut 10 circles from each crust with a 3-1/2 inch round cookie or biscuit cutter, spacing the cutouts closely. Spoon a generous tablespoon beef filling in center of each circle, leaving 1/4-inch border around edge. Moisten edge of dough with water; fold pastry over filling to form half-circle. Press edge together with fork to seal. Place on baking sheet. Bake in 400°F oven 14 to 16 minutes or until pastry is golden brown. Serve as above. Makes 30 appetizers.

Favorite recipe courtesy of **The Beef Checkoff**

Cashew Chicken Dijon
(pictured below)

2 cups MINUTE® White Rice, uncooked
2 tablespoons vegetable oil, divided
1 medium green bell pepper, cut into strips
1 medium red bell pepper, cut into strips
1 pound boneless skinless chicken breasts, cut into thin strips
1 cup low-sodium chicken broth
1/4 cup Dijon mustard
1 teaspoon cornstarch
1/4 cup cashews, coarsely chopped

Prepare rice according to package directions. Heat 1 tablespoon oil in large skillet over high heat. Add bell peppers; cook and stir until crisp-tender. Remove from skillet; cover to keep warm. Add remaining 1 tablespoon oil and chicken to skillet; cook and stir until chicken is cooked through. Remove from skillet; cover to keep warm. Mix broth, mustard and cornstarch. Add to skillet; cook on medium-high heat until thickened, stirring constantly. Return chicken and peppers to skillet; cook and stir 2 minutes or until heated through. Stir in cashews. Serve over rice.   *Makes 6 servings*

Tip: Cut chicken into strips while still slightly frozen.

Cashew Chicken Dijon

Porcupine Meatballs

(pictured below)

1 tablespoon butter or margarine
1 small onion, chopped
1 pound lean ground beef*
1 cup MINUTE® White Rice, uncooked
1 egg, lightly beaten
1 small packet meatloaf seasoning
1/4 cup water
1 jar (15-1/2 ounces or larger) spaghetti sauce

Or substitute ground turkey.

Melt butter in small skillet over medium-high heat. Add onion; cook and stir until tender. Place onion, meat, rice, egg and seasoning in large bowl. Add water; mix until well blended. Shape into medium-sized meatballs. Pour spaghetti sauce into skillet. Bring to a boil. Add meatballs; return to a boil. Reduce heat to low; cover. Simmer 15 minutes or until meatballs are cooked through.

Makes 4 servings

Tip: Round out each serving with 1/2 cup hot cooked rice and a serving of your kids' favorite vegetables.

Porcupine Meatballs

Shrimp Scampi Angel Hair Pasta with Lemon and Pine Nuts

1 carton (12 ounces) SEAPAK® Shrimp Scampi—Authentic Garlic and Butter
12 ounces angel hair pasta, dry
Finely grated zest and juice of 1 lemon
1/2 cup fresh flat-leaf parsley leaves, roughly chopped
1/3 cup pine nuts, toasted
Kosher salt and freshly ground black pepper

Boil large pot of cold water and salt it generously. Add the pasta and cook, stirring occasionally until al dente, 4 to 5 minutes. Drain the pasta reserving about 1 cup of the cooking water.

Prepare the shrimp in a large skillet according to package directions.

Stir the lemon zest and juice into the shrimp. Add the pasta, reserved pasta water, parsley and pine nuts, and toss in the skillet to coat the pasta evenly.

Divide shrimp and pasta among warm pasta bowls and serve. Season with salt and pepper.

Makes 4 servings

Country French Pizza

1 tablespoon vegetable oil
1 package SIMPLY POTATOES® Diced Potatoes with Onion
1/2 teaspoon dried basil leaves
1 package (14 ounces) 12-inch pre-baked Italian pizza crust
1 cup chopped ham
1 jar (7-1/2 ounces) marinated artichokes, drained, chopped
1 medium tomato, chopped
1 cup CRYSTAL FARMS® Shredded Mozzarella cheese

1. Heat oven to 425°F. In 12-inch nonstick skillet heat oil over medium-high heat. Add Simply Potatoes® and basil. Cover; cook 12 to 14 minutes, stirring occasionally, until Simply Potatoes® are tender and browned.

2. Place pizza crust on ungreased cookie sheet. Top crust with cooked Simply Potatoes®, ham, artichokes, tomatoes and cheese. Bake 10 to 12 minutes or until cheese is melted.

Makes 6 servings

Herb and Lemon-Scented Tilapia

Herb and Lemon-Scented Tilapia

(pictured above)

1 cup minced fresh Italian parsley
1/2 cup minced fresh chives
3/4 teaspoon salt, divided
1/2 teaspoon pepper, divided
1 large lemon
1 pound tilapia fillets (large fillets if available)
  Butter- or olive-oil-flavored nonstick cooking spray
4 tablespoons butter, divided

1. Combine parsley, chives, 1/2 teaspoon salt and 1/4 teaspoon pepper on a platter. Grate peel from lemon over herbs. Toss to combine. Reserve lemon.

2. Spray tilapia fillets with nonstick cooking spray. Press fillets into herb mixture to coat both sides.

3. Melt 2 tablespoons butter in large skillet over medium heat. Add tilapia. Cook 3 to 4 minutes per side or until fish flakes easily when tested with fork. Transfer to serving platter. Keep warm.

4. Add remaining 2 tablespoons butter to skillet; melt over low heat. Cut lemon in half; squeeze juice from one half into skillet. Stir remaining 1/4 teaspoon salt and 1/4 teaspoon pepper into lemon-butter mixture. Pour over fish. Slice remaining lemon half for garnish. Serve immediately.

Makes 4 servings

Glazed Corned Beef

(pictured at right)

1 uncooked corned beef brisket (about
    2 pounds), rinsed
3/4 cup apricot jam
2 tablespoons brown sugar
1/2 teaspoon cayenne pepper

1. Preheat oven to 350°F. Place corned beef in roasting pan. Cover with foil. Bake 45 minutes.

2. Combine jam, brown sugar and cayenne pepper in small bowl. Reserve half of mixture; set aside. Uncover corned beef; brush with 2 tablespoons of mixture. Roast 20 minutes; brush with another 2 tablespoons jam mixture. Roast additional 20 minutes or until tender.

3. Cut into thin slices to serve. Serve with reserved glaze. *Makes 6 to 8 servings*

Pepperoni Pizza Quiche

1 package (8 ounces) shredded Italian blend
    cheese, divided
2 ounces thinly sliced pepperoni (about 20 to
    30, 1-1/2 to 2-inch diameter slices), cut into
    quarters, divided
1 unbaked 9-inch (4 cup volume) frozen pie shell
1 can (12 fluid ounces) NESTLÉ® CARNATION®
    Evaporated Milk
3 large eggs, beaten
2 tablespoons all-purpose flour
1 teaspoon dried basil leaves
1/8 teaspoon garlic powder

PREHEAT oven to 350°F.

SPRINKLE *1 cup* cheese and *half* of pepperoni pieces onto bottom of pie shell.

WHISK evaporated milk, eggs, flour, basil and garlic powder in medium bowl until blended. Pour mixture into pie shell. Sprinkle with remaining cheese. Decorate top with remaining pepperoni pieces and any other topping you like. Place quiche on baking sheet (if pie pan is made of aluminum foil).

BAKE for 40 to 45 minutes or until knife inserted near center comes out clean. Cool for 5 minutes before serving. *Makes 8 servings*

Tip: Choose 1/4 cup of any of your favorite toppings (such as chopped onions, red or green peppers or sliced black olives) and add as topping with the remaining pepperoni pieces.

Chipotle Shrimp & Pineapple Kabobs

1 cup LAWRY'S® Baja Chipotle Marinade With
    Lime Juice, divided
1-1/2 pounds large shrimp, peeled and deveined
1 can (20 ounces) DOLE® Pineapple Chunks,
    drained
1 medium red onion, cut into chunks
2 red or green bell peppers, cut into chunks

• Pour 3/4 cup baja marinade over shrimp in large sealable plastic bag. Refrigerate and marinate for 30 minutes.

• Remove shrimp from baja marinade and plastic bag; discard marinade.

• Thread shrimp, pineapple chunks, onion and bell peppers onto skewers.

• Grill or broil 8 minutes turning and brushing with reserved baja marinade or until shrimp turns pink. Discard any remaining marinade.

Makes 4 to 6 servings

Cheesy Ham and Macaroni

1 (1.8 ounce) package white sauce mix
2 cups milk
1/2 cup grated Parmesan cheese
1/2 cup cubed American cheese
1/8 teaspoon ground pepper
7 ounces macaroni, cooked according to
    package directions, drained
1-1/2 cups diced fully cooked ham
1 cup frozen green peas, thawed

In a large saucepan, stir together white sauce mix and milk.* Following package directions, cook until thickened. Stir in cheeses and pepper. Add macaroni, ham and peas; cook, stirring until heated through. Serve hot. *Makes 6 servings*

*If you want to make a white sauce from scratch, melt 3 tablespoons butter in a saucepan. Stir in 1/4 cup flour and cook until mixture bubbles. Stir in 2 cups milk and cook, stirring until thickened.

Favorite recipe from **National Pork Board**

Glazed Corned Beef

Caribbean Glazed Swordfish with Grilled Pineapple Chutney

(pictured at right)

1/2 cup *Frank's® RedHot®* Cayenne Pepper Sauce or *Frank's® RedHot®* XTRA Hot Cayenne Pepper Sauce
1/4 cup packed light brown sugar
1 teaspoon dried thyme leaves
1/2 teaspoon ground allspice
2 tablespoons olive oil
4 swordfish steaks, 1-inch thick, seasoned with salt and pepper to taste
Grilled Pineapple Chutney (recipe follows)

1. Whisk together *Frank's® Redhot®* Sauce, sugar, thyme and allspice. Reserve 3 tablespoons mixture for Grilled Pineapple Chutney.

2. Mix oil into remaining spice mixture; thoroughly baste fish.

3. Place fish on well-greased grill. Cook, covered, over medium-high direct heat for 10 to 15 minutes until opaque in center, turning once. Serve with Grilled Pineapple Chutney. *Makes 4 servings*

Grilled Pineapple Chutney

1/2 of a fresh pineapple, peeled and sliced 1/2-inch thick
1 red or orange bell pepper, cut into quarters
2 tablespoons minced red onion
1 tablespoon minced candied ginger
1 tablespoon minced cilantro leaves

Grill pineapple and bell pepper about 10 minutes over medium direct heat until lightly charred and tender. Coarsely chop and place in bowl. Add reserved 3 tablespoons hot sauce mixture, onion, ginger and cilantro. Toss to combine.

Makes 3 cups

helpful hint

To ripen a pineapple, keep at room temperature for up to 5 days. To store ripe pineapple, refrigerate, tightly wrapped, for up to 3 days. A medium pineapple (about 3 pounds) makes about 3 cups cubed pineapple.

Teriyaki Rib Dinner

1 package (about 15 ounces) refrigerated fully cooked pork back ribs in barbecue sauce
2 tablespoons vegetable oil
1 large onion, thinly sliced
4 cups frozen Japanese-style stir-fry vegetables
1 can (8 ounces) pineapple chunks, undrained *or* 1 cup diced fresh pineapple
1/4 cup hoisin sauce
2 tablespoons cider vinegar

1. Remove ribs from package; reserve remaining barbecue sauce. Cut into individual ribs; set aside.

2. Heat oil in Dutch oven over medium-high heat. Add onion; cook and stir 3 minutes or until softened. Add vegetables; cook and stir 4 minutes.

3. Add ribs, reserved sauce, pineapple with juice, hoisin sauce and vinegar to vegetable mixture; mix well. Cover; cook 5 minutes or until hot.

Makes 4 servings

Cheeseburger Potatoes

1 package SIMPLY POTATOES® Homestyle Slices
2 to 3 tablespoons olive oil
1/2 teaspoon salt
1 pound lean ground beef
1/2 cup chopped onion
1/2 cup ketchup
1 teaspoon Worcestershire sauce
1 cup (4 ounces) CRYSTAL FARMS® Finely Shredded Cheddar cheese
1 cup chopped tomatoes
1/4 cup chopped pickles

1. Heat oven to 425°F. Place Simply Potatoes® in single layer on 15×10×1-inch baking pan. Drizzle with oil; sprinkle with salt. Gently turn Simply Potatoes® to coat evenly with oil. Bake 25 to 30 minutes, turning occasionally, until Simply Potatoes® are crisp and golden brown.

2. Meanwhile, cook ground beef and onion in 10-inch skillet over medium heat until beef is browned. Drain grease. Reduce heat to low; add ketchup and Worcestershire sauce. Cook until heated through.

3. To serve, divide Simply Potatoes® evenly onto 4 dinner plates. Top potatoes with one-fourth meat mixture, 1/4 cup cheese, 1/4 cup tomatoes and 1 tablespoon pickles. *Makes 4 servings*

Caribbean Glazed Swordfish with Grilled Pineapple Chutney

Grilled Fish Tacos

Grilled Fish Tacos

(pictured above)

3/4 teaspoon chili powder
  1 pound skinless mahi mahi, halibut or tilapia
    fillets
1/2 cup salsa, divided
  2 cups packaged coleslaw mix or shredded
    cabbage
1/4 cup sour cream
1/4 cup chopped fresh cilantro, divided
  8 (6-inch) corn tortillas, warmed

1. Prepare grill for direct cooking. Sprinkle chili powder over fish. Spoon 1/4 cup salsa over fish; let stand 10 minutes. Meanwhile, combine coleslaw mix, remaining 1/4 cup salsa, sour cream and 2 tablespoons cilantro in large bowl; mix well.

2. Grill fish, salsa side up, over medium heat, covered, 8 to 10 minutes without turning or until fish is opaque in center. Slice fish widthwise into thin strips or cut into chunks. Fill warm tortillas with fish and coleslaw mixture. Garnish with remaining cilantro.   *Makes 4 servings*

Asian Beef
with Mandarin Oranges

2 tablespoons vegetable oil
2 pounds boneless beef chuck, cut into 1/2-inch
    strips
1 small onion, thinly sliced
1 small green bell pepper, sliced
1 package (about 3 ounces) shiitake mushrooms,
    sliced
1 bunch bok choy, chopped
1 can (5 ounces) sliced water chestnuts, drained
1/3 cup soy sauce
2 teaspoons minced gingerroot
1/4 teaspoon salt
2 tablespoons cornstarch
1 can (11 ounces) mandarin oranges, drained
    and syrup reserved
2 cups beef broth
6 cups steamed rice

SLOW COOKER DIRECTIONS

1. Heat oil over medium-high heat. Working in batches, brown beef on all sides. Transfer browned beef to 4-quart slow cooker.

2. Add onion to same skillet. Cook and stir over medium heat until softened. Add green pepper, mushrooms, bok choy, water chestnuts, soy sauce, gingerroot and salt. Cook and stir until bok choy is wilted, about 5 minutes. Spoon mixture over beef.

3. Whisk together cornstarch and reserved mandarin orange syrup in medium bowl until blended. Stir in broth; pour over ingredients in slow cooker. Cover and cook on LOW 10 hours or on HIGH 5 to 6 hours or until beef is tender.

4. Stir in mandarin oranges. Serve over rice.
Makes 6 servings

helpful hint

Browning meats and poultry before cooking in the slow cooker is not necessary but can enhance the flavor and appearance of the finished dish.

Orange and Maple Glazed Roast Turkey

(pictured at bottom right)

1 small turkey (10 pounds), thawed if frozen
1/2 cup water
  Vegetable oil
1/4 cup (1/2 stick) butter
1/2 cup orange juice
2 tablespoons maple syrup
1/2 teaspoon chili powder
1/4 teaspoon salt
1/8 teaspoon pepper
1 cup chicken broth, divided
1 to 2 teaspoons all-purpose flour

1. Preheat oven to 325°F. Remove any packets from turkey cavity. Tuck ends of turkey drumsticks into cavity; tuck tips of wings under turkey.

2. Place turkey on rack in shallow roasting pan; add water to pan. Lightly brush turkey with oil; cover loosely with heavy-duty foil. Roast turkey 1 hour and 15 minutes. Remove foil and roast, uncovered, 1 hour.

3. Melt butter in small saucepan over medium heat. Stir in orange juice, maple syrup, chili powder, salt and pepper; bring to a simmer. Remove turkey from oven; generously brush glaze over turkey.

4. Roast 30 to 45 minutes or until turkey is golden brown and meat thermometer inserted into thickest part of thigh registers 165°F. Remove turkey to serving platter; cover loosely with foil. Set aside 15 to 20 minutes.

5. Skim fat from roasting pan. Place pan on stovetop over medium heat. Pour in 3/4 cup chicken broth, scraping up browned bits on bottom of pan. Stir flour and remaining 1/4 cup chicken broth in small cup until smooth. Add to roasting pan. Cook and stir over low heat until slightly thickened. If gravy is too thick, add additional broth or water. Slice turkey; serve with gravy.   *Makes 8 servings*

helpful hint

Thaw frozen poultry in the refrigerator, never at room temperature. Overnight thawing should be long enough for most chicken parts. For whole turkeys, allow 1 day of thawing for every 4 pounds.

Chicken A L'Orange

1 can (6 ounces) frozen unsweetened orange
  juice concentrate
1/2 cup water
1 tablespoon unsalted margarine
4 (4 ounces each) skinless chicken breast halves,
  bone-in
2 tablespoons MRS. DASH® Extra Spicy
  Seasoning Blend
1 large orange, cut into 1/4-inch slices
1 tablespoon cornstarch

1. Mix orange juice concentrate with water and set aside.

2. Melt margarine in large nonstick skillet over medium heat; brown chicken breasts on both sides.

3. Sprinkle each breast with MRS. DASH® Extra Spicy; top with one slice of orange. Reduce heat; pour half of orange juice mixture into skillet. Cover and cook, simmering for 15 to 20 minutes or until chicken juices run clear. When done, remove chicken to serving plate; keep warm. Discard orange slices.

4. Whisk cornstarch into remaining juice and stir mixture into skillet. Cook 1 to 2 minutes over low heat until slightly thickened.

5. To serve, pour sauce over chicken and garnish with remaining orange slices.   *Makes 4 servings*

Orange and Maple Glazed Roast Turkey

Chicken-Orzo Skillet

(pictured at right)

1 tablespoon olive oil
1 teaspoon Greek seasoning *or* 1 teaspoon
    oregano plus dash garlic powder
1/2 teaspoon grated lemon peel
1/2 teaspoon pepper
4 boneless skinless chicken breasts (about
    1-1/2 pounds), cut into 1-inch cubes
1 can (14-1/2 ounces) chicken broth
1-1/4 cups uncooked orzo pasta
6 ounces Greek green olives, drained
4 garlic cloves, minced
1/2 cup crumbled feta cheese
2 cups packed torn stemmed spinach

1. Heat large nonstick skillet over medium heat.
Add oil, seasoning, lemon peel and pepper. Cook
and stir just until fragrant. Add chicken. Cook and
stir 4 minutes. Stir in broth, orzo, olives and garlic.
Bring to a boil over high heat. Reduce heat and stir.
Simmer, partially covered, 15 minutes or until pasta
is just tender, stirring occasionally.

2. Stir in cheese. Place spinach on top of mixture.
Cover; let stand 2 to 3 minutes or until spinach
wilts. Stir to mix in spinach. Top with additional
cheese. *Makes 4 servings*

Quick & Crispy Mac & Cheese

1-1/3 cups *French's*® Cheddar or Original French
    Fried Onions
1 (10-3/4 ounce) can CAMPBELL'S® Condensed
    Cream of Celery Soup
1-1/4 cups milk
3 cups cooked elbow pasta (2 cups uncooked)
2 cups shredded Cheddar or cubed American
    cheese
1 cup diced cooked ham
1/2 cup frozen peas

1. Heat oven to 350°F. Crush French Fried Onions in
plastic bag.

2. Combine soup and milk in 2-quart baking dish.
Stir in pasta, cheese, ham and peas. Top with
crushed onions.

3. Bake 30 minutes or until heated through.
Makes 4 servings

BBQ Pulled Pork
with Cola BBQ Sauce

1 tablespoon seasoned salt
1 tablespoon brown sugar
1/2 teaspoon ground black pepper
1 (7 pound) Boston butt (bone-in pork shoulder
    roast)
Cola BBQ Sauce (recipe follows)
Hamburger buns

1. Combine seasoned salt, sugar and pepper. Rub
mixture into pork. Place meat into large resealable
plastic food storage bag. Refrigerate 3 hours.
Meanwhile, prepare Cola BBQ Sauce; reserve.

2. Transfer pork to rack in disposable foil pan.
Add enough water to just cover rack. Prepare grill
for indirect heat, setting temperature to medium/
medium-low (300°F). Cook pork in pan on covered
grill for 4 to 6 hours until internal temperature
reaches 195°F and meat is fall-off-the-bone tender.
Transfer to cutting board and let rest 15 minutes.

3. Wearing clean rubber gloves, remove and discard
fat and bone. Tear meat into long shreds, or chop
coarsely, if desired. In saucepan, heat 4 cups
shredded meat with 2 cups Cola BBQ Sauce. Serve
on hamburger buns. *Makes 14 cups pulled pork*

Tip: Leftover pulled pork can be portioned into
plastic bags and frozen. Reheat with additional
barbecue sauce and serve in wraps, tacos, nachos,
tostadas and enchiladas. Also great in soups,
stews and chili or as a topping on pizza.

Cola BBQ Sauce

2 tablespoons butter or vegetable oil
1 medium onion, finely chopped
1 clove garlic, minced
1-1/2 cups *Cattlemen's*® Award Winning Classic
    Barbecue Sauce or *Cattlemen's*® Authentic
    Smoke House Barbecue Sauce
1 (12 ounce) can cola soda
1/3 cup *French's*® Worcestershire Sauce

1. Melt butter in large skillet. Add onion and garlic;
cook 5 minutes over medium heat just until tender.

2. Add remaining ingredients. Heat to boiling.
Reduce heat; simmer, uncovered, 25 minutes until
sauce reduces to 2 cups, stirring occasionally.
Makes about 2 cups

Jerk Pork and Sweet Potato Stew

(pictured at right)

2 tablespoons all-purpose flour
1/4 teaspoon salt
1/4 teaspoon pepper
1-1/4 pounds pork shoulder, cut into bite-size pieces
2 tablespoons vegetable oil
1 large sweet potato, peeled and diced
1 cup corn
1/4 cup minced green onions, divided
1/2 medium scotch bonnet chile or jalapeño pepper,* cored, seeded and minced
1 garlic clove, minced
1/8 teaspoon ground allspice
1 cup chicken broth
1 tablespoon lime juice
2 cups cooked rice

Scotch bonnet chiles and jalapeño peppers can sting and irritate the skin, so wear rubber gloves when handling and do not touch your eyes.

SLOW COOKER DIRECTIONS

1. Combine flour, salt and pepper in large resealable food storage bag. Add pork; shake well to coat. Heat oil in large skillet over medium heat. Working in batches, add pork in single layer; brown on all sides, about 5 minutes. Transfer to 4- or 5-quart slow cooker.

2. Add sweet potato, corn, 2 tablespoons green onions, chile, garlic and allspice. Stir in broth. Cover and cook on LOW 5 to 6 hours.

3. Stir in lime juice and remaining 2 tablespoons green onions. Serve with rice.   *Makes 4 servings*

helpful hint

Always taste the finished slow cooker dish before serving. Adjust the seasoning to your preference. Seasoned herb blends, freshly ground pepper, lemon or lime juice, hot pepper sauce or minced fresh herbs perk up the flavor of your slow-cooked meal.

Pineapple Apricot Glazed Ham

1 can (20 ounces) DOLE® Pineapple Slices
1 (5-1/2-pound) ham
  Whole cloves
1 cup apricot jam or pineapple-apricot jam, divided
2 tablespoons balsamic or red wine vinegar
2 tablespoons honey
1 teaspoon cornstarch
1/8 teaspoon ground cinnamon

• Drain pineapple; reserve 3/4 cup juice. Chop 4 pineapple slices into small pieces; set aside.

• Score top of ham in diamond pattern, making 1/4-inch deep cuts. Insert cloves into each diamond. Place in shallow baking pan. Brush with 1/4 cup jam; cover with foil.

• Bake ham according to package directions. Arrange 6 pineapple slices on top of ham during the last 30 minutes of baking. Brush pineapple and ham with another 1/4 cup jam and continue baking.

• Combine reserved juice, vinegar, honey, cornstarch, cinnamon and remaining 1/2 cup jam in medium saucepan. Bring to boil. Reduce heat; cook and stir 2 minutes or until slightly thickened.

• Stir chopped pineapple into sauce; heat through. Serve warm over ham slices.   *Makes 16 servings*

All-in-One Burger Stew

1 pound ground beef
2 cups frozen Italian-style vegetables
1 can (14-1/2 ounces) diced tomatoes with basil and garlic
1 can (14-1/2 ounces) beef broth
2-1/2 cups uncooked medium egg noodles
  Salt and pepper

1. Brown beef in Dutch oven or large skillet 6 to 8 minutes over medium-high heat, stirring to separate meat. Drain fat.

2. Add vegetables, tomatoes and broth; bring to a boil over high heat.

3. Add noodles; reduce heat to medium. Cover and cook 12 to 15 minutes or until noodles have absorbed liquid and vegetables are tender. Season with salt and pepper.   *Makes 6 servings*

Southern Border Meat Loaf

Southern Border Meat Loaf

(pictured above)

    1 pound ground beef
1/2 cup cornmeal
1/2 cup finely chopped yellow onion
1/4 cup chopped fresh cilantro leaves
    1 can (4 ounces) chopped mild green chiles
    2 egg whites *or* 1 egg
1-1/2 teaspoons ground cumin
1/4 teaspoon salt
1/4 teaspoon pepper
    1 can (8 ounces) tomato sauce, divided
    2 tablespoons ketchup

1. Preheat oven to 350°F. Combine beef, cornmeal, onion, cilantro, chiles, egg whites, cumin, salt, pepper and half of tomato sauce in mixing bowl; mix well. Combine remaining tomato sauce and ketchup in a small bowl.

2. Place meat mixture on rimmed baking sheet coated with nonstick cooking spray; shape into 6×9-inch oval. Top with tomato sauce mixture. Bake 55 minutes or until cooked through (160°F).

3. Let stand 5 minutes before slicing.

Makes 4 servings

helpful hint

Leftover meat loaf is a great start for meals later in the week. Slices make terrific sandwiches. Or, combine meat loaf crumbles with spicy canned tomatoes or your favorite pasta sauce for tasty chili or pasta meals.

Baked Fusilli with Roasted Vegetables

1 large eggplant, cut in half
3 medium red bell peppers, cut in half
1 large sweet onion, cut into quarters
2 tablespoons olive oil
1 container (15 ounces) ricotta cheese
  Salt and pepper
1 package (about 16 ounces) fusilli pasta,
  cooked and drained
3 cups (12 ounces) shredded mozzarella cheese
1/2 cup grated Parmesan cheese

1. Preheat oven to 375°F. Line 2 baking sheets with foil. Place eggplant, peppers and onion, cut side down, on prepared baking sheets. Brush with oil; roast 30 minutes or until tender. Let cool; cut vegetables into bite-size pieces.

2. Combine ricotta and vegetables in large bowl; season with salt and pepper. Add pasta; stir just until combined.

3. Spoon half of pasta mixture into 13×9-inch baking dish. Sprinkle with half of each cheese. Repeat layers. Bake 25 minutes or until cheese begins to brown. *Makes 6 to 8 servings*

Turkey Cutlets Diane

1 package (about 1 pound) PERDUE® FIT 'N
  EASY® Fresh Skinless & Boneless Thin-Sliced
  Turkey Breast Cutlets
  Salt and black pepper to taste
2 tablespoons butter or margarine
2 tablespoons minced shallots
1/2 cup chicken broth or water
1 tablespoon Worcestershire sauce
1 teaspoon Dijon mustard

Season cutlets with salt and pepper. In large heavy skillet over medium-high heat, melt butter. Add shallots; sauté 1 minute. Add cutlets; sauté 1 to 2 minutes on each side or until lightly browned. Stir in remaining ingredients; cook 1 minute longer. Serve cutlets accompanied by pan sauce.
Makes 4 servings

Pineapple Teriyaki Chicken Kabobs

(pictured below)

1 can (20 ounces) DOLE® Pineapple Chunks
3/4 cup LAWRY'S® Teriyaki Marinade With
  Pineapple Juice
1 teaspoon Dijon-style mustard
4 (1-1/2- to 1-3/4-pound) boneless, skinless
  chicken breasts, cut into 1-inch pieces
2 red or green bell peppers, cut into 1-1/2-inch
  pieces
1 zucchini cut into 1/2-inch-thick slices
12 wooden skewers (12 inches long) soaked in
  water

• Drain pineapple; reserve 2 tablespoons juice.

• Combine pineapple juice, teriyaki marinade and mustard. Set aside 1/4 cup for grilling. Pour remaining marinade into sealable plastic bag; add chicken pieces, bell peppers and zucchini. Refrigerate and marinate for 30 minutes.

• Remove chicken and vegetables from plastic bag and discard marinade.

• Thread bell pepper, pineapple chunks, chicken and zucchini onto skewers. Brush with reserved marinade.

• Grill or broil 10 to 15 minutes, turning and brushing occasionally with teriyaki marinade, or until chicken is no longer pink. Discard any remaining marinade. *Makes 4 servings*

Pineapple Teriyaki Chicken Kabobs

Turkey Pot Pie Casserole

(pictured at right)

Nonstick cooking spray
2 pounds turkey breast, cut into 1-inch cubes
6 tablespoons butter
2/3 cup all-purpose flour
1/2 teaspoon ground sage
1/2 teaspoon ground thyme
1-1/2 cups chicken broth
1 cup milk
1 bag (16 ounces) frozen soup vegetables (carrots, potatoes, peas, celery, green beans, corn, onions and lima beans)
1 teaspoon salt
1/2 teaspoon pepper
1 container (8 ounces) refrigerated crescent roll dough

1. Preheat oven to 375°F. Coat 13×9-inch baking dish with cooking spray; set aside. Coat large nonstick skillet with cooking spray; heat over medium heat. Working in batches, brown turkey on all sides. Transfer to platter.

2. Melt butter in skillet until foamy. Whisk in flour, sage and thyme. Cook and stir 5 minutes. Slowly whisk in broth and milk. Cook, whisking constantly, about 5 minutes or until thickened.

3. Stir in turkey, vegetables, salt and pepper. Cook, stirring frequently, 5 to 7 minutes or until thick and creamy. Spoon mixture into prepared dish. Unroll crescent roll dough. Place over top of casserole. Bake 15 minutes or until top is golden brown.

Makes 6 servings

Classic Beef Stroganoff

1 cup MINUTE® White Rice, uncooked
1 tablespoon vegetable oil
1 cup chopped onion
1 pound lean ground beef
2 cups sliced mushrooms
1 can (14-1/2 ounces) beef broth
1 can (10-3/4 ounces) cream of mushroom soup
1 tablespoon Worcestershire sauce
1/2 cup sour cream

Prepare rice according to package directions. Heat oil in medium skillet over medium-high heat. Add onion; cook and stir 3 minutes. Add beef and brown; drain excess fat. Add mushrooms, broth, soup and Worcestershire sauce. Bring to a boil and simmer 5 minutes. Stir in sour cream. Serve over rice.

Makes 4 servings

Mediterranean Meatloaf

1/4 cup sun-dried tomatoes (about 1 ounce)
1 package (10 ounces) frozen chopped spinach, thawed and drained
1/2 cup chopped onion
1/4 cup crumbled feta cheese
1-1/2 pounds lean ground turkey
1 cup QUAKER® Oats (quick or old fashioned, uncooked)
1 teaspoon garlic powder
1 teaspoon dried oregano
1/2 teaspoon salt (optional)
1/4 teaspoon black pepper
1/2 cup milk

1. Heat oven to 400°F. Soften tomatoes according to package directions. Set aside.

2. Cook and stir spinach and onion in small skillet over low heat 4 to 5 minutes or until onion is tender. Remove from heat; cool slightly. Stir in cheese. Set aside.

3. Combine turkey, oats, garlic powder, oregano, salt, if desired, pepper, milk and reserved tomatoes in large bowl; mix lightly but thoroughly. Shape 2/3 of turkey mixture into 9×6-inch loaf and place on rack of broiler pan. Make deep indentation down center of loaf, leaving about 1-1/2 inches around edges of loaf. Fill with spinach mixture. Top with remaining turkey mixture. Seal edges to completely enclose filling.

4. Bake 30 to 35 minutes or until meat juices run clear. Let stand 5 minutes before slicing.

Makes 6 servings

helpful hint

Chewy and sweet sun-dried tomatoes add a rich tomato flavor to many dishes. They are also a great garnish. The dried variety must be softened in water before using them. Sun-dried tomatoes are also available packed in olive oil.

Turkey Pot Pie Casserole

Herb-Roasted Chicken and Corn Bread Dressing

(pictured at right)

CHICKEN

- 1/2 cup chopped fresh parsley
- 2 teaspoons grated lemon peel
- 2 tablespoons lemon juice
- 1 teaspoon dried thyme
- 3/4 teaspoon dried sage
- 1/2 teaspoon dried rosemary
- 1/2 teaspoon salt
- 1/4 teaspoon pepper
- 1 chicken (3-1/2 to 4 pounds)
- 1 cup water

DRESSING

- Nonstick cooking spray
- 4 ounces bulk sausage
- 1 cup finely chopped onion
- 2 medium stalks celery with leaves, thinly sliced
- 1 medium red bell pepper, diced
- 1 can (14-1/2 ounces) chicken broth
- 2 cups corn bread stuffing mix
- 1/2 teaspoon poultry seasoning

1. Preheat oven to 450°F. Adjust oven rack to lowest position. Combine parsley, lemon peel, lemon juice, thyme, sage, rosemary, salt and pepper in small bowl; mix well.

2. Separate chicken skin from meat by sliding fingers under skin. Spread parsley mixture evenly over chicken; cover with skin. (If skin tears, use toothpicks to hold skin together.) Place on rack in roasting pan, breast side up. Roast 20 minutes. Add water to pan. Roast 40 minutes or until meat thermometer inserted into thickest part of thigh registers 165°F. Remove from oven; let stand 15 minutes before slicing.

3. Meanwhile, coat large nonstick skillet with cooking spray. Heat over medium-high heat. Add sausage; cook 3 minutes or until cooked through, stirring to break up meat. Set aside on plate.

4. Add onion, celery and bell pepper to skillet. Cook and stir over medium heat 7 minutes or until celery is tender. Add broth. Bring to a boil. Remove from heat. Add sausage, stuffing mix and poultry seasoning; mix well. Serve with chicken.

Makes 6 servings

Variation: Add 1 garlic clove, minced, to parsley mixture.

Beef and Cabbage à la Mexicana

- 1 head cabbage, separated into individual leaves
- 1 box (about 10 ounces) Spanish-style rice mix, plus ingredients to prepare
- 2 pounds ground beef
- 1 cup Italian-style bread crumbs
- 1 cup chopped onion
- 1 cup chopped green bell pepper
- 2 eggs
- 1 tablespoon Worcestershire sauce
- 1 teaspoon taco seasoning
- 1 garlic clove, minced
- Salt and pepper
- 1 bottle (about 32 ounces) tomato juice

SLOW COOKER DIRECTIONS

1. Bring water to a boil in large saucepan. Drop cabbage leaves into boiling water for 3 minutes or until tender. Remove from water with slotted spoon; drain and set aside. Prepare Spanish rice according to package directions; set aside.

2. Mix together ground beef, bread crumbs, onion, bell pepper, eggs, Worcestershire sauce, taco seasoning and garlic in large bowl. Season with salt and pepper.

3. Place one cabbage leaf on plate. Spread 1/2 cup beef mixture and 1/4 cup Spanish rice evenly onto leaf; roll up and secure with toothpick. Place seam side down in slow cooker. Repeat with remaining cabbage leaves, beef mixture and rice. Pour tomato juice over cabbage bundles. Cover and cook on HIGH 4 to 6 hours.

Makes 6 servings

helpful hint

Slow cooker recipes provide a range of cooking times in order to account for variables such as the amount of ingredients in the slow cooker. To ensure the dish is done, measure the temperature of the ingredients in the center of the food. It should be at least 165°F.

Herb-Roasted Chicken and Corn Bread Dressing

Black Bean Cakes

Black Bean Cakes

(pictured above)

1 can (15 ounces) black beans, rinsed and
    drained
1/4 cup all-purpose flour
1/4 cup chopped fresh cilantro
2 tablespoons plain yogurt or sour cream
1 tablespoon chili powder
2 garlic cloves, minced
    Nonstick cooking spray
    Salsa

1. Place beans in medium bowl; mash with fork or
potato masher until almost smooth, leaving some
beans in larger pieces. Stir in flour, cilantro, yogurt,
chili powder and garlic.

2. Spray large nonstick skillet with cooking spray;
heat over medium-high heat. For each cake, drop
2 heaping tablespoonfuls bean mixture into skillet;
flatten to form cake. Cook 6 to 8 minutes or until
lightly browned, turning once. Serve with salsa.

Makes 4 servings

Chicken Carbonara Risotto

1 tablespoon vegetable oil
1 pound boneless skinless chicken breasts,
    cut into strips
1 can (10-3/4 ounces) condensed cream of
    chicken soup
1-1/2 cups milk
1 cup frozen peas
2 cups MINUTE® White Rice, uncooked
1/4 cup real bacon bits
1/4 cup grated Parmesan cheese*

*Or substitute grated Romano cheese.

Heat oil in large skillet over medium-high heat. Add
chicken; cook and stir 4 to 5 minutes or until cooked
through. Add soup, milk and peas; bring to a boil.
Stir in rice; cover. Reduce heat to medium-low;
simmer 5 minutes. Stir in bacon bits and Parmesan
cheese. *Makes 4 servings*

Pepper and Swiss Chard Turkey Stir-Fry

1 pound turkey cutlets or slices, cut into
    1/4-inch strips
1/2 teaspoon salt
1/4 teaspoon black pepper
1 tablespoon olive oil, divided
1 red bell pepper, cut into 1/4-inch strips
1 yellow bell pepper, cut into 1/4-inch strips
1 pound Swiss chard, stalks removed and
    coarsely chopped
2 tablespoons balsamic vinegar
2 tablespoons sugar

1. In medium bowl, combine turkey, salt and black
pepper. In large nonstick skillet, over medium-high
heat, sauté turkey in 2 teaspoons oil 4 to 5 minutes
or until turkey is no longer pink in center. *Do not
overcook.* Remove turkey from pan; set aside.

2. Add remaining 1 teaspoon oil to skillet and sauté
bell peppers 2 minutes. Gently fold in Swiss chard.

3. In small bowl, combine vinegar and sugar; stir
into vegetable mixture. Reduce heat to medium and
stir-fry 2 to 3 minutes or until vegetables are tender.
Return turkey strips to pan and heat well. Serve
immediately. *Makes 4 servings*

Favorite recipe from **National Turkey Federation**

Cranberry-Glazed Pork and Sweet Potatoes

2 teaspoons vegetable oil
4 pork chops, bone-in, 1 inch thick (about
     2-1/2 pounds)
1/4 teaspoon salt
1 cup chicken broth
1/3 cup maple syrup
1/4 cup orange juice
1/2 teaspoon ground cinnamon
1/2 teaspoon pepper
1/4 teaspoon ground allspice
     Pinch crushed red pepper flakes
4 cups peeled sweet potatoes, cut into
     2-inch cubes
1-1/2 cups fresh cranberries

1. Heat oil in large nonstick skillet over medium-high heat. Sprinkle pork chops with salt. Cook 4 minutes per side or until browned on both sides. Transfer chops to plate.

2. Add broth to skillet, stirring to scrape up any browned bits. Stir in syrup, juice, cinnamon, pepper, allspice, pepper flakes and potatoes. Bring to a boil.

3. Return chops to skillet. Reduce heat. Cover; simmer 15 to 20 minutes or until potatoes are tender and chops are barely pink in center. Transfer chops and potatoes to plate; keep warm.

4. Add cranberries to skillet. Bring to a boil over high heat. Reduce heat to medium. Cook, stirring frequently, about 6 minutes or until liquid is almost syrupy and reduced to 1 cup. Serve pork chops and potatoes with sauce.   *Makes 4 servings*

Slow Cooked Chicken Ratatouille

3 to 4 pound chicken, cut into serving pieces
1 can (14.5 ounces) diced tomatoes, drained
1 cup white mushrooms, quartered
1/2 cup LAWRY'S® Italian Garlic Steak Marinade
     With Roasted Garlic & Olive Oil
1 small zucchini, cut into 1/4-inch pieces
1 small onion, sliced
1 medium green bell pepper, cut into 1-inch
     pieces
1/2 teaspoon LAWRY'S® Seasoned Salt

In slow cooker, arrange chicken, then add remaining ingredients. Cook covered on high 4 to 6 hours or low 8 to 10 hours. Serve, if desired, over hot cooked rice.   *Makes 10 servings*

Easy Santa Fe Style Stuffed Peppers

(pictured below)

1 cup MINUTE® Brown Rice, uncooked
     Nonstick cooking spray
1 pound lean ground beef*
1 package (10 ounces) frozen whole-kernel corn
1-1/2 cups chunky salsa
4 large bell peppers, tops and seeds removed
1 cup shredded Colby and Monterey Jack cheese

Or substitute ground turkey.

Prepare rice according to package directions. Preheat oven to 425°F. Spray large nonstick skillet with nonstick cooking spray. Add meat and brown over medium heat; drain excess fat. Stir in corn, salsa and rice. Pierce peppers with fork or sharp knife; place in baking dish. Fill peppers with meat mixture. Cover with foil. Bake 20 minutes. Uncover. Sprinkle with cheese before serving.

Makes 4 servings

Easy Santa Fe Style Stuffed Peppers

Roasted Pepper Picante Chicken

(pictured at right)

- 4 ounces uncooked egg noodles
  Nonstick cooking spray
- 1 pound chicken tenders, cut into bite-size pieces
- 1/2 cup mild or medium picante sauce
- 1/2 cup chopped roasted red bell peppers
- 1/4 cup water
- 1/2 teaspoon ground cumin
- 3/4 cup (3 ounces) shredded cheddar cheese

1. Cook noodles according to package directions; drain.

2. Meanwhile, coat medium nonstick skillet with cooking spray; heat over medium-high heat. Add chicken. Cook and stir 2 minutes. Add picante sauce, peppers, water and cumin. Bring to a boil. Reduce heat to medium-low. Cover; simmer 10 minutes or until slightly thickened. Serve over noodles. Sprinkle evenly with cheese.

Makes 4 servings

Turkey Pizzas

- 6 ounces ground turkey
- 1 package (11 ounces) refrigerated French bread dough
- 1/2 cup spaghetti sauce
- 1 to 2 teaspoons dried oregano *or* 1 tablespoon chopped fresh oregano
- 1/2 cup (2 ounces) shredded mozzarella cheese
- 17 slices turkey pepperoni, quartered
- 2 tablespoons grated Parmesan cheese

1. Preheat oven to 350°F. Coat nonstick baking sheet with nonstick cooking spray; set aside.

2. Heat medium skillet over medium-high heat. Add turkey. Cook, stirring to break up meat, until cooked through.

3. Unroll dough onto work surface. Cut into 6 squares. Place squares on prepared baking sheet. Spoon 1 tablespoon spaghetti sauce on each square; spread evenly to within 1/2 inch of edges. Top evenly with turkey, oregano, mozzarella and pepperoni.

4. Bake 17 minutes or until edges are lightly browned. Sprinkle with Parmesan cheese.

Makes 6 servings

Just Peachy Peanutty Pork

- 6 boneless chops (about 1-1/2 pounds), trimmed and cut into 4×1×1-inch strips
- 1/4 cup peanut butter
- 1/4 cup peach jam
- 1-1/2 cups shredded coconut
- 3/4 cup graham cracker crumbs
- 2 teaspoons curry powder
- 1 teaspoon ground ginger
- 1/2 teaspoon ground black pepper

Heat oven to 400°F. Spray a 15×10×1-inch baking pan with nonstick cooking spray. In small saucepan, stir peanut butter and jam over low heat until melted; remove from heat. Add pork and toss to coat. In a large resealable plastic bag, combine coconut, cracker crumbs, curry powder, ginger and pepper; shake well to blend. Add pork to bag, a few pieces at a time; shake to coat.* Place pork in prepared pan and bake 8 minutes. Turn and bake 8 minutes more until coconut is lightly toasted. Serve with hot cooked rice or couscous and chutney, if desired. *Makes 6 servings*

*Coconut/crumb mixture can be placed in a large shallow dish, pork added then turned to coat.

Favorite recipe from **National Pork Board**

Lemony Chicken and Rice

- 1 tablespoon olive oil
- 1 pound boneless chicken thighs, chopped
- 2 cups water
- 1 package (6 ounces) chicken-and-vegetable rice blend
- 1/2 teaspoon dried oregano
- 1/4 teaspoon dried rosemary
- 2 cups small broccoli florets
- 3 tablespoons butter, softened
- 2 to 3 teaspoons grated lemon peel
- 3 tablespoons lemon juice
- 1/4 teaspoon salt

Heat large saucepan over medium-high heat. Add oil and chicken. Cook and stir until chicken just begins to brown. Add water; bring to a boil. Stir in rice blend and contents of seasoning packet, oregano and rosemary. Add broccoli. Return to a boil. Reduce heat; simmer 2 minutes. Remove from heat. Stir in butter, lemon peel, lemon juice and salt. Cover; let stand 5 minutes or until liquid is absorbed. *Makes 4 servings*

Oven-Fried Chicken Tenders

Oven-Fried Chicken Tenders

(pictured above)

    3/4 cup vegetable oil
      1 cup buttermilk
      1 egg, beaten
      1 cup all-purpose flour
      2 to 3 teaspoons Cajun seasoning
    3/4 teaspoon paprika
    1/2 teaspoon garlic powder
  1-1/2 pounds chicken tenders
        Salt and pepper

1. Place large roasting pan on rack of cold oven. Add oil. Heat oven to 425°F.

2. Meanwhile, whisk together buttermilk and egg in medium bowl until well blended. Combine flour, Cajun seasoning, paprika and garlic powder in shallow baking dish or pie plate. Coat each chicken tender with flour mixture. Dip each into buttermilk mixture. Coat each again with flour mixture. Place on plate in single layer. (If chicken begins to absorb flour, coat with flour mixture again.)

3. Place coated chicken tenders in heated oil in roasting pan in oven. Bake 6 minutes. Turn. Bake 6 to 7 minutes more or until golden and no longer pink in center. Place tenders on serving platter. Season with salt and pepper.   *Makes 4 servings*

Chicken, Hummus and Vegetable Wraps

(pictured on page 126)

    3/4 cup hummus
      4 (8- to 10-inch) sun-dried tomato or spinach
        wraps, or whole-wheat flour tortillas
      2 cups shredded rotisserie chicken breast or
        chopped cooked chicken breast
        Chipotle hot sauce or Louisiana-style hot sauce
        (optional)
    1/2 cup matchstick or thinly sliced carrots
    1/2 cup chopped unpeeled cucumber
    1/2 cup thinly sliced radishes
      2 tablespoons chopped fresh mint or basil

Spread hummus evenly over wraps all the way to edges. Arrange chicken over hummus; sprinkle with hot sauce, if desired. Top with carrots, cucumber, radishes and mint. Roll up tightly. Cut in half diagonally.   *Makes 4 servings*

Variation: Substitute alfalfa sprouts for the radishes.

Cumin-Rubbed Steaks with Avocado Salsa Verde

      2 beef shoulder center steaks (ranch), cut 1 inch
        thick (about 8 ounces *each*)
      2 teaspoons ground cumin
    3/4 cup prepared tomatillo salsa
      1 small avocado, diced
      2 tablespoons chopped fresh cilantro

1. Press cumin evenly onto beef steaks. Heat large nonstick skillet over medium heat until hot. Place steaks in skillet; cook 13 to 16 minutes for medium rare to medium doneness, turning occasionally.

2. Meanwhile, combine salsa, avocado and cilantro in small bowl.

3. Carve steaks into slices; season with salt, as desired. Serve with salsa.   *Makes 4 servings*

Tip: Two beef top loin (strip) steaks, cut 1 inch thick, may be substituted for shoulder center steaks. Cook 12 to 15 minutes, turning occasionally.

Favorite recipe courtesy of **The Beef Checkoff**

Marmalade-Glazed Ham Steak

(pictured on page 126)

1/4 cup orange marmalade
1 tablespoon Dijon mustard
1/8 teaspoon chili powder
1/3 cup orange juice
1-1/2 teaspoons vegetable oil
1 (1-pound) ham steak (hickory-smoked, bone-in, partially cooked)

1. Combine marmalade, mustard and chili powder in small bowl. Stir in juice.

2. Heat oil in large nonstick skillet over medium heat. Add ham. Cook 3 minutes on 1 side. Turn ham. Spoon half of marmalade mixture over ham. Cook 3 minutes. Transfer ham to cutting board. Cut into 4 servings. Transfer to serving plates.

3. Pour remaining marmalade mixture into skillet. Increase heat to medium-high. Boil 2 minutes or until thickened. Serve with ham.

Makes 4 servings

Note: To prepare ham on the grill, use half the marinade for basting during the last 2 minutes of grilling and serve the remainder with the ham.

Teriyaki Steak with Crunchy Onions and Peppers

4 (1-inch) thick boneless top loin steaks
3/4 cup low sodium teriyaki sauce
2 tablespoons butter
1 (10-ounce) package sliced mushrooms
1 large red bell pepper, cut into strips
1-1/3 cups *French's*® French Fried Onions

1. Marinate steaks in teriyaki sauce for 30 minutes or up to 3 hours in refrigerator.

2. Melt butter in skillet. Cook mushrooms until golden brown. Add bell pepper and cook 3 minutes until tender. Keep warm.

3. Grill steaks over high heat 15 minutes for medium doneness.

4. Place steak on serving plates. Stir French Fried Onions into mushroom-pepper mixture. Serve over steaks.

Makes 4 servings

Tip: For extra crispiness, microwave French Fried Onions for 1 minute. Steaks may also be broiled.

Stir-Fried Mu Shu Pork Wraps

(pictured below)

1 tablespoon dark sesame oil
1 red bell pepper, cut into short thin strips
1 small pork tenderloin (3/4 pound), cut into strips
1 medium zucchini or summer squash, or combination, cut into strips
3 garlic cloves, minced
2 cups packaged coleslaw mix or shredded cabbage
2 tablespoons hoisin sauce
4 (10-inch) wraps made with olive oil
1/4 cup plum sauce

1. Heat oil in large deep nonstick skillet over medium-high heat. Add bell pepper; cook and stir 2 minutes. Add pork, zucchini and garlic; cook and stir 4 to 5 minutes or until pork is cooked through and vegetables are crisp-tender. Add coleslaw mix; cook and stir 2 minutes or until wilted. Add hoisin sauce; cook and stir 1 minute.

2. Heat wraps according to package directions. Spread plum sauce down centers of wraps; top with pork mixture. Roll up tightly; cut diagonally in half.

Makes 4 servings

Stir-Fried Mu Shu Pork Wraps

Roasted Chili Turkey Breast with Cilantro-Lime Rice

(pictured at right)

TURKEY
1-1/2 tablespoons chili powder
2 teaspoons dried oregano
1-1/2 teaspoons ground cumin
1/2 teaspoon crushed red pepper flakes
1/2 teaspoon salt
1/2 teaspoon pepper
1 bone-in turkey breast with skin (5 pounds)

RICE
2 medium red bell peppers, chopped
2-1/2 cups water
1-1/2 cups quick-cooking brown rice
1/2 teaspoon ground turmeric (optional)
1 cup chopped green onions
1/2 cup chopped fresh cilantro
3 tablespoons olive oil
1 tablespoon grated lime peel
2 to 3 tablespoons lime juice
3/4 teaspoon salt

1. Preheat oven to 325°F.

2. Combine chili powder, oregano, cumin, pepper flakes, salt and pepper in small bowl. Separate turkey skin from meat by sliding fingers under skin. Spread chili mixture evenly over meat; cover with skin. (If skin tears, use toothpick to hold skin together.)

3. Coat roasting pan and rack with nonstick cooking spray. Place turkey breast on rack in roasting pan, breast side up. Roast 1 hour and 30 minutes or until meat thermometer reaches 165°F.

4. Remove from oven. Cover loosely with foil; let stand 10 to 15 minutes.

5. To prepare rice, combine bell peppers, water, rice and turmeric, if desired, in large saucepan. Bring to a boil. Reduce heat. Cover; simmer 10 minutes or until liquid has evaporated. Remove from heat. Stir in green onions, cilantro, oil, lime peel, lime juice and salt. Serve rice with turkey.

Makes 12 servings

helpful hint

Chili powder contains dried chiles and may include salt, cumin, cayenne pepper, oregano and spices. Adjust seasonings in your recipe depending on the type of chili powder you choose.

Cheddar Tuna Noodles

8 ounces egg noodles, cooked and drained
2 tablespoons butter
1/2 cup chopped onion
1/2 cup chopped celery
2 tablespoons all-purpose flour
1/2 teaspoon salt
1/4 teaspoon crushed red pepper flakes
2 cups milk
2 cans (6 ounces each) white tuna packed in water, drained and flaked
1 cup frozen peas
1/2 cup (2 ounces) shredded cheddar cheese

1. Preheat oven to 375°F. Spray 9-inch square baking dish with nonstick cooking spray.

2. Melt butter in large skillet over medium heat. Add onion; cook and stir 3 minutes. Add celery; cook and stir 3 minutes. Sprinkle flour, salt and red pepper flakes over vegetables; cook and stir 2 minutes. Gradually whisk in milk; bring to a boil. Cook and stir 2 minutes or until thickened. Remove from heat.

3. Combine noodles, white sauce, tuna and peas in prepared baking dish; toss well to coat. Sprinkle with cheese. Bake 20 to 25 minutes or until bubbly.

Makes 4 to 6 servings

Grilled Chicken Thighs

8 boneless, skinless chicken thighs
3 tablespoons MRS. DASH® CHICKEN GRILLING BLENDS™
4 tablespoons red wine vinegar
2 tablespoons tomato paste
2 tablespoons honey
1 to 2 tablespoons water

1. Lay chicken thighs side-by-side in large glass casserole. Score each thigh 2 to 3 times using sharp knife.

2. Combine MRS. DASH® Chicken Grilling Blends™, vinegar, tomato paste, honey and water. Set aside 1/4 cup. Pour remaining marinade over chicken; marinate in refrigerator at least 1 hour.

3. Preheat grill to medium heat.

4. Brush thighs with reserved marinade and grill 10 minutes on each side. *Makes 4 servings*

Roasted Chili Turkey Breast with Cilantro-Lime Rice

Cranberry Chutney Glazed Salmon

(pictured at right)

1/2 teaspoon salt
1/2 teaspoon ground cinnamon
1/4 teaspoon cayenne pepper
4 skinless salmon fillets (5 to 6 ounces each)
1/4 cup cranberry chutney
1 tablespoon white wine vinegar or cider vinegar

1. Preheat broiler or prepare grill for indirect cooking. Combine salt, cinnamon and pepper in cup. Sprinkle over salmon. Combine chutney and vinegar in small bowl; brush evenly over each salmon fillet.

2. Broil 5 to 6 inches from heat source or grill over medium-hot coals on covered grill 4 to 6 minutes or until salmon is opaque in center.

Makes 4 servings

Variation: If cranberry chutney is not available, substitute mango chutney. Chop any large pieces of mango.

Iron Range Pot Roast

1 (3-pound) boneless pork shoulder (Boston Butt) roast
2 teaspoons Italian seasoning
1 teaspoon fennel seed, crushed
1 teaspoon salt
1/2 teaspoon celery seed
1/2 teaspoon ground black pepper
2 large potatoes, peeled and cut into 3/4-inch slices
4 cloves garlic, peeled and sliced
3/4 cup beef broth (or water)

SLOW COOKER DIRECTIONS
Mix together seasonings and rub over all surfaces of pork roast. Brown roast in small amount of oil in large skillet over medium-high heat, turning often to brown evenly. Place potatoes and garlic in 3-1/2- to 4-quart slow cooker; pour broth over and top with browned pork roast. Cover and cook on LOW for 8 to 9 hours, until pork is very tender. Slice pork to serve with vegetables and juices.

Makes 6 to 8 servings

Favorite recipe from **National Pork Board**

Family-Favorite Roast Chicken

1 (4-1/2-pounds) roasting chicken
1/4 teaspoon black pepper
1/8 teaspoon salt
1 medium lemon, washed
4 ounces (1/2 of 8-ounce package) PHILADELPHIA® Cream Cheese, softened
1 tablespoon Italian seasoning
1/2 cup KRAFT® Zesty Italian Dressing

PREHEAT oven to 350°F. Rinse chicken; pat dry with paper towel. Use the tip of a sharp knife to separate the chicken skin from the meat in the chicken breast and tops of the legs. Sprinkle chicken both inside and out with the pepper and salt. Place in 13×9-inch baking dish.

GRATE the lemon; mix the peel with cream cheese and Italian seasoning. Use a small spoon or your fingers to carefully stuff the cream cheese mixture under the chicken skin, pushing the cream cheese mixture carefully toward the legs, being careful to not tear the skin.

CUT the lemon in half; squeeze both halves into small bowl. Add dressing; beat with wire whisk until well blended. Drizzle evenly over chicken. Place the squeezed lemon halves inside the chicken cavity. Insert an ovenproof meat thermometer into thickest part of 1 of the chicken's thighs.

BAKE 1 hour 30 minutes or until chicken is no longer pink in center (165°F), basting occasionally with the pan juices.

Makes 8 servings.

Crispy Onion Tilapia Fillets

3 cups *French's*® French Fried Onions
1 tablespoon minced cilantro
1 teaspoon grated lime zest
1/2 teaspoon paprika
1/4 cup flour
4 (1/2-inch thick) tilapia or red snapper fillets, split in half lengthwise if large
2 eggs, beaten

1. Place French Fried Onions, cilantro, lime zest and paprika in plastic bag. Crush onions with hands or rolling pin; shake to combine.

2. Place flour in another plastic bag. Add fillets; shake to coat. Dip fillets into egg; then into onion crumbs. Place on baking sheet. Bake at 400°F for 15 minutes or until fish flakes easily with fork.

Makes 4 servings

Chipotle-Rubbed Flank Steak

(pictured at right)

> 1 packet (1.25 ounces) ORTEGA® Smokey Chipotle Taco Seasoning Mix, divided
> 1/2 cup water
> 1/4 cup REGINA® Red Wine Vinegar
> 1-1/2 to 2 pounds flank steak
> 1 tablespoon olive oil
> 1 small onion, diced
> 1 tablespoon ORTEGA® Fire-Roasted Diced Green Chiles
> 1 cup ORTEGA® Garden Salsa
> Juice from 1/2 lime

Combine one-half of seasoning mix, water and vinegar in shallow dish. Add steak and turn to coat well. Marinate 15 minutes in refrigerator. Turn over and marinate 15 minutes longer.

Heat oil in small saucepan over medium heat. Add onion; cook and stir 5 minutes or until translucent. Stir in chiles and salsa; cook and stir over low heat 5 minutes.

Sprinkle remaining seasoning mix over both sides of steak. Broil or grill steak over high heat 5 minutes on each side, or to desired doneness. Let stand 5 minutes before slicing against grain. To serve, drizzle on sauce and lime juice.

Makes 4 to 6 servings

Tip: For a less formal meal, create flavorful tacos instead. Simply serve the steak and sauce in soft tortillas, and garnish with shredded lettuce, diced tomatoes and shredded cheese, if desired.

Sausage Pizza Pie Casserole

> 8 ounces mild Italian sausage, casings removed
> 1 package (13.8 ounces) refrigerated pizza dough
> 1/2 cup tomato sauce
> 2 tablespoons chopped fresh basil *or* 2 teaspoons dried basil
> 1/2 teaspoon dried oregano
> 1/4 teaspoon crushed red pepper flakes
> 3 ounces whole mushrooms, quartered
> 1/2 cup thinly sliced red onion
> 1/2 cup thinly sliced green bell pepper
> 1/2 cup seeded diced tomato
> 1/2 cup sliced pitted black olives
> 8 slices smoked provolone cheese
> 2 tablespoons grated Parmesan and Romano cheese blend

1. Preheat oven to 350°F. Coat 13×9-inch baking dish with nonstick cooking spray. Heat large skillet over medium-high heat. Add sausage; cook until browned, stirring frequently to break up meat. Drain fat.

2. Line prepared dish with pizza dough. Spoon sauce evenly over dough; sprinkle with basil, oregano and pepper flakes. Layer with sausage, mushrooms, onion, bell pepper, tomato, olives and provolone cheese. Roll down sides of crust to form rim. Bake 20 to 25 minutes or until crust is golden brown. Sprinkle with cheese blend; let stand 5 minutes before serving. *Makes 4 to 6 servings*

Spicy Oat-Crusted Chicken with Sunshine Salsa

SUNSHINE SALSA
> 3/4 cup prepared salsa
> 3/4 cup coarsely chopped orange sections

CHICKEN
> 2 tablespoons canola oil
> 1 tablespoon margarine, melted
> 2 teaspoons chili powder
> 1 teaspoon garlic powder
> 1 teaspoon ground cumin
> 3/4 teaspoon salt
> 1-1/2 cups Quick QUAKER® Oats, uncooked
> 1 egg, lightly beaten
> 1 tablespoon water
> 4 boneless, skinless chicken breast halves (about 5 to 6 ounces each)
> Chopped fresh cilantro (optional)

1. Combine salsa and orange sections in small bowl. Refrigerate, covered, until serving time.

2. Heat oven to 375°F. Line baking sheet with aluminum foil. Stir together oil, margarine, chili powder, garlic powder, cumin and salt in flat, shallow dish. Add oats, stirring until evenly moistened.

3. Beat egg and water with fork until frothy in second flat, shallow dish. Dip chicken into egg mixture, then coat completely in seasoned oats. Place chicken on foil-lined baking sheet. Pat any extra oat mixture onto top of chicken.

4. Bake 30 minutes or until chicken is cooked through and oat coating is golden brown. Serve with salsa. Garnish with cilantro, if desired.

Makes 4 servings

Chipotle-Rubbed Flank Steak

Deliciously Italian Rigatoni

8 ounces uncooked rigatoni
1 pound ground beef
3 cloves garlic, minced
1 teaspoon cayenne pepper, divided
1 teaspoon Italian seasoning
1 teaspoon onion salt
3/4 teaspoon sugar
1 can (8 ounces) tomato sauce
1 can (6 ounces) tomato paste
1/2 cup water
2 tablespoons olive oil
2 tablespoons flour
2-1/2 cups milk
1-1/2 cups Italian blend of 6 cheeses or any combination of mozzarella, smoked provolone, Parmesan, Romano, fontina and asiago
1/2 cup freshly grated Parmesan cheese
Parsley, chopped

Cook pasta according to package directions; drain.

In a large skillet over medium heat, brown ground beef; drain. Add garlic, 3/4 teaspoon cayenne pepper, Italian seasoning, onion salt, sugar, tomato sauce and paste and water; heat through.

In a saucepan, mix oil with flour, 1/4 teaspoon cayenne pepper and milk. Bring to a boil, stirring with whisk until smooth. Add Italian cheese and blend until smooth. Pour cheese sauce over drained pasta. Pour into 13×9-inch baking pan coated with nonstick cooking spray. Spread tomato/meat sauce over pasta. Sprinkle with Parmesan cheese and parsley. Bake in a preheated 350°F oven for 30 minutes. *Makes 8 servings*

Note: Can be prepared in advance and refrigerated; bake until heated through.

Favorite recipe from **North Dakota Wheat Commission**

Beef Stew

Beef Stew

(pictured above)

1 medium onion, chopped (about 1/2 cup)
1 cup baby carrots
2 cups sliced celery
1 pound red potatoes, scrubbed and cubed
2 pounds beef stew meat, cut into chunks
2 teaspoons dried thyme leaves
1 can (14-1/2 ounces) HUNT'S® Diced Tomatoes
3/4 cup water
1 can (6 ounces) HUNT'S® Tomato Paste

1. Place onion evenly over the bottom of 3-1/2-quart or larger **CROCK-POT®** slow cooker. Add the following ingredients in this order: carrots, celery, potatoes and beef. Sprinkle with thyme. Pour diced tomatoes and water over the top of beef.

2. Cover and cook on LOW setting for 8 to 10 hours until meat is tender. Stir in tomato paste; cover.

3. Cook 10 minutes on HIGH setting.
Makes 6 servings

helpful hint

The flavor of freshly grated Parmesan cheese is far superior to pre-grated Parmesan. Domestic and imported varieties are sold in chunks and wedges at supermarkets, and they can be quickly grated by hand with a box, rotary or microplane grater.

Chicken & Sage Risotto

4 cups chicken broth
8 tablespoons I CAN'T BELIEVE IT'S NOT
   BUTTER!® Mediterranean Blend spread,
   divided
1 small yellow onion, chopped
1 small yellow bell pepper, chopped
1 cup arborio rice
1 clove garlic, chopped
2 cups cut-up cooked chicken
1/2 cup grated Parmesan cheese
2 teaspoon chopped fresh sage or 1/2 teaspoon
   dried sage leaves, crushed

1. In 2-quart saucepan, heat broth over high heat
just to a simmer. Reduce heat to low and cover.

2. Meanwhile, in 3-quart saucepan, melt
6 tablespoons I CAN'T BELIEVE IT'S NOT BUTTER!®
Mediterranean Blend spread over medium heat and
cook onion and yellow pepper, stirring occasionally,
5 minutes or until tender. Add rice and garlic and
cook, stirring frequently, 2 minutes. Stir in hot broth
and bring to a boil over high heat.

3. Reduce heat and simmer covered, stirring
occasionally, 25 minutes or until almost all liquid
is absorbed and rice is creamy and tender. Stir in
chicken and cook covered, stirring occasionally,
2 minutes or until heated through. Stir in cheese,
sage and remaining 2 tablespoons Mediterranean
Blend. Serve immediately and sprinkle with
additional grated Parmesan cheese, if desired.

Makes 4 servings

Slow Cooker
Turkey and Dressing

1 pound BOB EVANS® Sage or Original Recipe
   Sausage Roll
1 package (6 ounces) herb seasoned cubed
   stuffing
2 cups chicken broth, divided
1/2 cup dried cranberries
2 sweet potatoes, peeled and cut into 2 inches
   pieces
1 pound turkey breast cutlets

In large skillet over medium heat, crumble and cook
sausage until brown. Stir in stuffing, 1-1/2 cups
broth and cranberries. Set aside. Place sweet
potatoes into crock pot. Place turkey on top. Add
1/2 cup chicken broth. Pour sausage mixture over
turkey. Cover and cook on low 4 to 6 hours.

Makes 4 servings

Double Cheeseburger Tortillas

(pictured below)

1 tablespoon vegetable oil
1 onion, diced
1 pound lean ground beef
1/2 teaspoon salt
1/2 teaspoon black pepper
1 cup ORTEGA® Salsa
1 jar (10.75 ounces) ORTEGA® Salsa con Queso,
   divided
6 (8-inch) ORTEGA® Soft Flour Tortillas, warmed
3 to 4 tomatoes, sliced
1 cup shredded lettuce

Heat oil in medium skillet over medium heat. Add
onion; cook and stir 4 minutes or until translucent.
Add beef, salt and pepper; cook and stir, breaking
up meat, until browned. Stir in salsa and 1/2 cup
salsa con queso until well mixed. Reduce heat to
low; cook 5 minutes longer.

Place warmed tortilla on plate. Spread with 2 to
3 tablespoons salsa con queso. Top with one-
quarter of meat mixture. Arrange several slices of
tomato on top and sprinkle with 1/4 cup shredded
lettuce. Add another tortilla and layer with 2 to
3 tablespoons salsa con queso, one-quarter of meat
mixture, tomato and 1/4 cup lettuce. Top with third
tortilla. Repeat steps for second cheeseburger
tortilla. Cut layered tortillas in half to serve.

Makes 4 servings

Tip: For a great garnish, top the stacked tortillas
with a pickle and olive spiked with a toothpick to
resemble a real cheeseburger.

Double Cheeseburger Tortillas

Grilled Steak and Peppers
With Chile Lime Sauce

Grilled Steak and Peppers With Chile Lime Sauce

(pictured above)

1 cup LAWRY'S® Mexican Chile & Lime
    Marinade With Lime Juice
1-1/2 pounds boneless sirloin, skirt or flank steak
1/4 cup HELLMANN'S® or BEST FOODS® Real
    Mayonnaise
1/4 cup sour cream
1/4 teaspoon LAWRY'S® Garlic Salt
3 red, yellow and/or green bell peppers,
    quartered

1. In large resealable plastic bag, pour 1/2 cup LAWRY'S® Mexican Chile & Lime Marinade With Lime Juice over steak. Close bag and marinate in refrigerator 30 minutes.

2. In small bowl combine Mayonnaise, sour cream and LAWRY'S® Garlic Salt. Set aside.

3. Remove steak from Marinade, discarding Marinade. Grill steak and peppers, turning once and brushing with remaining 1/2 cup Marinade, to desired doneness. Let steak stand covered 10 minutes before slicing. Serve with mayonnaise mixture.   *Makes 6 servings*

Note: Also terrific with LAWRY'S® Steak & Chop Marinade With Garlic & Cracked Black Pepper or LAWRY'S® Mesquite Marinade With Lime Juice.

Creamy Pesto Garden Pasta

1 box (12 ounces) dry tri-color rotini or spiral shaped pasta

1 bag (16 ounces) frozen broccoli, cauliflower and carrot medley

1 can (12 fluid ounces) NESTLÉ® CARNATION® Evaporated Milk

2 cups (8-ounce package) shredded Italian cheese blend or Monterey Jack cheese

3 tablespoons jarred or refrigerated pesto with basil

1/4 teaspoon ground black pepper

2 cups (8 ounces) cooked ham, cut into 1/2-inch pieces

COOK pasta according to package directions, adding frozen vegetables to boiling pasta water for last 2 minutes of cooking time; drain. Return pasta and vegetables to cooking pot.

MEANWHILE, combine evaporated milk, cheese, pesto and black pepper in medium saucepan. Cook over medium low heat, stirring occasionally, until cheese is melted. Remove from heat.

POUR cheese sauce over pasta and vegetables. Add ham; stir until combined.   *Makes 6 servings*

Boursin® Beef with Mushrooms

10 ounces mushrooms

2 shallots

1 small onion

2 tablespoons sunflower oil

2 tablespoons crème fraîche

1 package BOURSIN® pepper, crumbled

20 ounces of beef fillet (or any other tender cut)

1 ounce butter

Salt

1 tablespoon lemon juice

1 pinch paprika

4 sprigs flat leaf parsley

Wash the mushrooms, remove the stalk ends, and slice. Peel the shallots and onion and slice thinly. Fry the mushrooms, shallots and onion gently for 5 minutes in oil in a large saucepan. Add the crème fraîche and the crumbled BOURSIN® pepper. Stir together, cover, and leave to cook gently over a very low heat for 5 minutes. Cut the meat into slices and fry in butter for 3 minutes over high heat in a frying pan. Season lightly with salt and add the meat to the mushroom sauce. Add the lemon juice and stir for 2 minutes. Sprinkle with paprika and parsley and serve with peas or rice.   *Makes 4 servings*

Mu Shu Meatball Wraps

(pictured below)

MEATBALLS

1 pound lean ground turkey or lean ground beef

3/4 cup QUAKER® Oats (quick or old fashioned, uncooked)

1/2 cup finely chopped water chestnuts

1/3 cup chopped green onions

1 clove garlic, minced

1 teaspoon finely chopped fresh ginger or 1/4 teaspoon ground ginger

1/4 cup light soy sauce

1 tablespoon water

WRAPS

3/4 cup prepared plum sauce

6 (10-inch) flour tortillas, warmed

1-1/2 cups coleslaw mix or combination of shredded cabbage and shredded carrots

1. Heat oven to 350°F. Combine all meatball ingredients in large bowl; mix lightly but thoroughly. Shape into 24 (1-1/2-inch) meatballs; arrange on rack of broiler pan.

2. Bake 20 to 25 minutes or until centers are no longer pink (170°F for turkey; 160°F for beef).

3. To prepare wraps, spread plum sauce on flour tortilla; add about 1/4 cup coleslaw mix and 4 hot meatballs. Fold sides of tortilla to center, overlapping edges; fold bottom and top of tortilla under, completely enclosing filling. Repeat with remaining ingredients. Cut wrap in half to serve.   *Makes 6 servings*

Mu Shu Meatball Wraps

Indian-Style Apricot Chicken

(pictured at right)

6 chicken thighs, rinsed and patted dry
1/4 teaspoon salt
1/4 teaspoon pepper
1 tablespoon vegetable oil
1 large onion, chopped
2 garlic cloves, minced
2 tablespoons grated gingerroot
1/2 teaspoon ground cinnamon
1/8 teaspoon ground allspice
1 can (14-1/2 ounces) diced tomatoes
1 cup chicken broth
1 package (8 ounces) dried apricots
1 pinch saffron threads (optional)
Hot basmati rice
2 tablespoons chopped fresh parsley (optional)

SLOW COOKER DIRECTIONS

1. Coat 5-quart slow cooker with nonstick cooking spray.

2. Season chicken with salt and pepper. Heat oil in large skillet over medium-high heat. Brown chicken on all sides. Transfer to slow cooker.

3. Add onion to skillet. Cook and stir 5 minutes or until translucent. Stir in garlic, gingerroot, cinnamon and allspice. Cook and stir 15 to 30 seconds or until fragrant. Add tomatoes and broth. Cook 2 to 3 minutes or until heated through. Pour into slow cooker.

4. Add apricots and saffron, if desired, to slow cooker. Cover and cook on LOW 5 to 6 hours or on HIGH 3 to 3-1/2 hours or until chicken is tender. Serve with basmati rice; garnish with chopped parsley.   *Makes 4 to 6 servings*

Note: Use skinless chicken thighs, if desired. To skin chicken easily, grasp skin with paper towel and pull away. Repeat with fresh paper towel for each piece of chicken, discarding skins and towels.

helpful hint

Basmati is a fragrant, long-grained rice which was originally grown in the foothills of the Himalayas and served in India. Today, basmati is easy to find in most supermarkets and some varieties are grown in the U.S.

Sesame Beef with Pineapple-Plum Sauce

1 pound beef flank steak
3 tablespoons soy sauce, divided
3-1/2 teaspoons cornstarch, divided
2 teaspoons grated gingerroot
2 garlic cloves, minced
1/8 teaspoon crushed red pepper flakes
1 package (12 ounces) fresh refrigerated pineapple spears or chunks*
1 tablespoon sesame seeds
1 tablespoon vegetable oil
1/4 cup minced green onions, plus additional for garnish
1/4 cup thinly sliced red bell pepper
1/4 cup chicken broth
2 tablespoons plum sauce

Fresh pineapple spears packed in plastic containers can be found in supermarket produce departments. If unavailable, use 1-1/2 cups canned pineapple chunks packed in unsweetened juice.

1. Cut flank steak lengthwise in half, then widthwise into thin slices.

2. Stir 2 tablespoons soy sauce into 1-1/2 teaspoons cornstarch in medium bowl until well blended. Add steak, gingerroot, garlic and red pepper flakes; toss to coat. Let stand 30 minutes. Drain pineapple, reserving juice. Stir 2 tablespoons pineapple juice into remaining 2 teaspoons cornstarch in small bowl; mix well. Cut pineapple spears into chunks.

3. Toast sesame seeds in large heavy skillet over medium-low heat about 3 minutes or until golden. Immediately remove from skillet; set aside.

4. Heat oil in same skillet over medium-high heat. Working in batches, cook beef about 2 minutes per side or until browned and barely pink in center.

5. Stir pineapple juice-cornstarch mixture; add to skillet with 1/4 cup green onions, bell pepper, broth, plum sauce and remaining 1 tablespoon soy sauce. Cook and stir 1 minute or until sauce thickens. Stir in pineapple chunks; cook and stir until heated through. Sprinkle with sesame seeds; garnish with additional green onions.   *Makes 4 servings*

Linguine with Herbs, Tomatoes and Capers

(pictured at right)

1 package (9 ounces) refrigerated fresh linguine
2 tablespoons olive oil
2 cups chopped tomatoes
2 garlic cloves, minced
1/4 cup finely chopped green onions
3 tablespoons capers
2 tablespoons finely chopped fresh basil
1/4 teaspoon salt
1/8 teaspoon pepper
1/2 cup grated Parmesan cheese (optional)

1. Cook linguine according to package directions; drain well.

2. Meanwhile, heat oil in large skillet over medium-high heat. Add tomatoes and garlic; cook 3 minutes or until tomatoes begin to break down and soften, stirring frequently. Stir in green onions, capers and basil. Season with salt and pepper.

3. Add linguine to skillet; toss with tomato mixture. Sprinkle with cheese, if desired.

Makes 6 servings

Moroccan Brisket With Onions & Apricots

2 large onions, sliced into wedges
2 teaspoons ground coriander (optional)
2 teaspoons ground cumin
1/2 teaspoon ground cinnamon
1/2 teaspoon garlic powder
3-pound boneless beef brisket
1 cup dried apricots
1-3/4 cups SWANSON® Beef Broth (Regular, 50% Less Sodium or Certified Organic)
2 tablespoons honey

1. Place the onions into a 6-quart slow cooker.

2. Combine the coriander, cumin, cinnamon and garlic powder in a small bowl. Rub the mixture onto the beef. Place the beef into the cooker. Place the apricots around the beef.

3. Stir the broth and honey in a small bowl. Pour over the beef. Cover and cook on LOW for 7 to 8 hours* or until the beef is fork-tender.

Makes 8 servings

*Or on HIGH for 4 to 5 hours.

Smoky Mexican Pork Stir Fry

1 small pork tenderloin (about 12 ounces)
4 slices bacon, diced
1 chipotle chile*
1 tablespoon vegetable oil
1 teaspoon ground cumin
1 teaspoon dried oregano
2 cloves garlic, crushed
1 red or green bell pepper, cut into thin strips
1 small onion, cut in half and thinly sliced
3 cups coarsely chopped romaine or iceberg lettuce

*If canned in adobo sauce, drain chile and chop; if dried, rehydrate in warm water, drain and chop.

Slice pork tenderloin in half lengthwise, then cut crosswise thinly. Toss pork, bacon and chipotle chile together in small bowl; set aside. Combine oil, cumin, oregano and garlic and heat in large nonstick skillet over medium-high heat. Add bell pepper and onion; stir-fry 2 to 3 minutes or until crisp-tender. Remove and reserve. In same skillet, stir-fry the pork, bacon and chile for 2 to 3 minutes until pork is just done and bacon is crisp. Return vegetables to skillet and heat through. Serve over lettuce.

Makes 4 servings

Note: Serve with hominy or rice and a sliced orange and red onion salad.

Favorite recipe from **National Pork Board**

helpful hint

Chipotle chiles are dried smoked jalapeño peppers. They have a smoky, sweet flavor. Chipotles can be found dried and canned in adobo sauce. When using canned chiles, you can increase the spicy flavor by adding 1 to 2 teaspoons of the adobo sauce or an additional chile to the recipe.

Linguine with Herbs, Tomatoes and Capers

Mexican Picadillo

Mexican Picadillo

(pictured above)

1 pound lean ground beef
3/4 cup diced onion
1 can (28 ounces) plum tomatoes, drained
1/2 cup seedless raisins
1/2 cup B&G® Pimento-Stuffed Olives, sliced
2 tablespoons REGINA® White Wine Vinegar
1 teaspoon ground cinnamon
1 teaspoon ground cumin
3/4 teaspoon ORTEGA® Chili Seasoning Mix
Salt and black pepper, to taste
10 ORTEGA® Taco Shells
1 cup shredded Cheddar cheese

Preheat oven to 225°F. Brown beef in medium skillet over medium heat. Add onions; cook and stir 5 minutes or until softened. Drain excess fat and discard. Add tomatoes, breaking up with wooden spoon. Stir in raisins, olives, vinegar, cinnamon, cumin, seasoning mix, salt and pepper. Bring mixture to a boil. Reduce heat; simmer, uncovered, 10 minutes.

Place taco shells on baking sheet; bake 5 to 10 minutes or until warmed. Fill shells with beef mixture and sprinkle with cheese.

Makes 4 to 5 servings

Tip: If you prefer soft flour tortillas, use them instead. Just spoon the filling down the center of the tortillas, add the cheese, roll up and enjoy!

Zucchini Parmigiana Casserole

1/2 cup all-purpose flour
3 eggs, beaten
2 cups Italian-seasoned bread crumbs
6 cups zucchini slices
1/2 cup olive oil
Salt and pepper
1 pound ground beef
1/2 pound bulk sausage
1 cup chopped onion
1 tablespoon minced garlic
1/4 cup chopped fresh basil
1/4 cup chopped fresh oregano
4 cups tomato sauce
2 cups (8 ounces) shredded mozzarella cheese
1/4 cup grated Parmesan cheese
4 tablespoons chopped fresh parsley

1. Preheat oven to 350°F. Place flour, eggs and bread crumbs in separate shallow bowls. Dip zucchini in flour, egg, then bread crumbs to coat. Heat oil in medium skillet over medium-high heat. Brown zucchini on both sides in batches; season with salt and pepper. Drain on paper towels. Discard oil.

2. Add ground beef, sausage, onion and garlic to same skillet. Cook until meat is cooked through, stirring to break up meat. Drain fat. Stir in basil and oregano.

3. Layer half of tomato sauce, half of zucchini, half of meat mixture, half of mozzarella and half of Parmesan in 4-quart baking dish. Repeat layers.

4. Bake 30 minutes or until heated through and cheese is melted. Top with parsley.

Makes 6 servings

helpful hint

Warm flour tortillas in the microwave or oven. It's important to keep them moist so they do not become stiff or dry. To microwave, place a tortilla on a plate and cover it with a damp paper towel. Stack additional tortillas on top, separated by damp towels. Microwave for 30 seconds to 1 minute. To warm in the oven, wrap the stack of tortillas in a damp dishtowel and then tightly in foil. Warm in a preheated 250°F oven for about 20 minutes.

Chicken & Bean Burritos

(pictured below)

1 can (10-3/4 ounces) CAMPBELL'S® Condensed Cheddar Cheese Soup
1 teaspoon garlic powder
2 tablespoons chili powder
2 pounds skinless, boneless chicken thighs, cut into 1-inch pieces
1 can (about 14 ounces) black beans, rinsed and drained
1 can (about 14 ounces) pinto beans, rinsed and drained
12 flour tortillas (8- to 10-inch), warmed
Chopped lettuce
Chopped tomato

1. Stir the soup, garlic powder, chili powder and chicken in a 3-1/2 to 4-quart slow cooker.

2. Cover and cook on LOW for 6 to 7 hours* or until the chicken is cooked through.

3. Mash the black and pinto beans with a fork in a medium bowl. Stir into the chicken mixture. Spoon about **1/2 cup** of the chicken mixture down the center of each tortilla. Top with the lettuce and tomato. Fold the tortillas around the filling.

Makes 12 burritos

*Or on HIGH for 3 to 4 hours.

Chicken & Bean Burritos

Minestrone Skillet Dinner

(pictured at right)

2 slices bacon, coarsely chopped
1 tablespoon olive oil
2 cups coarsely shredded or chopped cabbage
1 large zucchini, cut into 1/2-inch dice
1 medium onion, chopped
1 large stalk celery, chopped
1 garlic clove, minced
1 can (14-1/2 ounces) diced tomatoes
1 cup cooked macaroni
3/4 cup great northern beans, rinsed and drained
3/4 cup cooked diced carrots
1/2 teaspoon dried oregano
1/4 teaspoon dried thyme
1/4 teaspoon salt
2/3 cup shredded Parmesan cheese

1. Preheat oven to 350°F. Cook bacon in large ovenproof skillet over medium heat. Remove bacon; set aside on paper towels. Add oil to skillet; heat over medium-high heat. Add cabbage, zucchini, onion, celery and garlic. Cook and stir 10 minutes or until cabbage is crisp-tender.

2. Stir in tomatoes, macaroni, beans, carrots, oregano, thyme, salt and bacon. Simmer 5 minutes to blend flavors. Sprinkle cheese evenly over mixture. Place skillet in oven; heat 15 minutes or until hot. *Makes 6 servings*

Tip: For a vegetarian dish, omit the bacon and increase the olive oil to 1-1/2 tablespoons.

Beef and Broccoli Stir-Fry

2 cups MINUTE® Brown Rice, uncooked
1 pound beef flank steak, cut into strips
2 teaspoons cornstarch
1/4 cup orange juice
1 teaspoon ground ginger
1 tablespoon vegetable oil
1 package (10 ounces) frozen broccoli florets, thawed
1 can (8 ounces) sliced water chestnuts, drained
1/4 cup reduced-sodium soy sauce
1/4 cup dry-roasted peanuts (optional)

Prepare rice according to package directions. Place steak strips in medium bowl. Sprinkle with cornstarch; toss to coat. Add orange juice and ginger; stir until well blended. Heat oil in large nonstick skillet over medium-high heat. Add steak

mixture; stir-fry 4 to 5 minutes or until steak is cooked through. Reduce heat to medium-low. Add broccoli, water chestnuts and soy sauce; mix well. Cover; simmer 5 minutes or until thickened, stirring frequently. Serve over rice; sprinkle with peanuts, if desired. *Makes 4 servings*

Tip: To make slicing easier, place steak in freezer for 30 minutes to 1 hour before cutting into strips.

Grilled Salmon with Sweet-Heat Carrot-Pineapple Salsa

SALSA

1 cup finely chopped carrots
1/2 cup finely chopped red bell pepper
1/2 cup pineapple tidbits, well drained
1/4 cup chopped cilantro or mint
2 tablespoons chopped dried apricots
1 medium jalapeño pepper,* seeded and finely chopped
1 tablespoon lemon juice
1 teaspoon sugar
1/2 teaspoon grated orange peel

SALMON

4 salmon fillets (6 ounces each), skin removed
2 tablespoons olive oil
1/2 teaspoon ground cumin
Salt and pepper

*Jalapeño peppers can sting and irritate the skin, so wear rubber gloves when handling peppers and do not touch your eyes.

1. Prepare grill for direct cooking over medium-high heat. Combine salsa ingredients in medium bowl. Toss gently yet thoroughly, blending well; set aside.

2. Brush both sides of salmon with oil. Sprinkle evenly with cumin, salt and pepper.

3. Brush grill grid with oil. Place fillets on grid. Grill 5 minutes per side or until opaque in center. Serve with salsa. *Makes 4 servings*

Chicken and Bean Tostadas

Chicken and Bean Tostadas

(pictured above)

1 tablespoon vegetable oil
3/4 pound boneless skinless chicken breasts, cut
    into 3/4-inch pieces
1 green, red or yellow bell pepper, diced
1 cup chopped yellow onion
2 teaspoons ground cumin
1 cup chunky salsa, divided
1 can (15 ounces) refried beans
8 tostada shells
1/4 cup chopped fresh cilantro or green onions

1. Heat oil in large nonstick skillet over medium heat. Add chicken, bell pepper, onion and cumin. Cook, stirring occasionally, 6 minutes or until chicken is no longer pink. Stir in 3/4 cup salsa. Reduce heat; simmer 5 to 6 minutes or until chicken is cooked through.

2. Meanwhile, combine beans with remaining 1/4 cup salsa in small saucepan. Heat over medium heat until hot, stirring occasionally. Spread mixture over tostada shells. Top with chicken mixture and cilantro.   *Makes 4 servings*

Mexican Potato Sausage Casserole

12 ounces bulk pork sausage or lean ground beef
1/2 cup green bell pepper, chopped
  1 package SIMPLY POTATOES® Southwest Style
    Hash Browns
  1 cup (4 ounces) CRYSTAL FARMS® Shredded
    Cheddar cheese
  1 cup (4 ounces) CRYSTAL FARMS® Shredded
    Marble Jack cheese
  4 eggs
  1 cup milk
  1 medium tomato, seeded, chopped

1. Heat oven to 350°F. Spray 8- or 9-inch square baking dish with nonstick cooking spray.

2. In large skillet, cook sausage or beef and bell pepper until browned; drain. In baking dish, layer half the Simply Potatoes®, half the sausage or beef mixture and 3/4 cup of each cheese; repeat layers. Combine eggs and milk in medium bowl; beat well. Pour evenly over mixture; press lightly.

3. Cover with foil and bake 45 minutes. Uncover; add chopped tomato and remaining 1/2 cup cheese. Bake, uncovered, for an additional 10 to 15 minutes or until knife inserted in center comes out clean. Let stand 10 minutes before serving.

Makes 6 servings

All-Star Pork Meatballs

  1 pound ground pork
3/4 cup crushed corn flakes
  1 tablespoon onion flakes
1/2 teaspoon salt
1/8 teaspoon ground black pepper
  1 egg
1/4 cup ketchup
  3 tablespoons brown sugar
  1 teaspoon dry mustard

Heat oven to 375°F. In a large bowl, combine ground pork, corn flakes, onion flakes, salt, pepper and egg. In a small bowl stir together ketchup, brown sugar and dry mustard. Spoon 2 tablespoons of the ketchup mixture into the pork and mix well.

Spray muffin tin with vegetable cooking spray. Form 6 meatballs and place in muffin tin. Coat the top of each meatball with the remaining ketchup mixture. Bake for 30 minutes at 375°F., until nicely browned and glazed.   *Makes 6 servings*

Favorite recipe from **National Pork Board**

Oven-Fried BBQ Glazed Chicken

1 cup all-purpose flour
1 tablespoon LAWRY'S® Seasoned Salt
1 teaspoon LAWRY'S® Garlic Salt
1 teaspoon LAWRY'S® Seasoned Pepper
3 pounds chicken legs and/or bone-in chicken thighs
1 cup milk
1 cup barbecue sauce

1. Preheat oven to 425°F. Spray jelly roll pan with nonstick cooking spray; set aside.

2. In large resealable plastic bag, combine flour, LAWRY'S® Seasoned Salt, Garlic Salt and Seasoned Pepper. Dip chicken in milk, then add to bag; shake to coat. On prepared pan, arrange chicken skin-side up.

3. Bake, turning once, 35 minutes. Generously coat with barbecue sauce. Bake an additional 5 minutes or until chicken is thoroughly cooked.

Makes 8 servings

Penne with Sausage and Feta

6 ounces uncooked penne
Nonstick cooking spray
12 ounces mild Italian bulk sausage
1/4 teaspoon crushed red pepper flakes
2 cups packed spring greens or baby spinach leaves
1/2 cup roasted red peppers, cut into thin strips
24 pitted kalamata olives, coarsely chopped
1/4 cup chopped fresh basil
2 tablespoons olive oil
1 cup (4 ounces) crumbled feta cheese with tomatoes and basil
1/4 teaspoon salt

1. Cook penne according to package directions. Meanwhile, coat large skillet with cooking spray; heat over medium-high heat. Add sausage and pepper flakes. Cook until sausage is cooked through, stirring to break up meat. Drain fat.

2. Drain cooked penne. Add to skillet with sausage. Add greens, roasted peppers, olives, basil and oil. Toss gently until mixed well and greens have wilted slightly. Add feta and salt. Toss again.

Makes 6 servings

Note: If bulk sausage is not available, use regular sausage and remove casings.

Mozzarella-Pepper Sausage Skillet

(pictured below)

1 pound mild Italian sausage, casings removed
1 tablespoon olive oil
6 ounces sliced mushrooms
1 medium zucchini, thinly sliced
3/4 cup finely chopped onion
1 tablespoon dried basil
1 can (8 ounces) tomato sauce
1/2 cup plain bread crumbs
1/4 teaspoon salt
1 medium red bell pepper, cut into strips
1 medium green bell pepper, cut into strips
1-1/2 cups (6 ounces) shredded mozzarella cheese

1. Heat large nonstick skillet over medium-high heat. Add sausage; cook until browned, stirring to break up meat. Remove sausage with slotted spoon; drain on paper towels.

2. Add oil to skillet. Add mushrooms, zucchini, onion and basil; cook 5 minutes or until zucchini is soft, stirring frequently.

3. Return sausage to skillet. Add tomato sauce, bread crumbs and salt; mix well. Top mixture with bell pepper strips. Cover; simmer 25 minutes or until peppers are tender. Remove from heat. Top with cheese. Cover and let stand 2 to 3 minutes or until cheese is melted. *Makes 4 servings*

Mozzarella-Pepper Sausage Skillet

Pizza Casserole

(pictured at right)

2 cups uncooked rotini or other spiral pasta
1-1/2 to 2 pounds ground beef
1 medium onion, chopped
    Salt and pepper
1 can (15 ounces) pizza sauce
1 can (8 ounces) tomato sauce
1 can (6 ounces) tomato paste
1/2 teaspoon sugar
1/2 teaspoon garlic salt
1/2 teaspoon dried oregano
2 cups (8 ounces) shredded mozzarella cheese
12 to 15 slices pepperoni

1. Preheat oven to 350°F. Cook pasta according to package directions; drain and set aside.

2. Meanwhile, brown beef with onion 6 to 8 minutes in large skillet over medium-high heat, stirring to break up meat. Drain fat. Season beef with salt and pepper.

3. Combine pasta, pizza sauce, tomato sauce, tomato paste, sugar, garlic salt and oregano in large bowl. Add beef mixture; stir until blended.

4. Place half of mixture in ovenproof skillet or 3-quart baking dish; top with 1 cup cheese. Repeat layers. Arrange pepperoni slices on top. Bake 25 to 30 minutes or until heated through and cheese is melted.
Makes 6 servings

Sesame Salmon On A Raft With Grilled Vegetables

3/4 cup LAWRY'S® Sesame Ginger Marinade With Mandarin Orange Juice
2-1/2 pound salmon fillet
    Cedar plank
1/4 cup sliced green onions
1 tablespoon sesame seeds
1 teaspoon LAWRY'S® Garlic Salt
3 medium red, yellow and/or orange bell peppers, quartered
2 large onions, sliced into thick rounds
2 medium zucchini, cut into 3/8-inch thick diagonal slices
2 tablespoons BERTOLLI® CLASSICO™ Olive Oil

1. In large resealable plastic bag, pour LAWRY'S® Sesame Ginger Marinade With Mandarin Orange Juice over salmon; turn to coat. Close bag and marinate in refrigerator 30 minutes.

2. Grill cedar plank* 5 minutes; remove from grill. Remove salmon from Marinade, discarding Marinade. On charred side of cedar plank, arrange salmon skin-side-down. On cedar plank, grill salmon, covered, 10 minutes or until salmon flakes with a fork. Sprinkle with green onions and sesame seeds.

3. Meanwhile, in large bowl, toss vegetables with Olive Oil. Grill, turning once, 4 minutes or until vegetables are golden and tender; cut peppers. Serve grilled vegetables with salmon.
Makes 10 servings

Soak cedar plank in water at least 4 hours prior to grilling.

Grilled Spanish Skirt Steak with Salsa Picante

1/4 cup I CAN'T BELIEVE IT'S NOT BUTTER!® Mediterranean Blend spread
2 medium shallots or small onions, finely chopped
3 tablespoons red wine vinegar
2 tablespoons all-purpose flour
1/4 teaspoon salt
1/8 teaspoon ground black pepper
1-1/4 cups beef broth
2 tablespoons small capers, rinsed and drained
2 tablespoons finely chopped fresh parsley
1/4 cup heavy or whipping cream (optional)
1 pound skirt steak, grilled to desired doneness and sliced

In 2-quart saucepan, melt I CAN'T BELIEVE IT'S NOT BUTTER!® Mediterranean Blend spread over medium-high heat and cook shallots 1 minute, stirring occasionally. Stir in vinegar. Cook, stirring occasionally, 3 minutes. Stir in flour, salt and pepper. Cook 1 minute, stirring frequently. With wire whisk, stir in broth. Bring to a boil over high heat. Reduce heat to low and simmer, stirring occasionally, 3 minutes or until slightly thickened. Stir in capers and parsley, and then cream; heat through. Serve with steak.
Makes 4 servings

Hot & Bubbly Casseroles

Casseroles are perfect for make-ahead meals.

• To save time preparing future meals, double a casserole recipe and freeze half. With minimal additional effort, you've prepared two meals in the time it takes for one.

• If you're doubling a recipe and discover your largest mixing bowl is too small for all the ingredients, try using a roasting pan or a Dutch oven as a substitute.

• To prepare casseroles for individual servings, assemble the filling in small ovenproof ramekins or baking dishes (about 6 ounces each). Bake 5 to 10 minutes less than the baking time for the larger casserole.

Freezing Casseroles

• Unbaked casseroles that contain condensed canned soup freeze well.

• When using cheese for a topping, it is best to freeze an unbaked casserole without the cheese. Add it during the final 20 to 30 minutes of baking.

• Most casseroles are great candidates for freezing. When preparing a casserole for the freezer, line the baking dish with plastic wrap or heavy-duty aluminum foil, leaving several inches of overhang around the sides. Add the casserole ingredients, wrap tightly and freeze until firm. Lift the frozen casserole from the baking dish and store in a resealable plastic freezer bag. When ready to bake, remove the wrap and place the frozen casserole back into the original baking dish. Thaw in the refrigerator and bake as directed.

• Cool any baked casserole at least 2 hours before freezing.

The Right Dish

• The right size dish for a casserole allows about 1 inch between the ingredients and the top of the baking dish.

• A casserole dish that is too large can cause the food to dry out. A casserole dish that is too small creates messy spills in the oven.

• If you don't have the shape of casserole dish that is called for in a recipe, substitute a dish with the same volume in a different shape. To measure the volume of another dish, fill it with water, then measure the number of cups of water it takes to fill the dish. The amount will tell you the size of the dish.

• Common dish sizes: an 8- to 9-inch pie plate holds about 4 cups; an 8-inch square or an 11×7-inch dish holds about 6 cups; a 9-inch square dish (1-1/2 inches deep) holds about 8 cups; a 13×9-inch dish holds about 16 cups.

Casserole Toppers

Toppings add a delicious combination of creamy or crispy textures to a casserole.

• Homemade bread crumbs or croutons add a crispy texture and are a good use for leftover bread. Process stale bread in a food processor to make coarse crumbs.

• Crushed chips add a salty and crispy crunch and are a great way to use the crumbled bits that are always left in the bottom of the bag.

• Toasted sliced almonds add a wonderful nutty flavor.

• Shredded cheese provides two textures: soft and gooey or slightly crisp, depending on the length of cooking time.

Slow Cooker

Techniques and time-savers for preparing successful slow cooker dishes.

- Manufacturers recommend that slow cookers should be one-half to three-quarters full for the best results.

- To make cleanup easier, spray the inside of the slow cooker with nonstick cooking spray before adding any food.

- Keep a lid on it! Slow cookers can take as long as 30 minutes to regain heat lost when the cover is removed. Only remove the cover when instructed to do so in the recipes.

- Spin the cover until the condensation falls off. This will allow you to see inside the slow cooker without removing the lid, which delays the cooking time.

- Slow cooker recipes with raw meat should cook a minimum of 3 hours on LOW for food safety reasons.

- Do not cook whole chickens in the slow cooker because the chicken cannot reach a safe temperature quickly enough for food safety. Cut a whole chicken into quarters or parts.

- Dairy products should be added at the end of the cooking time because they will curdle if cooked in the slow cooker for a long time.

- For vegetables to cook properly, they need to be cut into uniform pieces in the size suggested in the recipes.

- Frozen meat and poultry should not be cooked in a slow cooker; always thaw such ingredients first.

Cooking with Ground Meats

Versatile ground meats are often the foundation for many casseroles.

- When browning ground meat, break it up into 3/4- to 1-inch pieces. The larger pieces will give the dish better flavor. Smaller crumbles become dry and retain less flavor.

- Cooking ground meat with dried seasonings adds more flavor to the finished dish than adding the seasonings to the sauce. Dried seasonings tend to release their flavors when heated over direct heat.

- For quicker thawing, always freeze fresh ground meats in small packages or patties.

- To properly thaw frozen meats, place them in the refrigerator overnight or thaw in the microwave before cooking. Use meat thawed in the microwave immediately.

- To brown 1 pound of ground meat using your microwave, place it in a microwavable colander set in a deep microwavable bowl. Cook on HIGH 4 to 5 minutes or until the meat is cooked through, stirring twice during cooking. Discard the drippings that accumulate in the bowl.

- If a recipe calls for ground turkey, ground beef or pork can be substituted. Ground turkey can also be used in place of ground beef or pork. Or, use half ground turkey and half ground beef or pork.

- Burgers, meat loaf and meatballs made with ground beef, pork or lamb should be cooked through and measure 160°F on an instant-read thermometer. Burgers, meat loaf and meatballs made with ground poultry should be cooked to 165°F.

Desserts

Blueberry Swirl Cheesecake

(pictured at left)

1 cup HONEY MAID® Graham Cracker Crumbs
1 cup plus 3 tablespoons sugar, divided
3 tablespoons butter or margarine, melted
4 packages (8 ounces each) PHILADELPHIA® Cream
    Cheese, softened
1 teaspoon vanilla
1 cup BREAKSTONE'S® or KNUDSEN® Sour Cream
4 eggs
2 cups fresh or thawed frozen blueberries

PREHEAT oven to 325°F. Mix crumbs, 3 tablespoons of the sugar and butter. Press firmly onto bottom of foil-lined 13×9-inch baking pan. Bake 10 minutes.

BEAT cream cheese, remaining 1 cup sugar and vanilla in large bowl with electric mixer on medium speed until well blended. Add sour cream; mix well. Add eggs, 1 at a time, beating on low speed after each addition just until blended. Pour over crust. Purée blueberries in a blender or food processor. Gently drop spoonfuls of puréed blueberries over batter; cut through batter several times with knife for marble effect.

BAKE 45 minutes or until center is almost set; cool. Cover and refrigerate at least 4 hours before serving. Store leftover cheesecake in refrigerator.   *Makes 16 servings.*

Substitution: Substitute 1 can (15 ounces) blueberries, well drained, for the 2 cups fresh or frozen blueberries.

Make It Easy: Instead of using a blender, crush the blueberries in a bowl with a fork. Drain before spooning over the cheesecake batter and swirling to marbleize as directed.

Clockwise from top left: *Blueberry Swirl Cheesecake, Lemony Pound Cake (p. 198), Coconut Brownie Bites (p. 204), Carrot Ginger Cupcakes (p. 186)*

Pistachio Strawberry-Cream Cupcakes

(pictured at right)

1 package (4-serving size) cook-and-serve vanilla pudding and pie filling mix
1-1/2 cups cake flour
3/4 teaspoon baking powder
1/4 teaspoon salt
1 cup (2 sticks) butter, softened
1-1/4 cups granulated sugar
4 eggs
1 tablespoon plus 1/2 teaspoon vanilla extract, divided
1/4 cup chopped pistachios
1 cup whipping cream
2 tablespoons superfine (instant-dissolve) sugar*
1/2 cup diced strawberries
9 strawberries, halved

Confectioners' sugar can be substituted for the superfine sugar.

1. Prepare pudding mix according to package directions. Pour into medium bowl; cover surface of pudding with plastic wrap. Refrigerate several hours or until chilled. (Filling may be prepared up to 1 day ahead.)

2. Preheat oven to 325°F. Line 18 standard (2-1/2-inch) muffin cups with paper baking cups.

3. Whisk together flour, baking powder and salt in medium bowl; set aside.

4. Beat butter and granulated sugar in large bowl with electric mixer at medium speed until light and fluffy. Add eggs, 1 at a time, beating well after each addition. Add flour mixture; beat at low speed until just combined. Add 1 tablespoon vanilla extract; beat at medium speed 30 seconds. Fold in pistachios.

5. Pour batter into muffin cups. Bake 20 to 25 minutes or until toothpick inserted into centers comes out clean. Cool cupcakes in pans on wire racks 10 minutes. Remove to racks; cool completely.

6. Beat whipping cream, superfine sugar and remaining 1/2 teaspoon vanilla extract in medium bowl with electric mixer at high speed until soft peaks form.

7. To serve, remove paper baking cups. Halve cupcakes horizontally. Fold diced strawberries into 1 cup pudding. (Reserve leftover pudding for another use.) Place dollop of pudding mixture onto each cupcake bottom; cover with tops. Garnish each with dollop of whipped cream mixture and strawberry half. *Makes 18 cupcakes*

Spiced Raisin Cookies with White Chocolate Drizzle

2 cups all-purpose flour
1-1/2 teaspoons ground cinnamon
1 teaspoon baking soda
1 teaspoon ground ginger
1/2 teaspoon ground allspice
1/4 teaspoon salt
1 cup sugar
3/4 cup butter, softened
1/4 cup molasses
1 egg
1 cup SUN-MAID® Raisins or Golden Raisins
4 ounces white chocolate, coarsely chopped

HEAT oven to 375°F.

COMBINE flour, cinnamon, baking soda, ginger, allspice and salt in small bowl. Set aside.

BEAT sugar and butter in large bowl until light and fluffy.

ADD molasses and egg; beat well.

BEAT in raisins. Gradually beat in flour mixture on low speed just until incorporated.

DROP dough by tablespoonfuls onto ungreased cookie sheets 2 inches apart. Flatten dough slightly.

BAKE 12 to 14 minutes or until set. Cool on cookie sheets 1 minute; transfer to wire racks and cool completely.

MICROWAVE chocolate in heavy, resealable plastic bag at high power 30 seconds. Turn bag over; heat additional 30 to 45 seconds or until almost melted. Knead bag with hands to melt remaining chocolate. Cut 1/8-inch corner off one end of bag. Drizzle cooled cookies with chocolate. Let stand until chocolate is set, about 20 minutes.

Makes about 2 dozen cookies

---

helpful hint

Ground spices can lose their flavor just sitting on a shelf in as little as a year. Always store your spices away from heat and light in tightly closed containers. If the spice smells musty or has no odor, it's time to replace it.

Pistachio Strawberry-Cream Cupcakes

Fluffy Peanut Butter Pie

(pictured at right)

1/4 cup (4 tablespoons) butter or margarine
2 cups finely crushed crème-filled chocolate
sandwich cookies (about 20 cookies)
1 (8-ounce) package cream cheese, softened
1 (14-ounce) can EAGLE BRAND® Sweetened
Condensed Milk (NOT evaporated milk)
1 cup smooth or crunchy peanut butter
3 tablespoons lemon juice
1 teaspoon vanilla extract
1 cup (1/2 pint) whipping cream, whipped

1. In small saucepan over low heat, melt butter; stir in cookie crumbs. Press crumb mixture firmly on bottom and up side of 9-inch pie plate; chill while preparing filling.

2. In large bowl, beat cream cheese until fluffy. Gradually beat EAGLE BRAND® and peanut butter until smooth. Add lemon juice and vanilla; mix well. Fold in whipped cream. Pour into crust.

3. Chill 4 hours or until set. Garnish as desired. Store leftovers covered in refrigerator.

Makes one (9-inch) pie

Carrot Ginger Cupcakes

(pictured on page 182)

1 pound carrots
3 cups all-purpose flour
1/3 cup pecan chips
2 teaspoons baking powder
1 teaspoon baking soda
1 teaspoon salt
1/2 teaspoon cinnamon
1 cup (2 sticks) plus 2 tablespoons butter
1-1/2 cups sugar
1 tablespoon honey
4 eggs
Peel of 2 oranges, grated
Juice of 1 orange
1 tablespoon vanilla extract
1-1/2 teaspoons grated gingerroot

ORANGE CREAM CHEESE FROSTING
1 package (8 ounces) cream cheese, softened
1/4 cup (1/2 stick) butter
2 teaspoons orange extract
1 teaspoon vanilla extract
Pinch salt
3-1/2 cups confectioners' sugar
Chopped pecans

1. Preheat oven to 350°F. Line 24 standard (2-1/2-inches) muffin cups with paper baking cups.

2. Grate carrots in food processor; drain excess juice. Set aside.

3. Whisk together flour, pecan chips, baking powder, baking soda, salt and cinnamon in large bowl. Set aside.

4. Beat butter, sugar and honey in medium bowl with electric mixer at medium speed until light and fluffy. Add eggs, 1 at a time, beating well after each addition. Add carrots, orange peel, orange juice, vanilla extract and gingerroot; mix well. Add flour mixture; mix until just combined. Do not overmix.

5. Spoon batter into muffin cups. Bake 20 to 25 minutes or until toothpick inserted into centers comes out clean. Remove from oven. Cool pans 10 minutes on wire racks. Remove cupcakes; cool completely on racks.

6. Prepare Orange Cream Cheese Frosting. Beat cream cheese, butter, orange extract, vanilla extract and salt in medium bowl with electric mixer at medium speed until light and fluffy. Add confectioners' sugar gradually, beating well after each addition. Cover and set aside.

7. Frost cooled cupcakes. Sprinkle with pecans. Refrigerate until ready to serve.

Makes 24 cupcakes

Crunchy Peppermint Candy Ice Cream

2 cups (1 pint) light cream
1 (14-ounce) can EAGLE BRAND® Sweetened
Condensed Milk (NOT evaporated milk)
1-1/4 cups water
1/2 cup crushed hard peppermint candy
1 tablespoon vanilla extract

1. Combine cream, EAGLE BRAND®, water, peppermint candy and vanilla in ice cream freezer container. Freeze according to manufacturer's instructions.

2. Garnish with additional crushed peppermint candy (optional). Store leftovers tightly covered in freezer.

Makes 1-1/2 quarts

Double-Chocolate Pecan Brownies

(pictured at right)

3/4 cup all-purpose flour
3/4 cup unsweetened cocoa powder
1/2 cup CREAM OF WHEAT® Hot Cereal (Instant, 1-minute, 2-1/2-minute or 10-minute cook time), uncooked
1/2 teaspoon baking powder
1-1/4 cups sugar
1/2 cup (1 stick) butter, softened
2 eggs
1 teaspoon vanilla extract
1/2 cup semisweet chocolate chips
1/2 cup pecans, chopped

1. Preheat oven to 350°F. Line 8-inch square baking pan with foil, extending foil over sides of pan; spray with nonstick cooking spray. Combine flour, cocoa, Cream of Wheat and baking powder in medium bowl; set aside.

2. Cream sugar and butter in large mixing bowl with electric mixer at medium speed. Add eggs and vanilla; mix until well combined.

3. Gradually add Cream of Wheat mixture; mix well. Spread batter evenly in pan, using spatula. Sprinkle chocolate chips and pecans evenly over top.

4. Bake 35 minutes. Let stand 5 minutes. Lift brownies from pan using aluminum foil. Cool completely before cutting.   *Makes 9 brownies*

Tip: For an even more decadent dessert, drizzle caramel sauce over the warm brownies and serve with mint chocolate chip ice cream.

Old-Fashioned Sour Cream Cookies

3 cups all-purpose flour
1 teaspoon WATKINS® Baking Powder
1/2 teaspoon baking soda
1/2 teaspoon salt
1 cup (2 sticks) butter, softened
1-3/4 cups sugar, divided
2 eggs
1 cup sour cream
2 teaspoons WATKINS® Clear Vanilla Extract
1/2 teaspoon WATKINS® Ground Cinnamon

Sift flour, baking powder, baking soda and salt into medium bowl. Beat butter, 1-1/2 cups sugar and

eggs in large bowl with electric mixer at medium speed until light and fluffy. Beat in sour cream and vanilla at low speed until smooth. Gradually beat in flour mixture until well combined. Refrigerate for at least 1 hour or until dough is firm enough to roll into balls.

Preheat oven to 350°F. Lightly grease cookie sheets. Combine remaining 1/4 cup sugar and cinnamon. Roll dough into 1-inch balls and place on prepared cookie sheets. Sprinkle lightly with cinnamon-sugar. Bake for 10 to 12 minutes or until bottoms are lightly browned. Remove cookies to wire rack to cool completely.   *Makes 5 dozen cookies*

Easy English Trifle

1 package (8 ounces) PHILADELPHIA® Cream Cheese, softened
2 cups cold milk, divided
1 package (4-serving size) JELL-O® Vanilla Flavor Instant Pudding & Pie Filling
1 package (10.75 ounces) pound cake, cut into 21 slices
1 package (10 ounces) frozen strawberries in syrup, thawed, drained and halved, syrup reserved
1/2 cup orange marmalade
2 cups thawed COOL WHIP® Whipped Topping

BEAT cream cheese and 1/2 cup of the milk in large bowl with electric mixer on medium speed 1 minute or until well blended. Add dry pudding mix and remaining 1-1/2 cups milk; beat on low speed 1 minute.

BRUSH both sides of pound cake slices with reserved strawberry syrup; set aside. Mix drained strawberries and marmalade. Place one-third of the cake slices on bottom of 2-quart clear glass serving bowl, cutting slices to fit. Layer with one-third each of the strawberry and pudding mixtures. Repeat layers 2 times. Cover surface with wax paper or plastic wrap.

REFRIGERATE several hours or until chilled. Top with whipped topping before serving. Store leftover dessert in refrigerator.
        Makes 14 servings, about 2/3 cup each.

Substitution: Substitute 50 NILLA Wafers for the pound cake.

Dutch Apple Dessert

(pictured at right)

5 medium apples, peeled, cored and sliced
1 (14-ounce) can EAGLE BRAND® Sweetened Condensed Milk (NOT evaporated milk)
1 teaspoon ground cinnamon
1/2 cup (1 stick) plus 2 tablespoons cold butter or margarine, divided
1-1/2 cups biscuit baking mix, divided
1/2 cup firmly packed brown sugar
1/2 cup chopped nuts
Ice cream (optional)

1. Preheat oven to 325°F.

2. In medium bowl, combine apples, EAGLE BRAND® and cinnamon.

3. In large bowl, cut 1/2 cup (1 stick) butter into 1 cup biscuit mix until crumbly. Stir in apple mixture. Pour into greased 9-inch square baking pan.

4. In small bowl, combine remaining 1/2 cup biscuit mix and brown sugar. Cut in 2 tablespoons butter until crumbly; add nuts. Sprinkle evenly over apple mixture.

5. Bake 1 hour or until golden. Serve warm with ice cream (optional). Store leftovers covered in refrigerator.   *Makes 6 to 8 servings*

Microwave Method: In 2-quart round baking dish, prepare as directed above. Microwave on HIGH (100% power) 14 to 15 minutes, rotating dish after 7 minutes. Let stand 5 minutes.

Ooey Gooey Krisper Bars

1 cup KARO® Light or Dark Corn Syrup
1 cup granulated sugar
1/2 teaspoon salt
1 cup crunchy or creamy peanut butter
5 cups crispy rice "or" corn flakes cereal
1 cup semi-sweet chocolate chips
1/2 cup peanut butter chips (optional)

Combine corn syrup, sugar and salt in a medium saucepan and cook over medium heat, stirring to dissolve sugar. (OR microwave on high (100%) for 2 to 2-1/2 minutes until syrup bubbles around the edge.)

Bring to a boil; add peanut butter and stir until blended. Remove from heat.

Stir in cereal. Pour into greased 9"×13" pan; pat with greased spatula or waxed paper to level.

Melt chocolate chips in small saucepan over low heat, stirring constantly. (OR microwave on medium-high heat (70%) for one minute. Stir, then microwave at additional 10- to 20-second intervals, stirring until smooth.) Spread over bars. If desired, melt peanut butter chips and use small spoon to dot or drizzle onto bars in any design you prefer. Cool and cut into squares.   *Makes 32 squares*

Apple-Oatmeal Spice Cookies

3/4 cup packed brown sugar
1/2 cup granulated sugar
1/4 cup (1/2 stick) margarine, softened
3/4 cup apple butter* or applesauce
2 egg whites or 1 egg
2 tablespoons milk
2 teaspoons vanilla
1-1/2 cups all-purpose flour
1 teaspoon baking soda
1 teaspoon ground cinnamon
1/2 teaspoon salt (optional)
1/4 teaspoon ground nutmeg (optional)
3 cups QUAKER® Oats (quick or old fashioned, uncooked)
1 cup diced dried mixed fruit or raisins

*Look for apple butter in the jam and jelly section of the supermarket.

1. Heat oven to 350°F. Lightly spray cookie sheets with nonstick cooking spray.

2. Beat sugars and margarine in large bowl until well blended. Add apple butter, egg whites, milk and vanilla; beat well. Combine flour, baking soda, cinnamon and, if desired, salt and nutmeg in medium bowl; mix well. Add to creamed mixture; mix well. Stir in oats and dried fruit; mix well. (Dough will be moist.)

3. Drop dough by rounded tablespoonfuls onto cookie sheets.

4. Bake 10 to 12 minutes or until edges are light golden brown. Cool 1 minute on cookie sheets. Transfer to wire rack; cool completely. Store tightly covered.   *Makes 32 cookies*

Dole Golden Layer Cake

Dole Golden Layer Cake

(pictured above)

1 can (20 ounces) DOLE® Crushed Pineapple, undrained
1-1/2 cups non-diary whipped topping, thawed
1 package (4-serving size) instant vanilla pudding and pie filling mix
1 (14- to 16-ounce) prepared pound cake
1/3 cup almond-flavored liqueur (or 1/3 cup pineapple juice and 1/2 teaspoon almond extract)
DOLE® Pineapple Slices (optional)
Sliced almonds, toasted (optional)

• Combine undrained pineapple, whipped topping and dry pudding mix. Let stand 5 minutes.

• Cut cake lengthwise into thirds. Drizzle with liqueur. Spread one-third pudding mixture over bottom layer of cake. Top with second layer. Repeat layering, ending with pudding.

• Chill 30 minutes or overnight. Garnish with pineapple and sprinkle with toasted, sliced almonds, if desired. *Makes 12 servings*

Carrot Cake with Creamy Frosting

3 cups all-purpose flour
1 tablespoon baking soda
1 tablespoon pumpkin pie spice
1 teaspoon salt
1 can (8 ounces) crushed pineapple in juice
2 cups sliced carrots (about 3 large carrots)
1 cup granulated sugar
1 cup packed brown sugar
4 eggs
3/4 cup vegetable oil
2/3 cup sour cream
1 tablespoon vanilla extract
1 cup shredded carrots
1 cup chopped pecans or walnuts, toasted* (optional)
Creamy Frosting (recipe follows)
Toasted coconut**

*To toast pecans, spread on baking sheet. Bake 5 to 7 minutes in preheated 350°F oven or until nuts are just beginning to darken and are fragrant.

**To toast coconut, spread in shallow baking pan. Bake in preheated 350°F oven 5 to 7 minutes or until golden brown, stirring occasionally.

1. Preheat oven to 350°F. Spray 9- or 10-inch bundt or angel food cake pan with nonstick cooking spray. Combine flour, baking soda, pumpkin pie spice and salt in large bowl. Drain pineapple; reserve juice for frosting.

2. Cook sliced carrots in boiling water 10 minutes or until tender; drain. Place in food processor; process until puréed. Add sugars; process until smooth. Add eggs, oil, sour cream and vanilla extract; process until blended.

3. Add carrot mixture to flour mixture; beat with electric mixer at medium speed 2 to 3 minutes or until blended. Fold in shredded carrots, drained pineapple and nuts, if desired.

4. Spoon batter into prepared pan. Bake 1 hour or until toothpick inserted near center comes out clean. Cool cake in pan on wire rack 10 minutes. Remove from pan; cool completely.

5. Meanwhile, prepare Creamy Frosting. Spread over top of cake. Garnish with toasted coconut.
Makes 24 servings

Creamy Frosting: Combine 1/2 package (8 ounces) softened cream cheese, 1/2 cup confectioners' sugar and 1 tablespoon reserved pineapple juice in medium bowl; beat until smooth and creamy.

French Apple Bread Pudding

(pictured below)

4 cups cubed French bread
1/2 cup raisins (optional)
3 eggs
1 (14-ounce) can EAGLE BRAND® Sweetened Condensed Milk (NOT evaporated milk)
3 medium apples, peeled, cored and finely chopped
1-3/4 cups hot water
1/4 cup (4 tablespoons) butter or margarine, melted
1 teaspoon ground cinnamon
1 teaspoon vanilla extract
Ice cream (optional)

1. Preheat oven to 350°F. Combine bread cubes and raisins (optional) in buttered 9-inch square pan.

2. In large bowl, beat eggs; add EAGLE BRAND®, apples, water, butter, cinnamon and vanilla. Pour evenly over bread cubes, moistening completely.

3. Bake 50 to 55 minutes or until knife inserted near center comes out clean. Cool slightly. Serve warm with ice cream (optional). Store leftovers covered in refrigerator.   *Makes 6 to 9 servings*

Fourth of July Cherry Pie

5 cups pitted Northwest fresh sweet cherries
2 tablespoons cornstarch
Pastry for 2-crust (9-inch) pie
2 tablespoons butter or margarine
1/3 cup sifted powdered sugar
1 tablespoon fresh lemon juice
1 teaspoon grated lemon peel

Preheat oven to 425°F.

Sprinkle cornstarch over cherries; toss to coat. Turn into pastry-lined 9-inch pie pan. Dot with butter. Roll remaining pastry into 10-inch circle. Cut into 3/4-inch-wide strips. Arrange lattice-fashion over filling; seal and flute edges. Bake 35 to 45 minutes or until filling bubbles. Combine powdered sugar, lemon juice and peel; drizzle over warm pie.   *Makes one (9-inch) pie*

Combination Method: Preheat oven to 425°F. Prepare pie as above in microwave/ovenproof pie plate. Microwave at HIGH 10 minutes or until filling bubbles; remove to conventional oven and bake 10 to 15 minutes or until crust is golden.

Favorite recipe from **Northwest Cherry Growers**

French Apple Bread Pudding

Brownie Apple Sauce Cake

(pictured at right)

    1/2 cup butter
      3 squares (1 ounce each) unsweetened chocolate
    1-1/2 cups MOTT'S® Apple Sauce
      1 cup sugar
      3 eggs, well beaten
      1 teaspoon vanilla extract
    1-1/2 cups all-purpose flour
      1 teaspoon baking soda
    1/2 teaspoon salt
    1/2 cup chopped walnuts
        Apple Cream Cheese Frosting (recipe follows)

1. Heat oven to 350°F. In large heavy saucepan, over low heat, melt butter and chocolate, stirring constantly. Remove from heat and cool. Blend apple sauce, sugar, eggs and vanilla into chocolate mixture. In large bowl, mix flour, baking soda and salt. With wooden spoon, stir in chocolate mixture until blended. Stir in walnuts.

2. Pour batter into 2 greased and floured 8-inch round cake pans. Bake 35 to 40 minutes or until toothpick inserted in center comes out clean. Cool in pans 10 minutes. Prepare Apple Cream Cheese Frosting. Remove cakes from pans; cool completely on wire racks. Fill and frost with Apple Cream Cheese Frosting. Garnish as desired.

Makes 12 servings

Apple Cream Cheese Frosting: In large bowl, beat 2 packages (8 ounces each) softened cream cheese and 1/2 cup softened butter until light and fluffy. Blend in 1 cup confectioners' sugar, 1/2 cup MOTT'S® Apple Sauce, 1/2 cup melted and cooled caramels and 1 teaspoon vanilla extract.

Chocolate Chunk Cookies

    2-3/4 cups flour
      1 teaspoon baking soda
    1/4 teaspoon salt
    3/4 cup butter or margarine, softened
    3/4 cup firmly packed brown sugar
    1/2 cup KARO® Light or Dark Corn Syrup
      1 egg
      1 teaspoon vanilla
      1 package (8 ounces) semi sweet chocolate, cut
          into 1/2-inch chunks, divided
      1 cup chopped pecans, divided

In bowl, combine flour, baking soda and salt. In mixing bowl with mixer at medium speed, beat butter and sugar until fluffy. Gradually beat in corn syrup. Beat in egg and vanilla. Gradually beat in flour mixture until just combined. Stir in half of the chocolate chunks and pecans.

Drop dough by rounded tablespoonfuls onto ungreased baking sheets. Sprinkle with remaining chocolate chunks and pecans.

Bake in 350°F oven 8 to 10 minutes or until lightly brown. Cool on wire rack.   *Makes 36 cookies*

Cranberry Apple Crisp

    1/2 cup KARO® Light Corn Syrup
    1/3 to 1/2 cup sugar
      1 teaspoon cinnamon
    1/2 teaspoon nutmeg
      5 to 6 cups cubed, peeled tart apples
      1 cup fresh or frozen cranberries
      3 tablespoons ARGO® or KINGSFORD'S® Corn
        Starch
      1 teaspoon grated orange peel

TOPPING
    1/2 cup walnuts or uncooked oats
    1/3 cup packed brown sugar
    1/4 cup flour
    1/4 cup (1/2 stick) margarine or butter

Preheat oven to 350°F.

In large bowl combine corn syrup, sugar, cinnamon and nutmeg. Add apples, cranberries, cornstarch and orange peel; toss to mix well. Spoon into shallow 2-quart baking dish.

TOPPING
Combine nuts, brown sugar and flour. With pastry blender or 2 knives, cut in margarine until crumbly. Sprinkle over cranberry mixture.

Bake 50 minutes or until apples are tender and juices that bubble up in center are shiny and clear. Cool slightly; serve warm.   *Makes 8 servings*

---

helpful hint

Fresh cranberries freeze very well. Purchase an extra bag when they are on sale during the holidays and store it in your freezer. When you're ready to use them simply rinse in a colander. No need to thaw.

Chocolate Mousse Cake Roll

(pictured at right)

Chocolate Mousse Filling (recipe follows)
4 eggs, separated
1/2 cup plus 1/3 cup granulated sugar, divided
1 teaspoon vanilla extract
1/2 cup all-purpose flour
1/3 cup HERSHEY'S Cocoa
1/2 teaspoon baking powder
1/4 teaspoon baking soda
1/8 teaspoon salt
1/3 cup water
Powdered sugar
HERSHEY'S Syrup

1. Prepare Chocolate Mousse Filling. Chill 6 to 8 hours or overnight.

2. Prepare cake.* Heat oven to 375°F. Line 15-1/2×10-1/2×1-inch jelly-roll pan with foil; generously grease foil.

3. Beat egg whites in large bowl until soft peaks form; gradually add 1/2 cup granulated sugar, beating until stiff peaks form. Beat egg yolks and vanilla in medium bowl on medium speed of mixer 3 minutes. Gradually add remaining 1/3 cup granulated sugar; continue beating 2 additional minutes.

4. Stir together flour, cocoa, baking powder, baking soda and salt; add to egg yolk mixture alternately with water, beating on low speed just until batter is smooth. Gradually fold chocolate mixture into beaten egg whites until well blended. Spread batter evenly in prepared pan.

5. Bake 12 to 15 minutes or until top springs back when touched lightly in center. Immediately loosen cake from edges of pan; invert onto clean towel sprinkled with powdered sugar. Carefully peel off foil. Immediately roll cake and towel together starting from narrow end; place on wire rack to cool completely.

6. Carefully unroll cake; remove towel. Gently stir filling until of spreading consistency. Spread cake with filling; reroll cake. Refrigerate several hours. Sift powdered sugar over top just before serving. Serve drizzled with syrup and garnished as desired. Cover; refrigerate leftover cake roll.

Makes 8 to 10 servings

*Cake may be prepared up to two days in advance. Keep cake rolled tightly and covered well so that it doesn't get dry.

Chocolate Mousse Filling

1/4 cup sugar
1 teaspoon unflavored gelatin
1/2 cup milk
1 cup HERSHEY'S SPECIAL DARK® Chocolate Chips or HERSHEY'S Semi-Sweet Chocolate Chips
2 teaspoons vanilla extract
1 cup (1/2 pint) cold whipping cream

1. Stir together sugar and gelatin in small saucepan; stir in milk. Let stand 2 minutes to soften gelatin. Cook over medium heat, stirring constantly, until mixture just begins to boil.

2. Remove from heat. Immediately add chocolate chips; stir until melted. Stir in vanilla; cool to room temperature.

3. Beat whipping cream in small bowl until stiff. Gradually add chocolate mixture, folding gently just until blended. Cover; refrigerate until ready to use.

Makes about 3 cups

Peanut Butter Cup Cookies

1-1/2 cups packed brown sugar
1 cup (2 sticks) margarine or butter, softened
3/4 cup peanut butter (not reduced-fat)
2 eggs
2 teaspoons vanilla
1-1/2 cups all-purpose flour
1/3 cup unsweetened cocoa powder
1 teaspoon baking soda
1/4 teaspoon salt (optional)
2 cups QUAKER® Oats (quick or old fashioned, uncooked)
1 package (9 ounces) miniature peanut butter cup candies, unwrapped, cut into halves or quarters (about 35 candies)

1. Heat oven to 350°F. Beat brown sugar, margarine and peanut butter until creamy. Add eggs and vanilla; beat well. Combine flour, cocoa powder, baking soda and salt, if desired, in small bowl; mix well. Add to creamed mixture; mix well. Stir in oats and candy; mix well.

2. Drop dough by level 1/4 cupfuls 3 inches apart onto ungreased cookie sheets. Bake 12 to 14 minutes or until cookies are slightly firm to the touch. (Do not overbake.) Cool 1 minute on cookie sheets. Transfer to wire racks; cool completely. Store tightly covered.

Makes 36 cookies

Banana Coconut Cream Pie

(pictured at right)

3 tablespoons cornstarch
1-1/3 cups water
1 (14-ounce) can EAGLE BRAND® Sweetened
    Condensed Milk (NOT evaporated milk)
3 egg yolks, beaten
2 tablespoons butter or margarine
1 teaspoon vanilla extract
1/2 cup flaked coconut, toasted
2 medium bananas
2 tablespoons lemon juice
1 (9-inch) prepared graham cracker or baked
    pie crust
    Whipped cream (optional)
    Additional toasted coconut for garnish
    (optional)

1. In heavy saucepan over medium heat, dissolve cornstarch in water; stir in EAGLE BRAND® and egg yolks. Cook and stir until thickened and bubbly. Remove from heat; add butter and vanilla. Cool slightly. Fold in coconut; set aside.

2. Peel and slice bananas into 1/4-inch-thick rounds. Toss banana slices gently with lemon juice; drain. Arrange bananas on bottom of crust. Pour filling over bananas.

3. Cover; refrigerate 4 hours or until set. Top with whipped cream and additional toasted coconut (optional). Store leftovers covered in refrigerator.

Makes one (9-inch) pie

Lemony Pound Cake

(pictured on page 182)

1 package (4-serving size) lemon-flavor gelatin
3/4 cup boiling water
1 package DUNCAN HINES® Moist Deluxe®
    Classic Yellow Cake Mix
4 eggs
3/4 cup vegetable oil
1 can (6 ounces) frozen lemonade concentrate,
    thawed
1/2 cup granulated sugar

1. Preheat oven to 350°F. Grease and flour 10-inch tube pan.

2. Dissolve gelatin in water in large mixing bowl; cool. Stir in cake mix, eggs and oil. Beat at medium speed with electric mixer for 2 minutes. Spoon into prepared pan. Bake 50 minutes or until toothpick inserted in center comes out clean. Mix lemonade

concentrate and sugar in small bowl. Pour over hot cake; cool in pan 1 hour. Remove from pan. Cool completely. *Makes 12 to 16 servings*

Tip: Serve this cake with fresh or thawed frozen strawberries for a special dessert.

Hershey's Brownies with Peanut Butter Frosting

1/2 cup (1 stick) butter or margarine
4 sections (1/2 ounce each) HERSHEY'S
    Unsweetened Chocolate Premium Baking
    Bar, broken into pieces
1 cup sugar
2 eggs
1 teaspoon vanilla extract
1/2 cup all-purpose flour
1/4 teaspoon baking powder
1/4 teaspoon salt
1/2 cup chopped nuts
    Peanut Butter Frosting (optional, recipe
    follows)

1. Heat oven to 350°F. Grease 8-inch square baking pan.

2. Melt butter and chocolate in medium saucepan over low heat. Remove from heat; stir in sugar. Beat in eggs and vanilla with wooden spoon. Stir together flour, baking powder and salt. Add to chocolate mixture, blending well. Stir in nuts. Pour batter into prepared pan.

3. Bake 30 to 35 minutes or until brownies begin to pull away from sides of pan. Cool completely in pan on wire rack. Frost with Peanut Butter Frosting, if desired. Cut into squares.

Makes about 16 brownies

Peanut Butter Frosting

1 cup powdered sugar
1/4 cup REESE'S® Creamy Peanut Butter
2 tablespoons milk
1/2 teaspoon vanilla extract

Combine all ingredients in small bowl; beat until smooth. If necessary add additional milk, 1/2 teaspoon at a time, until of desired consistency.

Makes about 3/4 cup

Walnut Caramel Triangles

(pictured at right)

> **2 cups all-purpose flour**
> **1/2 cup confectioners' sugar**
> **1 cup (2 sticks) cold butter or margarine**
> **1 (14-ounce) can EAGLE BRAND® Sweetened Condensed Milk (NOT evaporated milk)**
> **1/2 cup whipping cream**
> **1 teaspoon vanilla extract**
> **1-1/2 cups chopped walnuts**
> **Chocolate Drizzle (recipe follows)**

1. Preheat oven to 350°F. In medium bowl, combine flour and confectioners' sugar; cut in butter until crumbly. Press firmly on bottom of 13×9-inch baking pan. Bake 15 minutes or until lightly browned around edges.

2. In heavy saucepan over medium-high heat combine EAGLE BRAND®, whipping cream and vanilla. Cook and stir until mixture comes to a boil. Reduce heat to medium; cook and stir until mixture thickens, 8 to 10 minutes. Stir in walnuts.

3. Spread evenly over prepared crust. Bake 20 minutes or until golden brown. Cool. Garnish with Chocolate Drizzle. Chill. Cut into triangles. Store leftovers covered at room temperature.

Makes 4 dozen triangles

Chocolate Drizzle: Melt 1/2 cup semisweet chocolate chips with 1 teaspoon shortening. Carefully drizzle chocolate mixture over triangles with a spoon.

All-Chocolate Boston Cream Pie

> **1 cup all-purpose flour**
> **1 cup sugar**
> **1/3 cup HERSHEY'S Cocoa**
> **1/2 teaspoon baking soda**
> **6 tablespoons butter or margarine, softened**
> **1 cup milk**
> **1 egg**
> **1 teaspoon vanilla extract**
> **Chocolate Filling (recipe follows)**
> **Satiny Chocolate Glaze (recipe follows)**

1. Heat oven to 350°F. Grease and flour one 9-inch round baking pan.

2. Stir together flour, sugar, cocoa and baking soda in large bowl. Add butter, milk, egg and vanilla. Beat on low speed of mixer until all ingredients are moistened. Beat on medium speed 2 minutes. Pour batter into prepared pan.

3. Bake 30 to 35 minutes or until wooden pick inserted in center comes out clean. Cool 10 minutes; remove from pan to wire rack. Cool completely.

4. Prepare Chocolate Filling. Cut cake into two thin layers. Place one layer on serving plate; spread filling over layer. Top with remaining layer.

5. Prepare Satiny Chocolate Glaze. Pour onto top of cake, allowing some to drizzle down sides. Refrigerate until serving time. Cover; refrigerate leftover cake.

Makes 8 servings

Chocolate Filling

> **1/2 cup sugar**
> **1/4 cup HERSHEY'S Cocoa**
> **2 tablespoons cornstarch**
> **1-1/2 cups light cream**
> **1 tablespoon butter or margarine**
> **1 teaspoon vanilla extract**

Stir together sugar, cocoa and cornstarch in medium saucepan; gradually stir in light cream. Cook over medium heat, stirring constantly, until mixture thickens and begins to boil. Boil 1 minute, stirring constantly; remove from heat. Stir in butter and vanilla. Press plastic wrap directly onto surface. Cool completely.

Makes 8 servings

Satiny Chocolate Glaze

> **2 tablespoons water**
> **1 tablespoon butter or margarine**
> **1 tablespoon corn syrup**
> **2 tablespoons HERSHEY'S Cocoa**
> **3/4 cup powdered sugar**
> **1/2 teaspoon vanilla extract**

Heat water, butter and corn syrup in small saucepan to boiling. Remove from heat; immediately stir in cocoa. With whisk, gradually beat in powdered sugar and vanilla until smooth; cool slightly.

Makes 8 servings

Hermits

3. Bake 13 to 15 minutes or until set. Cool 5 minutes on cookie sheets. Remove to wire racks; cool completely.

4. Combine maple syrup, butter and maple flavoring in medium bowl. Add confectioners' sugar, 1/4 cup at a time, stirring until smooth. Spread glaze over cookies. Let stand 30 minutes or until set.

Makes about 4 dozen cookies

Brickle Bundt Cake

> 1-1/3 cups (8-ounce package) HEATH®
>   BITS 'O BRICKLE® Toffee Bits, divided
> 1-1/4 cups granulated sugar, divided
>   1/4 cup chopped walnuts
>   1 teaspoon ground cinnamon
>   1/2 cup (1 stick) butter, softened
>   2 eggs
> 1-1/4 teaspoons vanilla extract, divided
>   2 cups all-purpose flour
> 1-1/2 teaspoons baking powder
>   1 teaspoon baking soda
>   1/4 teaspoon salt
>   1 container (8 ounces) dairy sour cream
>   1/4 cup (1/2 stick) butter, melted
>   1 cup powdered sugar
>   1 to 3 tablespoons milk, divided

1. Heat oven to 325°F. Grease and flour 12-cup fluted tube pan or 10-inch tube pan. Set aside 1/4 cup toffee bits for topping. Combine remaining toffee bits, 1/4 cup granulated sugar, walnuts and cinnamon; set aside.

2. Beat remaining 1 cup granulated sugar and 1/2 cup butter in large bowl until fluffy. Add eggs and 1 teaspoon vanilla; beat well. Stir together flour, baking powder, baking soda and salt; gradually add to butter mixture alternately with sour cream, beating until blended. Beat 3 minutes. Spoon one-third of the batter into prepared pan. Sprinkle with half of toffee mixture. Spoon half of remaining batter into pan. Top with remaining toffee mixture. Spoon remaining batter into pan. Pour melted butter over batter.

3. Bake 45 to 50 minutes or until wooden pick inserted in center comes out clean. Cool 10 minutes; remove from pan to wire rack. Cool completely.

4. Stir together powdered sugar, 1 tablespoon milk and remaining 1/4 teaspoon vanilla. Stir in additional milk, 1 teaspoon at a time, until desired consistency; drizzle over cake. Sprinkle with reserved 1/4 cup toffee bits.

Makes 12 to 14 servings

Hermits

(pictured above)

> 6 tablespoons unsalted butter, softened
> 1/4 cup packed dark brown sugar
>   1 egg
>   1 package (about 18 ounces) yellow cake mix
>   with pudding in the mix
> 1/3 cup molasses
>   1 teaspoon ground cinnamon
> 1/4 teaspoon baking soda
> 3/4 cup raisins
> 3/4 cup chopped pecans
> 2-1/2 tablespoons maple syrup
>   1 tablespoon butter, melted
> 1/4 teaspoon maple flavoring
> 3/4 cup confectioners' sugar

1. Preheat oven to 375°F. Line cookie sheets with parchment paper.

2. Beat butter and sugar in large bowl with electric mixer at medium-high speed until well blended. Beat in egg. Add cake mix, molasses, cinnamon and baking soda; beat just until blended. Stir in raisins and pecans. Drop batter by rounded tablespoonfuls 1-1/2 inches apart on prepared cookie sheets.

Sweet Potato Pie

(pictured below)

1 pound sweet potatoes,* boiled and peeled
1/4 cup (4 tablespoons) butter or margarine
1 (14-ounce) can EAGLE BRAND® Sweetened
   Condensed Milk (NOT evaporated milk)
2 eggs
1 teaspoon grated orange rind
1 teaspoon vanilla extract
1 teaspoon ground cinnamon
1 teaspoon ground nutmeg
1/4 teaspoon salt
1 (9-inch) unbaked pie crust

For best results, use fresh sweet potatoes.

1. Preheat oven to 350°F.

2. In large bowl, beat sweet potatoes and butter until smooth. Add EAGLE BRAND®, eggs, orange rind, vanilla, cinnamon, nutmeg and salt; mix well. Pour into crust.

3. Bake 40 minutes or until golden brown. Cool. Garnish as desired. Store leftovers covered in refrigerator.   *Makes one (9-inch) pie*

Pineapple Upside-Down Minis

2 cans (20 ounces each) DOLE® Pineapple Slices
1/3 cup butter or margarine, melted
2/3 cup packed brown sugar
9 maraschino cherries, cut in half
1 package (18-1/4 ounces) yellow or pineapple-
   flavored cake mix

• Drain pineapple; reserve juice.

• Stir together melted butter and brown sugar. Evenly divide sugar mixture into 18 (2/3-cup) muffin cups, sprayed with nonstick vegetable cooking spray. Lightly press well-drained pineapple slices into sugar mixture. Place cherries in center of pineapple, sliced sides up.

• Prepare cake mix according to package directions, replacing amount of water called for with reserved juice. Pour 1/3 cup batter into each muffin cup.

• Bake at 350°F. for 20 to 25 minutes or until toothpick inserted in center comes out clean.

• Cool 5 minutes. Loosen edges and invert onto cookie sheets.   *Makes 18 servings*

Sweet Potato Pie

Tutti Fruiti Rice Cream

(pictured at right)

> 1 cup MINUTE® White Rice, uncooked
> 1 can (15 ounces) tropical fruit salad, drained
> 2 cups miniature marshmallows
> 1-1/2 cups frozen nondairy whipped topping, thawed
> 1/4 cup sugar
> Ground cinnamon (optional)

Prepare rice according to package directions. Cool. Toss with remaining ingredients. Chill. Sprinkle with cinnamon before serving, if desired.

Makes 4 servings

Tip: To sneak some whole-grain nutrition into your kids' diet, try substituting MINUTE® Brown Rice in dessert recipes. The flavor and texture will be just as appealing, and you'll feel even better about providing a second helping.

Coconut Brownie Bites

(pictured on page 182)

> 42 MOUNDS® or ALMOND JOY® Candy Bar Miniatures
> 1/2 cup (1 stick) butter or margarine, softened
> 1/2 cup packed light brown sugar
> 1/4 cup granulated sugar
> 1 egg
> 1 teaspoon vanilla extract
> 1-1/4 cups all-purpose flour
> 1/3 cup HERSHEY'S Cocoa
> 3/4 teaspoon baking soda
> 1/2 teaspoon salt

1. Remove wrappers from candies. Line 42 small muffin cups (1-3/4 inches in diameter) with paper bake cups.

2. Beat butter, brown sugar, granulated sugar, egg and vanilla in large bowl until well blended. Stir together flour, cocoa, baking soda and salt; gradually add to butter mixture, beating until well blended. Cover; refrigerate dough about 30 minutes or until firm enough to handle.

3. Heat oven to 375°F. Shape dough into 1-inch balls; place one ball in each prepared muffin cup. *Do not flatten.*

4. Bake 8 to 10 minutes or until puffed. Remove from oven. Cool 5 minutes. (Cookies will sink slightly.) Press one candy into each cookie. Cool completely in pan on wire racks. *Makes 3-1/2 dozen cookies*

Red Devil's Chocolate Cake

> Vegetable cooking spray
> 2-1/2 cups all-purpose flour
> 1/2 cup unsweetened cocoa
> 1-1/2 teaspoons baking soda
> 1/4 teaspoon salt
> 1 stick (1/2 cup) butter, softened
> 1-3/4 cups sugar
> 2 eggs
> 1 teaspoon vanilla extract
> 3 teaspoons grated orange peel
> 1-1/2 cups CAMPBELL'S® Tomato Juice
> 1 cup sweetened coconut, toasted

CREAMY ORANGE BUTTER FROSTING
> 6 tablespoons butter, softened
> 2 cups confectioners' sugar
> 2 tablespoons milk
> 1/4 teaspoon vanilla extract
> 1/8 teaspoon salt

1. Heat the oven to 350°F. Spray an 11-3/4×9-3/8×1/2-inch disposable aluminum pan or a 13×9×2-inch baking pan with cooking spray. Set aside.

2. Mix the flour, cocoa, baking soda and salt in a small bowl.

3. Beat the butter and sugar in a medium bowl with an electric mixer at medium speed until they're light and fluffy, occasionally scraping side of the bowl. Beat in the eggs, one at a time, beating well after each addition. Beat in the vanilla and **1 teaspoon** of the orange peel. Reserve the remaining peel for the frosting.

4. Reduce the speed to low. Add the flour mixture alternately with the tomato juice, beginning and ending with the flour mixture. Beat well after each addition, occasionally scraping bowl. Pour the batter into the prepared pan.

5. Bake for 30 to 35 minutes or until a toothpick inserted in center comes out clean. Cool the cake in the pan on a wire rack.

6. Prepare Creamy Orange Butter Frosting: Put the butter, sugar, milk, vanilla, salt and reserved orange peel in a medium bowl. Beat with an electric mixer at low speed until smooth. Increase the speed to medium, adding a little more milk if necessary, to make the frosting more spreadable.

7. Frost with Creamy Orange Butter Frosting and sprinkle with the coconut. Store the cake in the refrigerator. *Makes 12 servings*

New York-Style Strawberry Swirl Cheesecake

(pictured at right)

1 cup HONEY MAID® Graham Cracker Crumbs
3 tablespoons sugar
3 tablespoons butter, melted
5 packages (8 ounces each) PHILADELPHIA®
    Cream Cheese, softened
1 cup sugar
3 tablespoons flour
1 tablespoon vanilla
1 cup BREAKSTONE'S® or KNUDSEN® Sour
    Cream
4 eggs
1/3 cup SMUCKER'S® Seedless Strawberry Jam

PREHEAT oven to 325°F. Line 13×9-inch baking pan with foil, with ends of foil extending over sides of pan. Mix cracker crumbs, 3 tablespoons sugar and butter; press firmly onto bottom of prepared pan. Bake 10 minutes.

BEAT cream cheese, 1 cup sugar, flour and vanilla in large bowl with electric mixer on medium speed until well blended. Add sour cream; mix well. Add eggs, 1 at a time, mixing on low speed after each addition just until blended. Pour over crust. Gently drop small spoonfuls of jam over batter; cut through batter several times with knife for marble effect.

BAKE 40 minutes or until center is almost set. Cool completely. Refrigerate at least 4 hours or overnight. Lift cheesecake from pan using foil handles. Cut into 16 pieces to serve. Store leftover cheesecake in refrigerator.

Makes 16 servings, 1 piece each.

Substitution: Substitute 1 bag (16 ounces) frozen fruit, thawed, drained and puréed for the 1/3 cup jam.

Petite Macaroon Cups

1 cup (2 sticks) butter or margarine, softened
2 (3-ounce) packages cream cheese, softened
2 cups all-purpose flour
1 (14-ounce) can EAGLE BRAND® Sweetened
    Condensed Milk (NOT evaporated milk)
2 eggs, beaten
1-1/2 teaspoons vanilla extract
1/2 teaspoon almond extract
1-1/3 cups flaked coconut

1. In large bowl, beat butter and cream cheese until fluffy; stir in flour. Cover; chill 1 hour.

2. Preheat oven to 375°F. Divide dough into quarters. On floured surface, shape 1 quarter into a smooth ball. Divide into 12 balls. Place each ball in a 1-3/4-inch muffin cup; press evenly on bottom and up side of each cup. Repeat with remaining dough.

3. In medium bowl, combine EAGLE BRAND®, eggs and extracts; mix well. Stir in coconut. Fill muffin cups three-fourths full. Bake 16 to 18 minutes or until slightly browned. Cool in pans. Remove from pan using small metal spatula or knife. Store leftovers loosely covered at room temperature.

Makes 4 dozen cups

Chocolate Macaroon Cups: Beat 1/4 cup unsweetened cocoa powder into egg mixture; proceed as above.

Island Cookies

1-2/3 cups all-purpose flour
3/4 teaspoon baking powder
1/2 teaspoon baking soda
1/2 teaspoon salt
3/4 cup (1-1/2 sticks) butter, softened
3/4 cup packed brown sugar
1/3 cup granulated sugar
1 teaspoon vanilla extract
1 large egg
1-3/4 cups (11.5-ounce package) NESTLÉ® TOLL
    HOUSE® Milk Chocolate Morsels
1 cup flaked coconut, toasted, if desired
1 cup chopped walnuts

PREHEAT oven to 375°F.

COMBINE flour, baking powder, baking soda and salt in small bowl. Beat butter, brown sugar, granulated sugar and vanilla extract in large mixer bowl until creamy. Beat in egg. Gradually beat in flour mixture. Stir in morsels, coconut and nuts. Drop by slightly rounded tablespoon onto ungreased baking sheets.

BAKE for 8 to 11 minutes or until edges are lightly browned. Cool on baking sheets for 2 minutes; remove to wire racks to cool completely.

Makes about 3 dozen cookies

Note: NESTLÉ® TOLL HOUSE® Semi-Sweet Chocolate Morsels, Semi-Sweet Chocolate Mini Morsels, Premier White Morsels or Butterscotch Flavored Morsels can be substituted for the Milk Chocolate Morsels.

New York-Style Strawberry
Swirl Cheesecake

Layers of Love Chocolate Brownies

a time, beating well after each addition. Add vanilla extract; mix well. Gradually beat in flour mixture. Reserve *3/4 cup* batter. Spread *remaining* batter into prepared baking pan. Sprinkle pecans and white morsels over batter. Drizzle caramel topping over top. Beat *remaining* egg and *reserved* batter in same large bowl until light in color. Stir in semi-sweet morsels. Spread evenly over caramel topping.

BAKE for 30 to 35 minutes or until center is set. Cool completely in pan on wire rack. Cut into squares.   *Makes 16 brownies*

Layers of Love
Chocolate Brownies

(pictured above)

3/4 cup all-purpose flour
3/4 cup NESTLÉ® TOLL HOUSE® Baking Cocoa
1/4 teaspoon salt
1/2 cup (1 stick) butter, cut into pieces
1/2 cup granulated sugar
1/2 cup packed brown sugar
3 large eggs, *divided*
2 teaspoons vanilla extract
1 cup chopped pecans
3/4 cup NESTLÉ® TOLL HOUSE® Premier White
    Morsels
1/2 cup caramel ice cream topping
3/4 cup NESTLÉ® TOLL HOUSE® Semi-Sweet
    Chocolate Morsels

PREHEAT oven to 350°F. Grease 8-inch square baking pan.

COMBINE flour, cocoa and salt in small bowl. Beat butter, granulated sugar and brown sugar in large mixer bowl until creamy. Add *2 eggs,* one at

Date Bars

1 package (8 ounces) chopped dates
3/4 cup NESTLÉ® CARNATION® Evaporated Milk
2 tablespoons granulated sugar
1 teaspoon vanilla extract
1/2 cup (1 stick) butter or margarine, softened
1/2 cup packed light brown sugar
1 cup all-purpose flour
3/4 cup quick oats
1/2 teaspoon baking soda
1/2 teaspoon salt
1/2 teaspoon ground cinnamon

PREHEAT oven to 400°F. Grease 8-inch square baking pan.

COMBINE dates, evaporated milk, granulated sugar and vanilla extract in medium saucepan. Cook over medium-low heat, stirring occasionally, for 8 to 10 minutes or until thickened. Remove from heat.

BEAT butter and brown sugar in large mixer bowl until creamy. Beat in flour, oats, baking soda, salt and cinnamon. With floured fingers, press *half* of crust mixture onto bottom of prepared baking pan. Spread date filling over crust. Top with *remaining* crust.

BAKE for 20 to 25 minutes or until golden. Cut into bars. Serve warm.   *Makes 16 bars*

--- helpful hint ---

Dates, being mostly sugar, are super sweet, but they also have a good amount of protein and iron. Fresh dates can be found in specialty markets from late summer to fall. Dried whole dates are sold pitted and unpitted, and packaged chopped dates are sold in most supermarkets.

Triple-Chocolate Cupcakes

(pictured below)

1 package (18-1/4 ounces) chocolate cake mix
1 package (4 ounces) chocolate instant pudding
    and pie filling mix
1 container (8 ounces) sour cream
4 large eggs
1/2 cup vegetable oil
1/2 cup warm water
2 cups (12-ounce package) NESTLÉ® TOLL
    HOUSE® Semi-Sweet Chocolate Morsels
2 containers (16 ounces *each*) prepared frosting
    Assorted candy sprinkles

PREHEAT oven to 350°F. Grease or paper-line
30 muffin cups.

COMBINE cake mix, pudding mix, sour cream, eggs,
vegetable oil and water in large mixer bowl; beat on
low speed just until blended. Beat on high speed for
2 minutes. Stir in morsels. Pour into prepared muffin
cups, filling two-thirds full.

BAKE for 25 to 28 minutes or until wooden pick
inserted in centers comes out clean. Cool in pans
for 10 minutes; remove to wire racks to cool
completely. Frost; decorate with candy sprinkles.

Makes 30 cupcakes

Lemon-Lime Daiquiri Layered Dessert

2 cups lime sherbet, softened
1 package (8 ounces) PHILADELPHIA® Cream
    Cheese Spread
1 can (14 ounces) sweetened condensed milk
1/2 cup lemon juice
1 tub (8 ounces) COOL WHIP® Whipped
    Topping, thawed

LINE 9×5-inch loaf pan with foil. Spoon sherbet into
prepared pan; spread to form even layer in pan.
Freeze 10 minutes.

BEAT cream cheese spread in large bowl with
wire whisk until creamy. Gradually add sweetened
condensed milk and lemon juice, beating until
well blended. Stir in whipped topping; spread over
sherbet layer in pan.

FREEZE at least 3 hours or overnight. Invert loaf
onto a serving plate and remove foil. Garnish with
lemon and lime slices, if desired. Cut into 12 slices
to serve. Store leftover dessert in freezer.

Makes 12 servings.

Triple-Chocolate Cupcake

Dazzling Desserts

Even the most humble desserts can be dressed to impress. A little whipped cream, a few berries or a quick drizzle of chocolate is all it takes to go from simple to spectacular.

Chocolate, Chocolate, Chocolate

- **Small Chocolate Curls:** Pull a vegetable peeler across a 1-ounce square of chocolate. (Soften chocolate for a few seconds in the microwave if necessary.) Refrigerate the curls for about 15 minutes or until firm.

- **Large Chocolate Curls:** Melt 7 (1-ounce) squares of chocolate; let cool slightly. Pour the melted chocolate onto a cold baking sheet and spread

it out about 1/4 inch thick, into a 6×4-inch rectangle. Let the chocolate stand in a cool, dry place until set. (Do not refrigerate.) When the chocolate is just set, use a small metal pancake turner to form the curls. Hold the pancake turner at a 45° angle and scrape the chocolate into a curl. Use a toothpick or wooden skewer to transfer the curl to waxed paper. Store in a cool, dry place until ready to use.

- **Chocolate Shavings or Grated Chocolate:** Create chocolate shavings by dragging a vegetable peeler across a square of chocolate in short, quick strokes. For grated chocolate, working over waxed paper, rub chocolate across the rough surface

of a grater, letting the pieces fall onto the waxed paper. The large and small holes of the grater can be used, depending on the size of the chocolate pieces you want.

- **Chocolate-Dipped Garnishes:** Dip cookies, nuts or fruit halfway into melted chocolate, let excess drip off, then place them on waxed paper until the chocolate is set.

Chocolate Drizzle or Shapes

- For a quick decoration, use a fork or spoon to drizzle melted chocolate over cookies.

- For a more controlled drizzle, melt chocolate in a resealable plastic food storage bag, cut off a very tiny corner from the bag and drizzle

chocolate over desserts. Or, pipe chocolate from the bag in lines, squiggles, grids or patterns directly over cookies and bars, or on waxed paper. Let stand until firm. Then, gently peel off the paper and place on the dessert.

- If the chocolate glaze or melted chocolate is too thin, let it stand at room temperature until it thickens; if it is too thick, microwave it very briefly on LOW (30% power).

Cream & Sugar

- **Whipped Cream:** Chill the cream, bowl and beaters before whipping to get the most volume. For extra decadence, make chocolate whipped cream: stir 1 cup whipping cream into a mixture of 2 tablespoons each powdered sugar and cocoa powder until well blended. Refrigerate the mixture 30 minutes before whipping.

- **Powdered Sugar or Cocoa Powder:** Place the powdered sugar or cocoa powder in a small strainer and gently shake the strainer over the dessert. For fancier designs on cakes and brownies or bar cookies, place

a stencil, doily or strips of paper over the top of the dessert before dusting it with sugar or cocoa. Carefully lift off the stencil, doily or paper strips by holding the edges firmly and pulling straight up.

- **Powdered Sugar Glaze:** Powdered sugar glaze can be used for drizzling and decorating just like melted chocolate. Blend 1 cup powdered sugar and 5 to 6 teaspoons water or milk to create a simple glaze that looks and tastes great on a variety of cookies. (Add additional sugar if the glaze is too thin; stir in a small amount of liquid if the glaze is too thick.) Tint the glaze with a few drops of food coloring, if desired.

- **Sugars, Sprinkles or Candies:** Sprinkle cookies with coarse sugar, colored sugars or sprinkles before baking. Or, after baking, cakes and cookies can be frosted and then topped with colored sugar, sprinkles or candies. To decorate a cake, coat the side with sprinkles while the frosting is still soft.

Coconut & Nuts

- **Toasted Coconut or Nuts:** Spread coconut or nuts in a thin layer on an ungreased cookie sheet. Bake in a preheated 325°F oven 7 to 10 minutes or until golden, stirring occasionally to promote even browning and prevent burning. Allow coconut and nuts to cool before using. Toasted nuts will darken and become crisper as they cool. To decorate a cake, press the toasted coconut or nuts onto the side while the frosting is still soft.

- **Tinted Coconut:** Dilute a few drops of liquid food coloring with 1/2 teaspoon milk or water in a large bowl. Add 1 to 1-1/3 cups flaked coconut and toss with a fork until the

coconut is evenly tinted. To decorate a cake, press the tinted coconut onto the side while the frosting is still soft.

Fruity Frills

- **Citrus Knots:** Using a vegetable peeler, remove strips of peel from a lemon, lime or orange. If necessary, scrape the cut sides of the peel with a paring knife to remove any white pith. Cut the strips into 3-1/2×1/8-inch pieces. Tie each piece into a bow.

- **Citrus Twists:** Diagonally cut a lemon, lime or orange into thin slices. Cut a slit through each slice just to the center. Holding each slice with both hands, twist the ends in opposite directions. Place the slices on a plate or the dessert to secure them.

- **Fresh Berries:** Pile berries high inside the center of a bundt or tube cake to instantly dress it up, or sprinkle them over almost anything.

- **Strawberry Fans:** Place a strawberry on a cutting board with the pointed end facing you. Make 4 or 5 lengthwise cuts from just below the stem end of the strawberry to the pointed end. Fan the slices apart slightly, being careful to keep all of the slices attached to the cap.

- **Cherry Flower:** Cut the top of a maraschino or candied cherry into 6 wedges, being careful to leave the bottom half of the cherry uncut. Gently pull out the wedges to make flower petals. Place a tiny piece of candied fruit in the center.

Prepared Toppings

- For quick and easy decorating, try topping your dessert with red cinnamon candies, miniature marshmallows, jelly beans, nonpareils, gummy candies, chopped candied ginger or miniature chocolate chips. Use fudge, caramel or butterscotch ice cream topping for quick decorative drizzles.

The publisher would like to thank the companies and organizations listed below for the use of their recipes and photographs in this publication.

ACH Food Companies, Inc.

Courtesy of The Beef Checkoff

Bob Evans®

Cabot® Creamery Cooperative

California Olive Industry

Campbell Soup Company

Chef Paul Prudhomme's Magic Seasoning Blends®

Cherry Marketing Institute

ConAgra Foods, Inc.

Cream of Wheat® Cereal

Del Monte Corporation

Dole Food Company, Inc.

Duncan Hines® and Moist Deluxe® are registered trademarks of Pinnacle Foods Corp.

EAGLE BRAND®

Grandma's®, A Division of B&G Foods, Inc.

Heinz North America

The Hershey Company

Hormel Foods, LLC

Idaho Potato Commission

Jennie-O Turkey Store, LLC

JOLLY TIME® Pop Corn

©2009 Kraft Foods, KRAFT, KRAFT Hexagon Logo, PHILADELPHIA AND PHILADELPHIA Logo are registered trademarks of Kraft Foods Holdings, Inc. All rights reserved.

© Mars, Incorporated 2009

Michael Foods, Inc.

Michigan Apple Committee

Mott's® is a registered trademark of Mott's, LLP

Mrs. Dash® SALT-FREE SEASONING BLENDS

National Honey Board

National Pork Board

National Turkey Federation

Nestlé USA

Newman's Own, Inc.®

Norseland, Inc.

North Carolina SweetPotato Commission

North Dakota Wheat Commission

Northwest Cherry Growers

Ortega®, A Division of B&G Foods, Inc.

Pacific Northwest Canned Pear Service

Peanut Advisory Board

Perdue Farms Incorporated

The Quaker® Oatmeal Kitchens

Reckitt Benckiser Inc.

RED STAR® Yeast, a product of Lasaffre Yeast Corporation

Riviana Foods Inc.

Sargento® Foods Inc.

SeaPak Shrimp Company®

Stonyfield Farm®

Sun•Maid® Growers of California

Unilever

U.S. Highbush Blueberry Council

USA Dry Pea & Lentil Council

USA Rice Federation®

Veg•All®

Watkins Incorporated

Wisconsin Milk Marketing Board

General Index

Alphabetical Index

METRIC CONVERSION CHART

VOLUME MEASUREMENTS (dry)

$1/8$ teaspoon = 0.5 mL
$1/4$ teaspoon = 1 mL
$1/2$ teaspoon = 2 mL
$3/4$ teaspoon = 4 mL
1 teaspoon = 5 mL
1 tablespoon = 15 mL
2 tablespoons = 30 mL
$1/4$ cup = 60 mL
$1/3$ cup = 75 mL
$1/2$ cup = 125 mL
$2/3$ cup = 150 mL
$3/4$ cup = 175 mL
1 cup = 250 mL
2 cups = 1 pint = 500 mL
3 cups = 750 mL
4 cups = 1 quart = 1 L

VOLUME MEASUREMENTS (fluid)

1 fluid ounce (2 tablespoons) = 30 mL
4 fluid ounces ($1/2$ cup) = 125 mL
8 fluid ounces (1 cup) = 250 mL
12 fluid ounces ($1 1/2$ cups) = 375 mL
16 fluid ounces (2 cups) = 500 mL

WEIGHTS (mass)

$1/2$ ounce = 15 g
1 ounce = 30 g
3 ounces = 90 g
4 ounces = 120 g
8 ounces = 225 g
10 ounces = 285 g
12 ounces = 360 g
16 ounces = 1 pound = 455 g

DIMENSIONS

$1/16$ inch = 2 mm
$1/8$ inch = 3 mm
$1/4$ inch = 6 mm
$1/2$ inch = 1.5 cm
$3/4$ inch = 2 cm
1 inch = 2.5 cm

OVEN TEMPERATURES

250°F = 120°C
275°F = 140°C
300°F = 150°C
325°F = 160°C
350°F = 180°C
375°F = 190°C
400°F = 200°C
425°F = 220°C
450°F = 230°C

BAKING PAN SIZES

Utensil	Size in Inches/Quarts	Metric Volume	Size in Centimeters
Baking or Cake Pan (square or rectangular)	$8 \times 8 \times 2$	2 L	$20 \times 20 \times 5$
	$9 \times 9 \times 2$	2.5 L	$23 \times 23 \times 5$
	$12 \times 8 \times 2$	3 L	$30 \times 20 \times 5$
	$13 \times 9 \times 2$	3.5 L	$33 \times 23 \times 5$
Loaf Pan	$8 \times 4 \times 3$	1.5 L	$20 \times 10 \times 7$
	$9 \times 5 \times 3$	2 L	$23 \times 13 \times 7$
Round Layer Cake Pan	$8 \times 1 1/2$	1.2 L	20×4
	$9 \times 1 1/2$	1.5 L	23×4
Pie Plate	$8 \times 1 1/4$	750 mL	20×3
	$9 \times 1 1/4$	1 L	23×3
Baking Dish or Casserole	1 quart	1 L	—
	$1 1/2$ quart	1.5 L	—
	2 quart	2 L	—